Wiccan

Beliefs & Practices

Why I Chose to Come Out of the Broom Closet

I elected to reveal my practice of witchcraft publicly simply because I personally feel that the time for intentionally hiding ourselves has come to an end. We are practitioners of a kind, gentle, and peace-loving religion. We are not the bloodthirsty or depraved, orgiastic fanatics all too often portrayed by the entertainment and news media. The general public has been misled about witchcraft for over a thousand years, and now with our numbers reaching an all-time high, possibly in excess of one million people worldwide, we need to stand up and set that record straight.

We are out there by the hundreds upon hundreds of thousands. We are in the arts, the sciences, and the humanities. We are law enforcement officers, engineers, builders, doctors, and farmers. We are a legally recognized religion under the protection of the First Amendment to the Constitution of the United States, and our isolation from the rest of the religious community should and must come to an end. With the phenomenal growth of witchcraft since the 1970s and with the free and easy interchange of information afforded to us by things like the Internet, that time will come to pass and it will happen soon. It may be happening now.

Wiccan

Beliefs & Practices

With
Rituals
for
Solitaries
&
Covens

Gary Cantrell

2003
Llewellyn Publications
St. Paul, Minnesota 55164-0383, U.S.A.

First Edition
Third Printing, 2003

Book design by Donna Burch
Cover art © Colin Sammuels/Photonica
Cover design by Lisa Novak
Editing by Andrea Neff

The story of the Louisiana Coven in chapter 10 is used by permission.

Library of Congress Cataloging-in-Publication Data
Cantrell, Gary, 1938–
    Wiccan beliefs & practices : with rituals for solitaries & covens / Gary Cantrell.— 1st ed.
        p. cm.
    Includes bibliographical references and index.
    ISBN 1–56718–112–0
        1. Witchcraft. 2. Covens. I. Title: Wiccan beliefs and practices. II. Title.

BF1572.C68 C36 2001
299—dc21   2001029073

Llewellyn Worldwide does not participate in, endorse, or have any authority or responsibility concerning private business transactions between our authors and the public.
    All mail addressed to the author is forwarded but the publisher cannot, unless specifically instructed by the author, give out an address or phone number.
    Any Internet references contained in this work are current at publication time, but the publisher cannot guarantee that a specific location will continue to be maintained. Please refer to the publisher's website for links to authors' websites and other sources.

Llewellyn Publications
A Division of Llewellyn Worldwide, Ltd.
P.O. Box 64383, Dept. 1-56718-112-0
St. Paul, MN 55164-0383, U.S.A.
www.llewellyn.com

Printed in the United States of America on recycled paper

Other Books by Gary Cantrell

Out of the Broom Closet
(Upublish, Inc., 1998)

Acknowledgments

Many thanks are due to my wife for her tireless efforts in proofreading the various versions of this manuscript and for her invaluable comments. I deeply appreciate her helping me bring this work to a successful conclusion. Many thanks also to the members of my Coven for taking their valuable time to read the finalized version of this manuscript and for their very insightful suggestions. Also, a special thank you to Miranda, High Priestess and Teacher, Circle of the Chalice and the Blade, who, whether she realized it or not, assured me that my feet were indeed firmly planted on the right path.

Contents

Tables and Figures

About the Author

Gary Cantrell is a Priest in an Eclectic-Celtic Path of Wicca and is currently High Priest of a small Coven. He has recognized the divinity of nature since the early 1970s, but did not fully realize that he had been unknowingly following the Pagan path until about 1991. He began a study of witchcraft in 1993, initiated as a witch and Priest of Wicca at Imbolc of 1995, and accepted the responsibilities of Coven High Priest in 1998. Soon to retire after forty years as an engineer in the aerospace industry, Gary now writes books on witchcraft and related subjects as a hobby.

This is the author's second book. His first effort, *Out of the Broom Closet*, described the pros and cons of making one's practice of witchcraft known to others outside of the Old Religion. In this first work, the author examines the emotional, spiritual, and legal rationale in making his own decision about this somewhat controversial topic, and presents the comments of others who have made this same decision.

The overall legality of Wicca as a recognized religion protected under various United States laws is also discussed. *Out of the Broom Closet* is available at amazon.com, Borders, Barnes & Noble, or can be ordered directly from the publisher at http://www.upublish.com/books/cantrell.htm.

In addition to authoring two books on the Craft, Gary has written several articles on Wicca published in local newspapers and in Pagan publications, and has been the featured guest on a Los Angeles–area television talk show to discuss *Out of the Broom Closet*.

He and his wife reside in the suburbs north of Los Angeles. They have a grown son and daughter, each with families of their own, and three grandchildren.

Preface

This book grew out of suggestions by friends and associates within the Craft to document techniques and rituals that could be used by either a small Coven or a Solitary practitioner of Wicca. In that sense, this is indeed a "how to" book on witchcraft. It is also somewhat autobiographical, as I describe many of my own thought processes and ritual development as my path through the Pagan life has led me from Solitary practitioner, to Priest of Wicca, and finally to the honor of Coven High Priest. To those of you who have read my other book, *Out of the Broom Closet*, some of the material presented here in the chapter on going public with your practice of witchcraft will be familiar.

Much of my approach to Craft rituals, rites, and theology has been influenced by various teachers as well as many other authors of Pagan and Wiccan works. While the words in this book are my own, aside from some of the ritual content suggested by other Wiccan friends, some of the wording you see herein may well reflect that outside influence.

Wiccan Beliefs & Practices is an attempt to put knowledge of Wiccan lore and ritual into a usable context for either Solitary practitioners of Wicca or small Covens of practitioners. Many other Craft instruction books dealing with Coven work, in particular those by the Farrars, tend to assume that the Coven is formally structured along the traditional Gardnerian or Alexandrian lines, with their initiatory and degree processes, and is composed of at least thirteen or more members. My own experience has taught me that this is frequently not the case. Many times a Coven will be formed with only a handful of members who may be much more eclectic than traditional.

Smaller groups of practitioners, and obviously the Solitaries who practice alone, occasionally have difficulty adapting rituals and rites written for larger groups since there are not always enough members to fill the myriad roles or positions involved in rituals that are sometimes described by other writers. In actuality, there is absolutely no reason why the Solitary practitioner cannot perform the same rituals that are done in a Coven environment. The rituals I describe in the appropriate chapters have been specifically designed for use by either the Solitary practitioner or a small Coven.

While I include considerable discussion on tools and rituals, including some basic spells, I will also be spending time defining Wicca and talking about our ethics. I believe that a firm understanding of these topics is necessary and even crucial to your understanding of Wiccan philosophy in general and in developing an understanding of your own personal goals as you set yourself on this Path. If you are willing to take the time and learn from the ground up and establish a firm understanding of Wicca as you go, you will be rewarded many times over in your growing relationship with our Lord and Lady.

Wiccan Beliefs & Practices was not designed to be a textbook on all things Wiccan, nor was it designed to even begin to cover details of all rites and rituals. There are simply too many of these, and their many variants would fill several volumes. I include the descriptive material in this text dealing with ritual work only to give you a starting or reference point in the development of your own set of rituals. The information presented here, if you are so inclined, will hopefully point you in a direction to uncover as much additional information as you wish. I only mean to offer some general guidelines in this book, not necessarily to provide step-by-step instructions. Your rites and rituals will be much more meaningful to you if you personally develop them at least in part, instead of simply copying someone else's words.

I think this book is as good a place as any for you to start your journey, in addition to several other books I have listed in the bibliography. Rest assured that my efforts as presented here represent only the first of many stepping stones on the way through Wicca, the Craft of the Wise, the Old Religion. Once you begin down this Path, I am convinced you will be rewarded beyond your wildest dreams. The choice to begin is yours and the door is open.

So my friends, I bid you welcome. May you always find peace, love, and joy in the world of the Craft. I wish you bright blessings, and may our Lord and Lady always be at your side.

1

Definitions

*B*efore starting down this rather detailed road of definitions, let me be perfectly clear and state that virtually any definition one can attach to the words *witch*, *witchcraft*, or *Wicca* is in many ways dependent on the person making that definition. My own experience has taught me that if you were to ask one dozen people who claim to be Wiccans exactly what that word means, you would probably get at least a half-dozen different answers, and each answer could probably be tied to some acceptable reference source.

This seeming discrepancy is not due to any attempt to mask the truth or to a lack of information among Wiccan practitioners, but is due in large part to the fact that our Craft is growing and diverging today at a phenomenal rate. Many of the newer Wiccan Paths, sometimes referred to as Neo-Wiccan, have evolved with their own definitions or interpretations of these basic words. Their definition of Wicca may not always coincide with that held by the older Anglo-centered, British Traditional forms of Wicca that originated in the United Kingdom.

There are many Traditions of the Old Religion and many Paths within each Tradition. They each differ sufficiently to make even some basic definitions somewhat open to the interpretation of the practitioner. The definitions I present in this chapter are essentially my own and are based on my research sources and my personal understanding of my chosen Tradition and Path, which is generally understood to be Eclectic-Celtic Wicca. These definitions may not reflect those of other Wiccans who follow other Traditions. They may use reference sources that differ from mine and may therefore arrive at definitions that differ from what I present here. Nonetheless, I believe the definitions and explanations I provide offer as good a beginning as any.

I want to be very clear at the start of this book that the comments, thoughts, and opinions you will read here regarding Wiccan theology, rituals, and such are mine as I understand them based on my own experience and learning. They reflect my interpretations of how I live and practice Wicca from the perspective of my own Tradition and Path and from my own sources of information. I am by no means touting the material in this book as being something that speaks for all Wiccans. I have no intention of making that claim, nor, I believe, should any other author. When I use the words *we* or *our* in this book, I am simply referring to Wiccans in general. The use of these words is not meant to imply that a statement under discussion is accepted exactly as I have written it by all who practice Wicca. There is indeed no "one and only way" to work the Craft and worship our deities. We all have some differing understanding or interpretation of many aspects of the

Old Religion, and each one of these interpretations is, by definition, the correct one for those who embrace it.

In any event, I encourage you to read what I present and use that information as a starting point in developing your own understanding of the Craft. Read as many sources as you can, do as much research as you can, and do not regard any one source as presenting the pure and unimpeachable truth over all others.

Wicca and Paganism

What does the word *Wicca* really mean, and where did it come from? Wicca is only one of many religions of the world that can be grouped under the umbrella of Paganism. So before we can define Wicca, we must first define the word *Pagan*. Pagan comes from the Latin word *pagani* or *paganus*, which translates into "hearth or home dweller," generally meaning a country person. In the days of the Roman Republic, the word *pagani* was somewhat derogatory in its application since those so addressed were considered "country cousins" and were usually thought of as being somewhat inferior to their more worldly, city-dwelling counterparts. With the expansion of Christianity, the word *Pagan* was redefined as one who worshipped the old gods and goddesses and did not seriously worship the new Christian god. In the early years of the Christian movement, being a Pagan had not yet taken on the ominous overtones of heathen or heretic that later lead to the persecutions and horrors of the Dark Ages, that period in history generally referred to as the Inquisition or the Burning Times.

The current definition of the word *Pagan* from *The American Heritage Dictionary of the English Language* is "a practitioner of any of the non-Christian, non-Muslim, or non-Jewish religions, typically holding a polytheist or pantheist doctrine, philosophy, or creed."[1] A Pagan is thus anyone who follows a religion other than the Christian, Muslim, or Jewish religions. This obviously includes such diverse religions as the Hindu, Taoist, Confucian, Buddhist, Pacific Islander, American Indian, and, of course, all the nature-oriented or Earth-worshipping god and goddess religions. According to information culled from both *The 1993 Encyclopedia Britannica* and the *The 1998 Cambridge Fact Finder*, the total of these so-defined Pagan religions accounts for approximately 50 percent of all the religious adherents in the world, which is, needless to say, a significant number of individuals.[2]

Figure 1 gives a general graphic representation of how Paganism, the Traditions of Wicca, and some of the various Paths within Wicca can be visualized from the standpoint of my own perspective and learning. Others may not agree with my arrangement of some of the figure components, disagreeing on how I have represented or depicted the relationships between some of the Traditions or Paths. I appreciate and understand this disagreement, since few of us will see these concepts in exactly the same way.

In any case, this figure is only meant to give some visual form to the concepts of Tradition and Path, and is obviously not meant to depict each and every form of Pagan Tradition or Wiccan Path. There are far too many of these to include in one simple graphic, and only a select few of the major Traditions and Paths are represented. Please note that the arrangement of figure 1 is alphabetical; there is no superiority implied by the order of appearance or by the absence of other major Pagan Traditions or Wiccan Paths.

That brings us back to the original question—what does Wicca mean? There are those who, with justification, may say that anyone who invokes a deity and addresses that deity

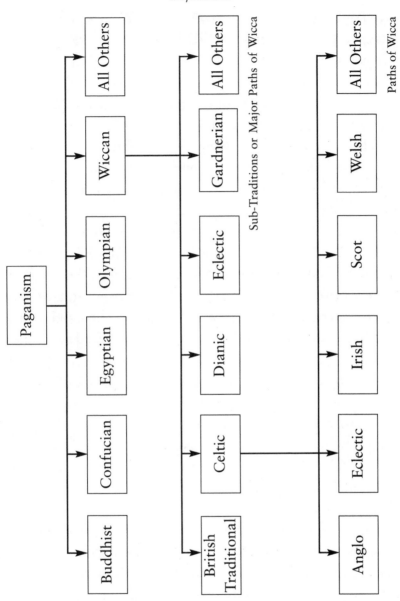

Figure 1. A Representation of Pagan Traditions and Paths.

through magick in order to bring about change is practicing witchcraft and is therefore a witch. Given that definition of witchcraft, one could assume the title of *witch* if magick were practiced by invoking a deity associated with virtually any theology, and no one could tell you that you were not practicing witchcraft as you understood it.

There are also those within Wicca who may not totally recognize your claim to be a witchcraft practitioner since that claim may fall outside of what their Tradition or Path may define or recognize as the practice of witchcraft. This may sound like splitting hairs, but I think it has some validity in that the title of *witch* and the understanding of what witchcraft is can be related directly to how one interprets the origin of those words. That is not to say that a person initiated as a witch under a theology outside of Wicca has no validity as a witch—far from it. I am only saying that the validity of one's claim to be a witchcraft practitioner may not necessarily be recognized by all those who practice under other Traditions or Paths of Wicca. This analysis, however, is probably more germane and firmly anchored to the teachings associated with the previously mentioned British Traditionals, such as the Gardnerian and Alexandrian Traditions, and much less so in the newer and generally more eclectic Craft Traditions that have evolved outside of that influence.

Many people feel that, technically, the word *witch* should be applied only to those practitioners of Paganism who follow one of the many Traditions of the Wiccan religion. The reason for this seems to be rooted in the derivation of the word *witch*. Some dictionaries and encyclopedias vary when defining its root source, with some listing it as a word of Germanic origin and others claiming it to be from Old English.

The 1999 World Book Encyclopedia defines *Wicca* as "the practice of witchcraft where-in most witches call their religion Wicca, from the Anglo-Saxon word meaning wisdom or wise, which is the root of such words as witch and wizard."[3] *The American Heritage Dictionary of the English Language* defines the word *witch* as "from the Middle English wicche, from Old English wicce (feminine) and wicca (masculine) meaning wizard or sorcerer, a believer or follower of Wicca, a Wiccan."[4] *The 1999 World Book Encyclopedia* defines the word *witch* as being "from the Old English word wicca, which is derived from the Germanic root wic, meaning to bend or to turn. By using magic, a witch is believed to have the ability to change or bend events. The word can be applied to a man or a woman."[5] The word *witch* thus seems to be able to claim a derivation from Wicca, meaning a practitioner of the Wiccan religion, a wise one, or one who can influence and change events. The words *witch* and *Wiccan* would thus appear to be interrelated, at least according to these reference sources.

Does this mean that only Wiccans are witches? Not necessarily, since we have already said that, in a broad sense, a witch is one who has the ability to influence events through magick and that this ability is not limited to Wiccans. That thought can probably be summarized with the statement that not all Pagans are witches, not all witches are Wiccans, but all Wiccans are witches. There are many differing Traditions of the Pagan religion involving rituals with magickal workings, and they may be performing witchcraft, but the practitioners of Wicca would seem to be witches and to be practicing witchcraft in the most literal sense of the word.

One can further bolster the argument relating the words *witch* and *Wiccan* by saying that the practice of Wicca brings with it an acceptance of all the ramifications inherent in magickal workings aimed at bringing about change. By that I mean that we who practice Wicca assume all the responsibilities and consequences of our actions commensurate with the Wiccan Law, also sometimes called the Wiccan Ethic. We understand this Law or Ethic and apply it to our daily lives. We fully appreciate the meaning of the Wiccan Rede and the Threefold Law, and we try our best to uphold the Old Code of Wiccan Chivalry. These concepts form the basis of the ethics of the Old Religion, which will be discussed in the next chapter.

There are other Pagan Traditions that practice magick to bring about change, but in some cases these Traditions may not embrace a recognition of the concept of "harm none" that is at the root of the Wiccan Law. In so doing, they may be working magick and effecting change, but may possibly be doing so in a form that is not acceptable to Wiccans, although they are in reality still practicing witchcraft. By making this statement, please remember that I am in no way implying that these other Pagan Traditions are in some way inferior to Wicca or that Wicca is the only way to practice Paganism or even witchcraft. All Pagan Traditions, or any religious traditions for that matter, are valid for their followers. If a spiritual path or path of enlightenment is appropriate to the practitioner, then it most certainly is proper and valid for those who practice it.

As always, one of the prime ingredients of adherence in any religious doctrine must be the spiritual and emotional awakening that comes from within the practitioner. This thought is exemplified by one line from *The Charge of the Goddess,* which states, "For if that which you seek, you find not within yourself, you will never find it without." Thus, if that awakening occurs within you, then the Path is a viable one, regardless of what others may think or assume about the "validity" of that Path. This is also true for the Solitary practitioner of Wicca, because all the teacher-student training and Coven initiations in the world will not make one iota of difference if the initiate is not fully and totally in tune with the Old Religion on a spiritual level. That is a decision the God and Goddess will make when They are good and ready to make it and, believe me, They will let you know when the time is right. It is not something novices can arbitrarily decide on their own, and it is not something that is automatically conferred simply due to the public rite of a Coven initiation.

Truly becoming a witch, be it done as a Solitary or in Coven, is a deeply moving and profound mental, spiritual, emotional, and sometimes even physical experience. It is an awareness of your connection to the God and Goddess, an awareness or maybe even a reawakening of your eons-old link through your ancestors to that wonderful and all-encompassing thing we call Nature. The feelings and emotions that will surge through you when you experience that awakening are impossible to describe with the written word. They will alter your heart and raise your soul. They will leave an everlasting mark on all who experience that awakening with an impact on your very psyche that is almost physical, and your life will be forever changed. Once you truly acknowledge and accept your rightful title of witch, regardless of how it is conferred, you will never again be the same.

Wicca makes no claims to be "the only way"; indeed, no religion can really make this claim, because all spiritual traditions or paths are meaningful and valid to their practitioners. Unfortunately, there are many religious or spiritual paths that do not share this concept and honestly believe they have the only meaningful or right avenue of religious pursuit. This type of myopic thinking can usually be found in the more fundamentalist or militant factions of most religions. It usually manifests eventually in such things as inquisitions, holy wars, or other attempts to impose the will of the (usually) minority fundamentalists on the rest of the adherents. Fortunately, Wicca does not make this claim; in fact, we refute it and fully support the concept that any religious path is by definition acceptable to the followers of that path.

Some Wiccans now recognize the many differing aspects of the Old Religion, even to the point of making the somewhat inflammatory statement that Wicca as we know it today has evolved far beyond the concepts described by Gardner and how it is practiced by Gardnerian or Alexandrian witches.

British Traditional Witch and High Priestess Raven Scott breaks from the more traditional school of thought and makes the analysis that common usage has somewhat changed the way we now see and understand Wicca and what it means to be Wiccan. Scott states, "Part of this change has been brought about by the very thing we actually desired to see, our formal recognition as an organized and accepted religion under the laws of the United States."[6]

Scott also accepts the fact that not all Wiccans may know the Mysteries and cherished beliefs of the British Traditionalists. She comments that "those newcomers to Wicca are discovering their own Mysteries to make either their own Traditions in their own way, or they are working the Craft as Solitaries and in so doing they have evolved multiple versions of Wicca."[7] I personally feel, as does Scott, that both versions of Wicca have a place in our Pagan society because both of them, the traditional and the new, enable us to connect with our ancestors and to find that divinity we seek. In the long run, isn't that what really matters?

Many of us have found something that speaks to the deepest and most emotional parts of our very inner selves, something that speaks to us across the gulf of thousands of years. What speaks to us was not called Wicca those thousands of years ago. There were no Gardnerians or Alexandrians at the building of Stonehenge, there was only the Craft of the Wise and it was simply there, as part of the everyday lives of our ancestors. That is the concept of the Old Religion that many of us embrace today. We choose to call our practice of that religion Wicca, and we choose to call ourselves witches.

I think that most practitioners of today's Craft realize that these new approaches have abandoned any deep or hidden content and instead embrace a totally open and visible path. I think we also understand that learning the ins and outs of the deeper meanings of our religion was never meant to be something that could be done quickly by just reading a few books. We can probably all agree here that a deeper understanding of the Craft does indeed require a program of dedication—it is not something that can be learned easily. On the other hand, the newer open or visible paths do lend themselves to a quick course of study. While they must, by definition, mask the deeper meanings of our religion, they still enable one to get a foothold as either a Solitary or as a member of a nontraditional Coven.

Summarizing these thoughts, we can probably make the assumption that the Craft of the Wise was originally formed around those deeper and hidden concepts; it was never intended to be a religion for an extended population. There was usually only one witch or healer in any given village who truly knew the Mysteries, and little thought was probably given to providing interpretations of the belief system beyond that necessary for communal rituals.

The result of this transition from the hidden to the open in the twentieth century is the fact that many seekers of Wicca have learned the religion essentially through books. Unfortunately, because of this, many of the deeper concepts may have been misunderstood or misinterpreted; thus, the Mysteries have been changed from that which was understood by the Traditionalists to that which is understood by the newcomers.

What we have postulated essentially recognizes the emergence of a different form of Wicca, a Wicca that is open, fluid, evolving, and dynamic. This new concept of Wicca sometimes causes serious concerns among traditionalist practitioners because it seems to strike at what they see as the very heart of Wicca; and we must realize that their viewpoint, as narrow as it may seem to some newcomers, does indeed have merit.

The Wicca I identify with is the practice of the Old Religion that recognizes the old gods and goddesses who have been with us for literally hundreds of thousands of years, only the names have changed. It is the Wicca that understands the balance in nature that gives us life, death, and rebirth, and it calls to me from the deepest parts of my very being. That is my version of Wicca. True, it may not be exactly the same Wicca as practiced by the traditionalists, but it is what calls to me. It is how I understand and worship the Old Ones, by embracing the divinity we call Nature in all her glorious manifestations.

Table 1 at the end of this chapter describes some of the better known Paths, some would say sub-Traditions, of Wicca It is a relatively short table, since it would be impossible to include each and every Path. I included the table only to give the novice reader a feel for the depth of the differing Paths. It is in no way intended to be a complete compilation of the major Paths of Wicca. If you are a practitioner of a Path that is not described in this table, then I apologize for my unintentional oversight. I have listed the various Paths alphabetically; their order of appearance is in no way to be construed as placing one over another in order of importance.

If you are just beginning a study of Paganism, you may need to evaluate many differing Traditions or Paths before finding the one for which you are looking. Your chosen Path in the Old Religion must be one that is uniquely suited to you as an individual and one that lets you speak to the Lord and Lady in your own fashion. That Path may lead you to teachers and a Coven relationship, or it may lead you down the Solitary path. Each has its own validity, and one must not be construed to be somehow superior to the other.

To those people who say that a Solitary is not a real witch, that a Solitary initiation into the Craft is not a real initiation, and only a Third Degree witch or an Elder can initiate another into the Craft, I take great exception. If a Solitary individual completes a reasonable course of study in the Wiccan religion, formally and without reservation dedicates and consecrates to the Lord and Lady, swears to defend Them and all those who love Them, and vows to follow the Wiccan Law, then that individual has indeed self-initiated. That initiation has been duly witnessed and accepted by the God and Goddess, and he or she has as much right to the title of witch as anyone initiated by any Coven High Priestess or High Priest in any Coven ritual.

As to the use of the word *self-initiate* as opposed to *self-dedicate*, I feel to some degree that this is simply a case of semantics. *The 1999 World Book Encyclopedia* defines the word *dedicate* as "the act or state of giving up wholly or earnestly to some person or purpose."[8] It defines the word *initiate* as "a formal admission into a group or society, or the ceremonies by which one is admitted to a group or society."[9] Whether you use the word *dedicate* or *initiate*, you are doing the same thing in either case. You are giving yourself wholly to a purpose (Wicca), and you are being admitted into that society (of Wicca) by a ceremony.

Having stated that Solitaries have exactly the same right to use the title of witch as any Coven initiate, it is important to realize that Solitary practitioners must by necessity obtain their information from existing written sources, either books or possibly from the Internet. Please be aware that not every written source available on our Craft is necessarily a "good" source. There are many published materials that contain errors or misinformation. This is usually not by design, but is usually due to conflicting opinions or philosophies between authors or, in some cases, is simply due to a lack of research by an author. Be aware of this and seek the opinions of others regarding the credibility of an author before totally accepting his or her word. Never assume any one author or teacher has the final and absolute answers to all your questions, and always know that there may be some kernel of wisdom in almost any source. If necessary, take what information you feel you can use, build on that, and leave the rest behind.

Most people knowledgeable in the Old Religion will also tell you that there is no "one and only true Path" of Paganism or Wicca. If you are unfortunate enough to come across a teacher or source that espouses this philosophy, run like hell because this is the last place a novice or seeker needs to be. There is no such thing as "the only way." As long as your path of study is built on a background of solid information, it is quite acceptable, if not necessary, to develop your own religious philosophy by taking the best parts of many others to form a new whole. The Path some identify as Eclectic-Celtic Wicca, which has taken what its practitioners believe to be the best from several Paths (Irish, Welsh, and Scot, and maybe even some Anglo-Roman influences), is exactly that and is perfectly acceptable. The main thing that matters in such an eclectic Path is the spiritual connection between you and the deities. As long as this connection is established, provides you with growth both spiritually and magickally, and is one in which you are comfortable, then go with it.

There is nothing wrong with changing your chosen Path later on. As your Craft knowledge expands over time, you may realize that there is some other Path within a Tradition, or maybe an entirely different Tradition, that seems more comfortable for you. If that happens, it is fully permissible to change direction and go with the new one—nothing is forever cast in stone. You are free to find the way most suited to you, be it as Solitary or in an established Tradition, but it must be one of your own choosing and one that ignites your own spirituality.

Let me be clear, however, about one very important point that every Solitary practitioner must take into account. I am in no way implying that a year and a day of self-study, followed by a self-initiation, automatically grants the Solitary immediate peerage and equality with those who have completed years of formal study with established teachers and attained the level of Third Degree in a structured Coven.

There are people in our religion who have dedicated their lives to learning the Craft. They have been taught by others who have similarly dedicated their lives to the study of our Craft, and many of them have gone on to accept the position of Coven High Priest or High Priestess. Some have also earned the right to the title of Elder, with all the respect due them that their hard-earned wisdom and education merits. These people are the ones you should seek if at all possible, for they are the teachers who can and will pass on to you knowledge that is virtually impossible to attain on your own from any book. I have been a Pagan for over thirty years and I marvel almost daily at the knowledge that I realize I have yet to uncover. The old axiom "the more you learn, the more you realize you don't know" is very true, believe me.

That leads us to a brief discussion of what constitutes a Wiccan Priestess or Priest. Generally speaking, Wicca does not embody the structure of clergy and congregation typically found in most religions. Any practitioner of the Craft who has initiated is considered a Priest or Priestess of Wicca. There is no overall governing body granting formal certification. That is not to say that these individuals have amassed sufficient skills or knowledge to become teachers, only that by the time of initiation these people have developed ritual skills and the affinity with our deities that essentially define the words *priest* and *priestess*.

As to High Priestess or High Priest, typically each Tradition will have its own requirements in both the time and skills needed before a Priest or Priestess can attain this position. It is a position of leadership within the Coven, and the individuals so designated will be responsible for leading all rituals and magickal rites. It is also a position of trust and responsibility, which will be discussed in more detail in chapter 2 on ethics.

What Does Wicca Really Embody?

Wicca is a religion rooted in the mists of Neolithic history. By whichever name you choose to call it—Wicca, the Old Religion, Witchcraft, or the Craft of the Wise—it is basically a fertility and agrarian religion. It is a religion of nature worship and the subsequent interaction with nature that is descended from that practiced by the Celtic clans of Western Europe and the indigenous peoples of the British Isles, the builders of such monuments as Stonehenge. The basics of what we today call Wicca can be found in the pantheons and theologies of both the Celts and British Islanders. Wicca by that very definition is thus an Anglo-European Pagan religion, and I personally feel that it is impossible to have a Wiccan Tradition such as Egyptian Wicca, Buddhist Wicca, or North American Indian Wicca. While the Egyptian, Buddhist, and North American Indian religions are obviously Pagan religions in their own right, they cannot be part of the Wiccan Tradition of Paganism.

That is not to say, of course, that one cannot extract elements of Wicca and somehow merge them with elements of something like Buddhism. I suppose that could be done, but such a conglomeration, even though it may be meaningful to its adherents, could not in reality be called Wicca since the theological concepts would in all probability be too far removed from Wicca as the rest of the Wiccan population understands it.

Just a few more words need to be said about the origin of Wicca. Although there is no question that Gerald Gardner should be credited with bringing our religion into the public eye in the twentieth century, he did not invent Wicca. It would be more correct to state that Gardner rediscovered it or possibly reinvented it by developing the Tradition that bears his name, Gardnerian Wicca, from which many of the present day myriad Wiccan Traditions may have themselves evolved. Gerald Gardner, Aleister Crowley, and Margaret Murray have all made an indelible contribution to the revival of the Wiccan religion it exists today, and their part in our evolution must never be forgotten.

The religion we know as Wicca was already thousands of years old before any of these contributors came on the scene. It is true that it was probably not called Wicca five thousand years ago. I am sure the rites and rituals practiced then were somewhat different from today's counterparts, but the religion we Wiccans practice at the dawn of the twenty-first century is indeed rooted in the earliest religious observances of our Neolithic ancestors. It is essentially the same age-old religion observing the same nature-driven ritual holidays and recognizing the eternal cycle of life, death, and rebirth. It is the same now as it was then.

As was discussed earlier, the definitions associated with our religion can be somewhat dependent on who you ask. Our religion is changing day by day. It is growing and expanding, which sometimes brings growing pains. There are many practitioners who have spent most of their lifetimes learning the intricacies of the Craft, studying for years before they would dare assume the mantle of *witch*, and who sometimes feel the old ways are being ignored and shunted aside by a new breed of practitioner. To a certain extent, this feeling may have some merit. There are probably too many "boilerplate" instruction books available on Wicca and witchcraft that take little or no time trying to impart what it means to be Wiccan. They jump instead directly into the mechanics of "how to be a witch" with no regard for the responsibility and understanding that must be inherent in that mantle.

As Wiccans, we acknowledge and worship the old gods and goddesses in a form both pleasing to Them and meaningful to us, and do so in a form that has remained essentially unchanged for thousands of years, regardless of the Tradition of the practitioner. We do not want to change the basics of that worship, because they are at the heart of what it means to be a Wiccan. Once you step out of that philosophy and develop a path of worship that fails to address those basics or subverts the old methods, you are no longer practicing Wicca. You may be practicing a Pagan religion and working some form of magick, but you are not practicing the Old Religion, you are not practicing Wicca.

Even given the somewhat diverse definitions of Wicca, we can still make the following general statements regarding the fundamental tenets that are at the heart of the religion with some degree of certainty. The religion of Wicca, the Old Religion, is a loving and peaceful Pagan religion of nature or Earth worship. It is tied to the phases of the moon and the seasons of the year as defined by both lunar and solar astronomical events. It is oriented generally toward agrarian fertility celebrations and recognizes both a female goddess and a male god as equal deities. Wicca is a spiritual awakening within one's self, recognizing the interrelationship between humankind and nature. It is first and foremost a veneration of our Lord and Lady, a deep and abiding understanding of the natural order of things, and an awareness of the religious and cultural significance of our special holidays. Only after all this is Wicca concerned with spells, magick, and the arts of divination.

Wicca teaches us that the Goddess and God are equal and exist together in each and everything in and on this Earth, including ourselves, so that we are part of the God and Goddess just as They are part of us. We and our deities are all linked together as part of the life force or cosmic energy that flows through all things, both animate and inanimate. The witch becomes in tune with this force, this energy, during rituals. It is the same force we tie into and manipulate for the creation of positive personal change through spells and magick.

Wicca is a religion based on harmony with nature and all aspects of the God and Goddess divinity. It is a veneration of our Earth. We understand that our world is in the midst of an ecological disaster in the making and that our atmosphere and our water have been polluted to the extent that major expenditures of effort and money are now required to even begin to repair the damage. Fortunately, some steps are finally being taken to stop the destruction of the ozone layer and to decrease the emissions of greenhouse gases that cause global warming. This does not mean the ecological battle is over—far from it—since the damage already done to our atmosphere and oceans will take years if not centuries to repair. While there may be no immediate solutions to these problems, they are issues of which we as Pagans and Wiccans must be acutely aware.

We understand and are in tune with the seasons, the natural order of changes in nature and in the universe. We recognize that death is part of life just as night is part of day, and that storms and monsoon rains are needed just as much as the warm spring mists and dry summer days. You cannot have one without the other. This concept of balance is carried forward in our understanding of the balance needed between male and female and our belief that our God and Goddess are always equal, even though one or the other may tend to dominate in some rituals.

Wicca is a peace-loving religion that exemplifies joy and harmony with all the manifestations of nature. We understand and recognize the relationship of humankind to the natural order of all things. We recognize divinity in everything both animate and inanimate, and embrace the God and Goddess equally in perfect love and perfect trust.

Wicca has its roots in a pre-industrial fertility or nature-oriented agrarian religion, and the seasonal festivals or other working meetings of witchcraft typically coincide with either the solar or lunar cycles of nature. These festivals and meetings, generally referred to as Sabbats and esbats, are further discussed in chapter 4.

A Wiccan Philosophy

What is a Wiccan's basic belief? Having previously made the case for Wicca being an esoteric, multifaceted, almost an ethereal concept, can we even answer this question? There may not be a single answer, but I believe we can at least address it. First of all, you must understand that how I define Wicca is based on the teachings and practices of my own Tradition. I am not implying that the thoughts and concepts in the following paragraphs are universally held by all Wiccans. In general, though, I believe you will find that most of the basic material being discussed herein is generally accepted in some form by the vast majority of those who practice Wicca.

You also need to understand that our religion is not specifically a goddess religion. It is a nature religion keyed to the natural order of events that is somewhat goddess-oriented due primarily to the unique position of the female in the birth cycle. We understand that obviously both male and female components are necessary for reproduction, but we also recognize the special place of the female in that cycle. When we discuss the Wiccan Sabbats later on, you will see that the Goddess is the dominant entity throughout all spring and summer rituals, with the God coming into prominence for the rituals of fall and winter; but even in those late-year celebrations and rites, the Goddess element is still present.

Like most religions of the world, the Pagan religions also have their own creation stories, those "in the beginning" stories that differ markedly from one Pagan religion to another. Although many similarities exist, there are significant differences between the creation stories of Buddhists, Native Americans, and Wiccans; and within the Wiccan religion, there are differences between the creation stories of the various Traditions.

If there is a basic creation story imbedded in most traditions of Wicca, it might be something as follows, and it does not differ that much from the basically accepted facts of evolutionary science. Generally speaking, we accept the fact that billions of years ago, according to astrophysical sciences, the entire universe was created in one split second by what is generally referred to as the Big Bang. This violent explosion of matter and antimatter expelled gases and dust particles at phenomenal speeds in all directions, a process that continues even today. As the eons passed, many of these particles of dust and stellar matter condensed and coalesced into larger and larger objects, finally forming into a multitude of stars and planetary systems. On many of these planetary systems, life began.

As Wiccans, we each have our own Tradition's view of this process and how life as we know it evolved; but I believe many of us consider that this Big Bang concept may have evolved from something similar to the ultimate cosmic orgasm between God and Goddess, eventually giving birth to every element and component of our universe. As time passed and life developed on myriad planets, it universally exhibited the balance and equality of male and female that is personified by the God and Goddess. On planet Earth, those early life forms began to recognize and accept the balance and divinity that is personified by what they choose to identify as *Nature*. The male and female balance was recognized by the most primitive of emerging life forms, and the acceptance of nature as a manifestation of the God and Goddess divinity began to emerge as a driving force in all sentient beings.

As time progressed, our ancestors moved out of their Paleolithic caves and built villages and cities, and they worshipped the God and Goddess as they saw Them existing in all things. They saw Nature as continuing year by year, ever renewing. This then could have been the beginning, the creation, of what we today call our Wiccan religion. From these basic concepts came the image of life ever-dying to be reborn, that which we understand as our "Wheel of the Year" and that which we identify as our "Mysteries."

The concept of the Wheel of the Year is woven into the fabric of most Traditions (see figure 2). Simply put, it is our calendar that defines the dates of our Sabbat rituals and shows those rituals to be repeating year after year, eternally. The Wheel tells us that the Wiccan year begins on the Sabbat of Yule when the Goddess gives birth to the God. The God grows strong through the spring and summer Sabbats of Ostara and Beltain when the God and Goddess unite and the Goddess becomes pregnant with the new God. The God begins his repose through the fall Sabbats of Lughnassadh and Mabon, finally dying on Samhain to be reborn at Yule, and the cycle begins again.

Interwoven with the Wheel of the Year are the Mysteries, those innermost parts of the theology of each Tradition that make it unique and special to its followers. The Mysteries are an integral part of each Wiccan Tradition, defining each and every one. They are a cyclical part of the Wheel of the Year, the cycle of nature, and they are the things that novices learn as the Tradition is studied, defining their Wiccan heritage and shaping their future. The concept of Wiccan Mysteries is discussed in more detail in chapter 4, although in a rather generic sense. Since this book has been written essentially to cut across Traditions and be as nontraditional as possible, I will leave it to each reader to identify, understand, and learn independently those things that form the Mystery of your chosen Tradition.

This concept of the eternal cycle of all things is at the heart of Wiccan philosophy, because it exemplifies our belief that all things must continue and that there must eventually be balance in all things. There can be no spring without winter, no rain without sun, no day without night, and no life without death. The Wheel of the Year and the Mysteries show us that all aspects of existence are cyclical and repeating, never to end, everlasting and eternal.

We thus recognize the existence of a supreme creator/creatrix from which all other things that Wiccans hold sacred have sprung. We believe that everything was created by an entity we call "the One," which is that primal and indefinable essence of the ultimate existence that is almost beyond comprehension and is at the heart of everything we identify as the spiritual beginning of us all. We perceive the One to be composed of equal elements of both male and female, which is personified as the Goddess and God divinity that bring the concept of balance to all we know as nature. The Goddess and God are knowable and generally within our reach, yet still beyond our real understanding. Their essence is always present in all things—in the sky, fields, streams, rivers, trees, flowers, and in all of us. We are and have always been part of the Goddess and God, and They are and have always been part of all of us.

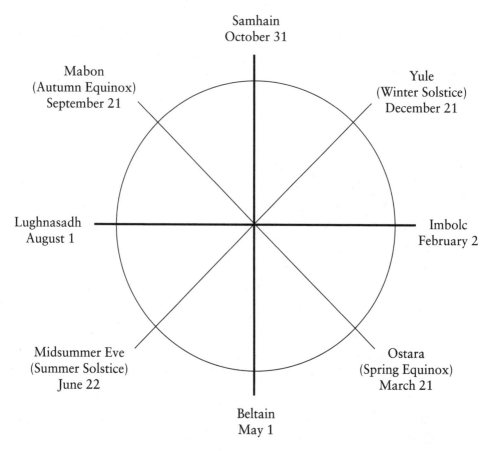

Figure 2. The Wheel of the Year.

To take this idea one step further, we also conceive of the many aspects of the God and Goddess that are represented by the actual named entities we invoke and address at our rituals and rites. We understand that our deities are not single individual entities. These thousands of aspects are each part of the essential personality of the God and Goddess, each unique and each directly addressable. When we do an invocation or a ritual spell casting, it is vitally important that we understand

exactly which personification or aspect of our particular deity
we wish to invoke. Each aspect of the God and Goddess deity
has a specific name, and these are the names we call at our
rites. In short, every God and Goddess of virtually any Wiccan Tradition have multiple aspects, each one of them available to the practitioner to be called on as necessary, and each
one unique.

We also understand that the domain of the Goddess is the
night sky. She is invoked each esbat as the Silver Lady of the
Night, the full moon, ruling the tides of oceans and the cycles
of women. She is the Triple Goddess as Her symbol moves
from young woman, to mature woman, to old Crone, to death
and rebirth, on a monthly cycle as represented by the phases
of the moon. As the Maiden, She brings a new beginning; as
the Mother, She represents the nourishment of birth; and as
the Crone, She is all wisdom and compassion. She rules over
all fertility, crops, and reproduction. She is the goddess of
fields, streams, woodlands, the sea, and of all small creatures.
She is fertility for all living things, giving birth and nourishing
the young, be they animal or vegetable. She is the mother of
us all, our creatrix, and in the end all will return to Her.

We understand that the domain of the God is the day sky.
He rules over all aspects of the hunt and is the consort of the
Goddess in reproduction, ever-dying and being constantly reborn to rise as Her son and Her lover. He is the fire lord of the
day, the blazing sun. He is the dispeller of the cold of winter
and the bringer of the warmth of summer. He is hunter, crafts-
man, warrior, shepherd, and lover. He is the Horned God of
forests and mountains, and defender of all creatures. He is the
nature force that impregnates Mother Earth. He is the wisdom
and empowerment of all physical laws. He is the father of us
all, our creator, and in the end all will return to Him.

Like the Goddess, the God can have many aspects, and, like Her, it is necessary to know and understand which of His aspects a practitioner is trying to call upon when ritual work is being done. Figure 3 is a graphical representation of these concepts. While this figure does not attempt to identify the many aspects our God and Goddess can represent, since that would be impossible in a single graphic, it does give a general idea of how we may view or interpret the interrelationships comprising a basic Wiccan theology. The figure boxes labeled "Aspects" could represent literally thousands of entities, each with a specific name and each with a specific responsibility within any number of pantheons.

Wicca, like all religions, addresses the issue of life after death. Unlike at least the Christian religions, however, Wicca does not endorse the concepts of heaven or hell with the corresponding one-time reward or punishment scenario—these are strictly parts of the Christian theology. Wiccan philosophy embraces the concept of multiple reincarnations. The physical body you presently inhabit is only a shell for the intellect, the soul, or the spirit; call it what you will. The physical demise of that material entity releases the spirit back to the place we call Summerland for a time of rejuvenation, reflection, and ultimately another incarnation of the physical self. This process of reincarnation is repeated for numerous lifetimes until a development of the spirit is reached where that spirit can truly merge with the male and female balanced creator/creatrix entity. We return to the God and to the Goddess. This is one of the basic truths of the Wiccan religion.

What really is Summerland? Many define it as the place of ultimate peace and contentment, the place of eternal springs and summers, of soft green grasses and gentle warm breezes, and of clear, cool waters. It is the ultimate paradise, a place

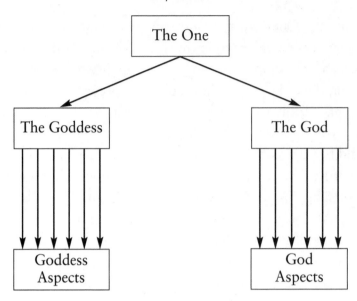

Figure 3. A Divinity Concept.

not of death but of life. The Romans called it Avalonia, from which comes the Avalon of Arthurian legend. The Norse call it Valhalla; North American Indians may call it the Last Hunting Ground; and some other Pagan religions may simply call it the Otherworld. We all have our definitions and our conceptions of what Summerland is, and they are mostly different, driven by our own desires and our understandings of the afterlife. It is therefore not readily definable in the written sense. It is a place in the hearts and minds of each of us, and its definitions vary with each of us. One thing is certain, though, in the philosophy of Wicca. We know that Summerland awaits us all as we pass from this incarnation, and we know also that Summerland is only the first step on our individual roads to immortality.

As Pagans, we understand that even as our physical bodies may cease to exist in what we may perceive as the present physical world, some of our essence will continue to inhabit that world even as our spirits journey through the gates of Summerland. This concept is beautifully represented in a prose that I have seen many times and in many forms, although each of the variations says essentially the same thing. I am unaware of the author of the original work so for purposes of this manuscript it is simply "Anonymous."

> *Do not grieve for me when I die, for I am still here.*
> *I will be in the evergreen trees of the forest.*
> *I will be in the flowers of the meadow.*
> *I will be in the spray of surf at the beach.*
> *I will be in the sigh of the wind on a warm summer*
>   *day.*
> *I will be in the waters of the rushing stream.*
> *I will be in the light of the sun, and of the full moon.*
> *I will be with the God and Goddess forever.*
> *I will be reborn.*
>
> *—Anonymous*

How often we may reincarnate, and how much time is spent in Summerland between incarnations is a matter of conjecture among various authors and Wiccan practitioners. My own past-life experiences let me subscribe to a break or space between incarnations of what appears to be at least several hundred years. How many incarnations we may experience probably depends on each individual spirit entity. Since the ultimate merging process is one of growth and experience, it is probably up to each one of us as individuals to determine how many incarnations we experience before final union with our God and Goddess.

Can the reincarnation process be cross-specie or cross-gender? I personally believe that it is not cross-specie. Once the cycle is begun as a human entity, it must continue in that vein to completion. As to cross-gender, I don't know. One can argue that in order to achieve the complete balance of male and female, which is emphasized in Wicca, one should experience existence as both sexes. So far, my personal past-life experiences have only reflected a male existence, as far as I can tell.

Wicca is more than a religion of nature ritual and reincarnation philosophy. It is also a religion of healing and change using a positive mental state and positive energy to achieve relief from both internal and external injuries or problems. This is the application of magick or spellcraft that we use to bring about these positive changes, a concept we will discuss in detail in chapter 6. The witch also understands and uses meditation techniques, as well as various herbs (either wild or cultivated) in conjunction with mainstream medical practices to help alleviate illness or injury. Our skills are meant to work in conjunction with modern medicine, not to replace it.

Chapter Summary

As we have discussed in this chapter, the definitions of *Pagan*, *Wiccan*, and *witch* vary among Pagans depending on the training and Pagan Tradition followed. Generally speaking, not all Pagans are Wiccans, not all Pagans are necessarily witches, and not all witches are Wiccans, but all Wiccans are indeed witches.

Regardless of whether we practice the Craft in Covens or as Solitaries, we practice it in a fully autonomous environment. We and we alone are totally responsible for the content and format of our rituals and rites and for how we establish a relationship with the Lord and Lady. There is no single individual appointed over us, no one empowered with the title of Grand

Pagan, King or Queen of all Witches, or Supreme Wiccan; nor is there an overall World Council of Witches passing laws and handing down directives to the rest of us. Even when a new Coven hives off from another and there is some allegiance between the two, that relationship is never such that one is subservient to the other.

There are, however, several loose confederations of Pagans such as the Covenant of the Goddess and some of the public awareness or public education organizations like the Pagan Educational Network. In these types of associations, Covens and Solitaries occasionally come together as both individuals and groups to celebrate a major Sabbat jointly or to address a common issue.

The upside to this autonomy is that we are indeed all fully independent in thought, word, and deed (at least within our own Tradition) to practice as we see fit. The downside is that it is difficult for us to organize into any really unified or cohesive whole if it becomes necessary to address a legal issue involving our rights, or even if one of us might be threatened. I strongly suggest that if you are practicing in a small Coven or as a Solitary that you at least make an effort to contact other Pagans in your area and develop some form of a relationship. This can usually be accomplished through a local Pagan or occult shop, or, failing that, try the Internet and search for like-minded groups within your geographical area.

It is important that you have some idea of where to go in order to resolve questions about the religion or just to be able to swap ideas and concepts with others, and to be made aware of possible antiwitch activities or pogroms; or, in the worst case, to have someplace to ask for help if that need should ever arise.

Since we are all fully autonomous, we are all free to interpret the guidelines of the Old Religion as we understand them and to worship the Old Ones in our own way. Others may disagree with our interpretations and even with some of our rituals, and it is fully their right to do so, be they novice or Elder; but any disagreement must be seen in the context of the other person's Tradition or Path, and no one, regardless of tenure in the Craft or position in their own Coven, is automatically endowed with infinite wisdom and infallible knowledge of all things Wiccan. No one has the right to tell other practitioners that they are "doing it all wrong"; in fact, I have known novices, those still in their first year and a day of study, who have demonstrated more Craft spirituality and magickal insight than some people who have been practicing the Craft for years.

We practice a very old religion, one that venerates life and understands the magickal relationship between ourselves and the divinity we call *Nature*, one that predates by thousands of years the advent of Gerald Gardner and the establishment of Gardnerian Wicca. Our religion is generically called witchcraft, although we who practice it today usually call it Wicca. No one, regardless of his or her professed Craft genealogy, has ownership of the word *witch* and can tell you that you cannot call yourself a witch or practice witchcraft unless you do so in a certain way. Practice the Craft in whatever way gives you a spiritual connection to the God and Goddess, and do it in such a way that you grow spiritually and magickally. Do all these things in conformance with the Wiccan Law, and you are indeed practicing witchcraft.

Wicca is a peaceful, nature-loving, and life-affirming religion with an inherent belief in the balance of nature, which can incorporate the practice of witchcraft in order to bring about a positive change in our lives or in our environment. We do not profess to be "the only way," and we understand that what is the right and sensible path for us may not be the right path for others. There are many religions in this world, and there are many Traditions within Paganism and many Paths within Wicca. Each one of them is meaningful and viable to its practitioners.

We honor and support all religions in the belief that religion is an individual choice and that each person must follow his or her own personal path of conviction. We do not disparage other religions or modes of worship, and we do not attempt to convert others to our way of thinking. Our way can only be attained through an individual's own initiative, never by proselytizing or recruitment.

Wicca is a peaceful and loving religion, and these concepts are incorporated into our rituals and daily activities. The tenet "Love is the Law and Love is the Bond" is fully understood and recognized by all practitioners of Wicca.

Table 1
Descriptions of Several Paths of Wicca

The material presented in this table was initially inspired by Raymond Buckland's book *Buckland's Complete Book of Witchcraft*, as well as by conversations with others in the Craft. While the material presented here is obviously not meant to give the reader a complete description of each Tradition listed, it should at least yield enough information to determine if a particular Tradition merits further investigation or study.

As noted before, this is only a sampling of some of Wicca's major Traditions, with their arrangement in this table being

purely alphabetical. There is no superiority or inferiority either expressed or implied by the order of appearance, or by
the lack of appearance, of a Tradition or Path.

1. Alexandrian

This is one of the Traditions generally grouped under the
heading of a "Brit Trad" or British Traditional form of Wicca.
This Tradition was originated in England by Alex Sanders in
the early 1960s, with its rituals being essentially a modifica-
tion of Gardnerian Wicca. A structured degree system of First
through Third Degree is used for advancement within the
Coven. Alexandrian Wicca is an initiatory Tradition and is
therefore not open to Solitaries.

2. British Traditional Witch (BTW)

This Tradition is essentially derived from Gardnerian principles
and has a strong Celtic component. This is a highly structured
Tradition with specific educational and training requirements
that need to be met for advancement within a Coven through a
degree process. This is an initiatory Tradition where an initiation is done only by an approved Elder, and the initiates can
typically trace their lineage back to the original Coven of Gerald Gardner; thus, BTW is not a Tradition open to the Solitary
practitioner. Some BTW Covens still tend to defend militantly
the use of the word *witch*. The believe this word is properly applied only to initiated members of this Tradition.

3. Celtic

This Tradition is a mix of the Kitchen Witch Path with the
very early Celtic pantheons of Scot, Irish, and Welsh, and
even having some Druid flavors. Anglo-Roman influences can
also be present in some Paths of Celtic Wicca. The emphasis is
on nature veneration and the elements identified as the An-

cient Ones or Old Ones, and it stresses the magickal properties of trees and plants. Celtic Wicca does not, however, have the firm connection to specific and holy groves, springs, or trees, as does the Druid Tradition, and is easily adaptable for Solitaries. The basic ritual structure and content of Celtic Wicca can generally be found, to some degree, in most Traditions. This may be one of the oldest Wiccan Traditions because of its broad influence across the entire Wiccan format.

4. Dianic

Developed by Margaret Murray in 1921, this Tradition is typically identified as a feminist Tradition. The focus of many Dianic Covens can be totally on the Goddess to the exclusion of the male God component, with all emphasis on "wimmin" or "womyn" only. This is generally an initiatory Tradition, but many individuals practice its tenets as Solitaries. Almost any Pagan Tradition can support a Dianic Path.

5. Eclectic

This Tradition is essentially a mix of various Paths wherein the worshipper selects what are considered the best parts of several Paths and combines them into a new whole, without following any specific or single Tradition or magickal practice. It is easily adaptable to the Solitary practitioner, but the downside to being totally eclectic is the obvious end result of developing a new concept of worship, one so new or different that it may no longer be considered Wiccan.

6. Gardnerian

This Tradition was founded by Gerald Gardner in the middle 1950s and is generally considered to be the starting Tradition of the modern witchcraft revival movement. Gardnerian Wicca is another of the British Traditionals and is highly structured, with firm requirements in both time and skills that have to be met for advancement through the various degrees. Self-initiation is not possible in Gardnerian Wicca; thus, it is not a viable Path for Solitaries.

7. Hereditary

This is a highly restrictive Tradition, since you must be able to trace your Wiccan ancestry back several generations in your genealogy. Teachings and initiations are done only by a living relative who was similarly instructed and initiated, and outsiders or nonfamily members are not considered for participation. It is ideal for Solitaries if you can meet these qualifications.

8. Kitchen Witch

This Tradition is devoted essentially to the practical or working end of the Old Religion, with emphasis on the use of plants and spells for such things as protection and healing. This Tradition may come closest to the generally understood meaning of what a witch is and does, and it was apparently practiced by the Neolithic inhabitants of most of Western Europe. This is also one of the Traditions most easily practiced by Solitaries, since the required education can be obtained from either self-teaching or can be learned from others.

9. Seax-Wica

This Tradition was founded by Raymond Buckland in the early 1970s as an offshoot of Gardnerian Wicca. Seax-Wica (that is the correct spelling of this Path) differs from Gardnerian primarily in its ability to accommodate the Solitary practitioner. There are no degrees in Seax-Wica, but emphasis is placed on skills learned either through instruction or self-instruction, and one can self-initiate.

10. Strega

This is an Italian Tradition, dating from about the middle of the fourteenth century A.D., that emphasizes worship of the Goddess in Her form of Aradia, daughter of Diana. Some of the Sabbat names in Strega may differ from those used in other Traditions of Wicca, although many of the same rites and festivals are celebrated.

11. Teutonic or Nordic

This Tradition is probably just as ancient a form of Wicca as the Celtic form, but it has its base in the Nordic countries of Europe, with emphasis on the Nordic pantheon more than on the British Isles or Celtic deities. This Tradition is typically more prevalent among some of the Germanic-speaking peoples such as the Dutch, Danes, Norwegians, Swedes, and Germans.

1. *The American Heritage Dictionary of the English Language*, 3rd ed., s.v. "pagan."
2. *The 1993 Encyclopedia Britannica*, s.v. "world religions"; *The 1998 Cambridge Fact Finder*, s.v. "religions."
3. *The 1999 World Book Encyclopedia*, s.v. "Wicca."
4. *The American Heritage Dictionary of the English Language*, 3rd ed., s.v. "witch."
5. *The 1999 World Book Encyclopedia*, s.v. "witch."
6. See Raven Scott, *Who Is Wiccan?*, http://annex.com/raven/wiccans.htm.
7. Ibid.
8. *The 1999 World Book Encyclopedia*, s.v. "dedicate."
9. Ibid., s.v. "initiate."

2

The Ethics of Wicca

*W*icca is beyond question a duly recognized religion under First Amendment protection of the United States Constitution as defined by federal law (*Dettmer v. Landon*)[1] and as upheld by the United States Congress with the repeal of the Helms Amendment.[2] Wicca has been identified as an acceptable religion for members of the U.S. Armed Forces, and our basic beliefs are explained in the *United States Military Chaplain's Manual*.[3] More details regarding the *Dettmer v. Landon* legal issue and the Helms Amendment are presented in chapter 8.

Wicca is thus an identifiable and recognized religion by any test one can apply to that terminology. As in most religions, Wicca has a concept of ethics, that code of behavior that is defined by *The American Heritage Dictionary* as "a branch of philosophy that attempts to help us understand which ways of life are worth following and which actions are right or wrong."[4] The word *ethics* is described by *The Concise Columbia Encyclopedia* as "the study of the general nature of morals and of the specific moral choices to be made by a person; or the moral philosophy, rules, or standards governing the conduct of a person or the members of a profession."[5]

The word *ethics* can also be described in a bit more detail as the study and evaluation of human conduct in the light of moral principles, something that may be viewed as an individual's or group's standard of conduct or as a body of social obligations and duties. These obligations and duties constitute what we sometimes call our conscience, our moral awareness of right and wrong, that innate set or sense of values that are derived from individual experience or group teachings. Idealists such as Plato have contended that there is an absolute good to which human activities aspire. That absolute good, sometimes referred to as an ethical criterion, can be based on religious absolutes or it can be independent of theological consideration and based solely on accepted social standards. The source of an ethical criterion can therefore be equated with religion, the state, or the good of a group as that group defines it.

Given these definitions and explanations of the word *ethics*, we can look at our religion and make the categorical statement that as practitioners of Wicca, we do indeed have a set of moral and spiritual values that precisely fit those definitions. We have a standard of ethics that governs our lives as witches both inside and outside of the Coven environment.

I briefly mentioned the subject of ethics in chapter 1, but it is a concept at the heart of our Wiccan belief system and I feel deeply that it is something that deserves considerable discussion. There is an excellent book by Robin Wood on the ethics of our religion titled *When, Why . . . If*. While it is not my intention to quote liberally from that particular work or paraphrase it in this chapter, I will be discussing the ethics of the Craft from my own perspective and training. In any event, I strongly recommend *When, Why . . . If* as mandatory reading for any novice or seeker.

The ethics of our religion are aptly incorporated into the Wiccan Law (also known as the Wiccan Ethic) as both the Wiccan Rede and the Rule of Three, which is also sometimes referred to as the Threefold Law. This rendition of the Wiccan Law as I show it here is in a considerably truncated form from the two much longer versions that are presented in appendix A. The factual origins of the two versions in appendix A are uncertain to me, but both conceivably date from the early twentieth century. Nonetheless, these words still form the cornerstone of Wiccan ethics:

> *Bide the Wiccan Law ye must,*
> *In perfect love and perfect trust.*
> *These eight words the Wiccan Rede fulfill,*
> *An ye harm none do as ye will.*
> *And ever mind the Rule of Three,*
> *What ye send out comes back to thee.*
> *Follow this with mind and heart,*
> *And merry ye meet and merry ye part.*

While there is little concrete evidence to suggest that the Wiccan Law is of any great antiquity, there is some indication that it may have had its actual beginning in book one of *Gargantua and Pantagruel*, written in 1532 by the French physician and humanist François Rabelais. In this book, Rabelais describes the laws that governed the manner of living of the Thelemites. Whether Rabelais' words actually inspired Crowley or Gardner, or any of those who preceded them, is a matter of conjecture. In any event, these eight lines of the Wiccan Law might be interpreted as the lynchpin of the Wiccan religion and are what I consider to be the basic building blocks of ethical witchcraft.

Now, I suppose there are people who will read that last sentence and see an oxymoron because they cannot understand that the practice of witchcraft can be ethical and utilize only rituals and magick aimed at positive changes; but that is truly the basis of our religion. We seek to harm none, including ourselves, and we seek never to attempt to make changes that could harm others in any way. Our understanding of the Wiccan Law and the oath we take at our initiation expressly forbid us from doing anything else.

This is one place where Wicca and some other Pagan religions can differ as to interpretation and application. I do not claim that all Pagan ritual magick adheres to the concepts of the Wiccan Law, only that we who follow and practice Wicca take every action within our power to do so. Wiccans take full responsibility for their actions. We are fully aware that we and we alone are responsible for any and all ramifications resulting from our magickal acts. This concept is part of what we are and of what we do, and it is what sets us somewhat apart from some of the other more aggressive or volatile Pagan religions. Wicca is not above or better than any of the other Pagan religions by any means, just simply different.

We who follow the Wiccan Path know and fully understand that the Wiccan Law is not a commandment nor is it a law in any legal sense. It is a law in the ethical sense, a guideline for our actions. While it may not be ancient and venerated, it still is the ethical guideline by which our practice of magick is driven. If we can somehow incorporate its tenets into our daily non-Craft lives as well, then so much the better.

As a guide, it may be followed more resolutely by some than others, and, when all is said and done, the concept of "harm none" as embodied in the Wiccan Rede will probably always be up to the interpretation and understanding of the practitioner. Personally, I interpret it exactly as written, without qualifications, and this interpretation has been a mainstay of my ethical practice of witchcraft since I first set foot on this path.

The Wiccan Rede

The Wiccan Rede, the fourth line of the Wiccan Law, states, "an ye harm none do as ye will," which means exactly that. The Rede is the inviolate rule of witchcraft as Wiccans understand it. We create the universe in which we live, and we all understand that our magick will have an effect on that universe. We understand that we are, each as individuals, responsible for our own actions. In following the Rede, we understand that we can work whatever magick or spell we feel necessary or appropriate, but we will never use those actions to cause distress or harm to come to others in any way that those individuals would not bring on themselves by their own actions. That is not to say we will not defend ourselves or our loved ones. Of course we will, and we can do so very effectively, but we will normally only take such actions in accordance with the "harm none" philosophy of Wicca. We can put up some pretty nasty magickal defenses, and if some aggressor happens to impale himself or herself on those defenses when attacking us, then any harm done to that aggressor was his or her own fault, not ours. By way of explanation, the word *an* as used in the Rede is an archaic representation of the modern word *if*, and *Rede* is an archaic expression meaning "council or guide."

As an example of "harm none," we would never wish a speeding motorist on the highway to have an accident; but there is nothing wrong with asking the deities to arrange for a police officer with a radar gun to appear under the next bridge. An action or spell used against a known predator or assailant would not be designed to injure or damage that person directly; but we could cast a spell to bind the individual's own conscious thought processes so that he or she inadvertently blunders into a situation where law enforcement authorities can make an arrest. In both these examples, it would be the culprit's own stupidity that became his or her undoing. We took no action and did no work to directly injure or harm either one.

As to the second part of the Rede, we understand the phrase "do as ye will" to mean essentially to work our rituals and magick in such a way as to accomplish our desired aims while not violating the "harm none" concept; in short, do the work to bring about only positive change in order to improve or better our lives or the lives of those who have asked us for assistance. That brings us to another understanding of how a Wiccan works magick under the "do as ye will" philosophy. We will not, without darned good reason, do magickal or spell work for individuals without their consent, and we will never do it against their will. To do so would be a violation of the heart of the Rede and would go against the basic tenets of our religion.

There is one example I can think of that would circumvent this doctrine. Let us assume that you have a close friend or relative who is deathly ill to the point of being unresponsive. If you had good reason to believe that the person would consent if he or she were able to communicate, and if you honestly felt your assistance necessary, then it would not be a violation of the Rede to take some magickal action on that person's behalf without obtaining his or her express consent. I must confess that I did this once, but only after a lot of soul searching and a lengthy meditation session with the Lady about why I felt it necessary to take that specific action. In my case, the results of the spell I worked were immediate and totally positive, so I assume that I chose the correct course of action; or, more correctly, it was chosen for me.

The Wiccan Rede thus forms one of the defining points of the Wiccan religion. It is a concept with which one must be totally familiar and in full agreement at all times. It is a keystone of the Wiccan Law and is one of the things that define us as practitioners of Wicca.

The Rule of Three

The Rule of Three, from the sixth line of the Wiccan Law, states, "what ye send out comes back to thee." This means essentially that whatever energy you send out in a spell, be it good or bad, will be returned to you threefold, or three times stronger. Why do we need this if we have already said that we follow the Rede? The Rule of Three is an adjunct or enforcement to the Rede in that it brings into play the concept of positive rewards for positive actions and negative results for negative actions. We are each responsible and accountable for our own actions.

In many cases, the effects of the Rule of Three may not be obvious to the recipient. For example, if someone representing a charity comes to my door asking for a financial contribution and I give them ten dollars, it does not necessarily mean that a week later my bank will discover a thirty-dollar error in my checking account in my favor. In actuality, my reward for this positive action could take many forms other than the obvious one of financial gain. Almost anything bringing me an emotional, mental, or physical reward at any time in the future could conceivably be linked to an effect of the Rule of Three caused by my positive action. Conversely, if a person violates the Wiccan Ethic by taking an action against another that is calculated to cause harm, it also does not follow that the perpetrator will quickly receive his or her own measure of harm three times in excess of what was sent out, or that it will be returned in exactly the same form.

The Rule of Three does not necessarily function in a linear, absolute, and immediate one-to-one correspondence of give and take, and it may only be obvious in hindsight much later that the Rule did indeed come into play in some form. In fact, the results may be totally transparent to the practitioner. By this I mean that if you send out energy with the express purpose of harming someone, it is quite possible that the measure of harm you will receive in return might be masked and not even recognized by yourself as such. It is conceivable that the Rule can act in such a way that you do not receive an obvious negative result, but that what could have been a very positive result is instead withheld from you.

By way of an illustration, let us assume that for some reason you did spell work specifically aimed at causing another person to have some negative event happen to him or her. It is guaranteed by the Rule of Three that, as a result of your action, you will experience some negative response in your life. This could be something that might be obvious, such as a stolen car or a series of injuries, or it might be transparent to you in that possibly something very good that was going to happen in your life simply does not happen. For example, suppose the next ticket due in the lottery quick-pick at your local supermarket was pre-ordained by powers beyond mortal control to be the winner of a multimillion-dollar jackpot. Instead of you buying that ticket and receiving instant wealth, let us further assume you somehow get sidetracked at the last minute just long enough for someone else to step into the checkout line ahead of you and purchase the winning ticket you were about to purchase. That person becomes the winner and not you. In this case, you have indeed been the recipient of at least three times the damage you attempted to cause, but do you know it? Quite possibly not. Even though the Rule has functioned, it may have happened in a manner that was not obvious to the recipient of the negative reaction.

This brings up the question of how long can one reasonably expect to wait before experiencing either a positive or negative reaction, which in turn leads us to a brief discussion of karma and karmic retribution or karmic debt. My own belief system tells me that the response to any good or bad act of mine will be experienced sometime in this present lifetime, I just do not know when or how. Personally, I do not believe in karmic retribution or in paying for the mistakes of this life in another, and I do not believe that we experience the horrors in one life that we had possibly inflicted on others in past lives. For example, I find it inconceivable that a child in this life suffers physical or emotional abuse because he or she was an abuser in a past life. This simply does not fit the overall love and trust concepts of Wicca as I understand those concepts.

Our reincarnation philosophy, as I have come to understand it, is a process of growth and learning. We reincarnate into the physical world, if we so choose, in a time and place suitable for our spiritual growth or maybe to function as guides or mentors to others. Our spiritual and emotional selves are constantly learning and expanding toward that ultimate union with the One, and I do not believe that a reincarnation into a realm of pain and suffering because of some karmic debt is part of that reincarnation process.

I fully believe that we will all experience the results of the Rule of Three on our actions in this life and that those results will not always be obvious to us, not even in hindsight. The Rule is always in effect; we may just not realize that it has impacted our lives.

The Wiccan Code of Chivalry

The Wiccan Code of Chivalry is a concept that is not specifically spelled out in the Wiccan Law, but is one that many of us have adopted as part of our way of life. It is sometimes referred to as the Old Code, and is essentially derived from the medieval knight's code of conduct. That code, as we envision it today, exemplifies a deep love of the Wiccan religion and of those who practice that religion. It is carried forth in some of the wording of an initiation wherein the initiate swears to defend the Lord and Lady and all those who love Them, in this life and all those sure to follow.

Implicit in the Code is also the promise to protect and assist those who may not be able to defend or care for themselves. This implication extends beyond the limits or confines of our Craft world. There may be those who need or seek our help who are not Pagan, but they are every bit as deserving of receiving it as any member in our Coven. We must never get so caught up in our own spiritual realm that we ignore others around us.

Ed Fitch, in his book *Magical Rites from the Crystal Well*, discusses the Old Code as it applies to Wicca in more detail than I wish to go into here, and there are many other sources that describe the code of chivalry of medieval knighthood in great detail. Any of these additional sources make worthwhile reading in order to better understand the Old Code and how it impacts our lives as Wiccans.

The Inviolate Circle

As you will learn later in this book, most of our ritual workings are done in a special space marked off as a Sacred Circle that is cast in a special way. This circle is purified and designated as a protected space for the practitioners and for whatever deities are invoked during the performance of a rite or ritual. The circle is, and must always be, a safe, sacred, and sacrosanct place. It is a place "between the worlds and between time" where spells of witchcraft are done and where the rituals or rites of our Craft are performed. It is a place of growth both spiritually and emotionally and a place where only perfect love and perfect trust are allowed to enter or to leave. Whatever is done or said inside the circle must never, under any circumstances, be revealed outside of that environment. It is crucially important in developing the trust between Coven members and the High Priestess or High Priest that all members of the Coven feel fully comfortable and secure in the knowledge that "what is said and done here will stay here."

This goes beyond the Mysteries of your Tradition, beyond keeping secret the names of your Coveners and never divulging that information without their express consent, or divulging any of your other oath-bound responsibilities. If your rituals are meaningful and truly bring you all closer to the Lord and Lady, a very special bond will quickly develop between all members of the Coven. That bond will allow you to express your innermost feelings without restraint and fear. It will allow you to sing, laugh, and cry. It will bring you a measure of relaxation, acceptance, and understanding that will transcend what you thought might have been previously possible. The circle is sacred and inviolate, and within it you will truly understand the Wiccan concept of perfect trust and perfect love.

I have seen this trust and love grow and mature in our own Coven as we have all grown closer together, and it is truly a wonderful experience. We are fortunate to work in a relatively small group, and the bond between all of us has strengthened quickly and deeply, much more so, I think, than would be possible in a larger Coven. A bond will develop in a group of any size, given time and given the understanding of all participants that the circle is indeed a safe and inviolate place, a place of love and trust.

The Right and Wrong of Our Craft

Generally speaking, there is no right or wrong way to practice the Old Religion. There are guidelines that point us in the right direction, but within these guidelines it is perfectly permissible to develop your own rhetoric, rituals, and concepts. That statement may fly in the face of the more traditional practitioners, but, given what was said in chapter 1 about the definitions of our Craft, I will stand by it. You are free to develop your own Tradition with its own set of Mysteries and rituals, and you are free to call it Wicca, if you so choose. Just be forewarned that there are those, with full justification in their own right, who will militantly disavow your practice as "not really Wiccan" unless you have experienced a traditional initiation into one of the fundamental or British Traditional forms of Wicca.

In the grand scheme of things, however, it simply does not matter. The only thing that matters is your spiritual connection to the Lord and Lady and to the Sabbat rituals that were practiced for thousands of years before Gerald Gardner and before the word *Wicca* came to be identified with the Craft of the Wise. Others may have their own Tradition of the Craft, and you may have yours, but we all, in our own way, have established a link with something that takes every one of us into the mists of prehistory. The deities are the same for all of us, and the method of ritual worship of Them is generally the same, only the names may be different. You still are a practitioner of the Old Religion, a practitioner of change through magick, a witch.

Since we have already spent considerable time discussing the positive philosophy of Wicca, it would probably be appropriate to attempt to dispel some of the negative stereotypes associated with our religion. Besides, it would be remiss of me not to include a brief discussion of what our Craft is *not*, contrary to opinions expressed in some of the popular press, the entertainment media, and as espoused by most Christian Fundamentalists. Once and for all, let us make very clear the fact that Wicca does not and never has embodied or exhibited any of the following characteristics:

1. Devil worship, Satanism, or "black masses"

In Wicca, there is no devil worship or the worship of devil figures such as Satan or the Antichrist, and there is no such thing as a black mass where Christian litanies are pronounced backward and Christian symbols are defamed. None of these practices exist, nor have they ever existed in Wicca. The devil and hell are parts of the Christian theology. They simply do not exist in Wicca, and these concepts have never been part of the Wiccan religion.

2. Bestiality or blood sacrifice

There is no sexual contact with animals or any other acts of bestiality in Wiccan ritual, and there is never any type of blood sacrifice at our rituals for any purpose. Various rites of bestiality supposedly conducted by witches during the Middle Ages were solely products of imagination. No Wiccan has ever conducted rites of bestiality. As far as animal sacrifice is concerned, a Wiccan venerates and celebrates life, and many of our Sabbat rituals are devoted to the concept of life everlasting. While some Pagan religions do perform ritual sacrifices of animals on occasion, this is not, nor has it ever been, a part of Wicca.

3. Acts of public sexual conduct

Wiccan rituals do not include orgies or public displays of overt sexual acts. While some witches do choose to practice skyclad (nude) for initiations or other specific rituals, this is done only with the full knowledge and consent of all members of the Coven. Since Wicca is essentially a fertility religion, there are some rituals or rites that do have an overt sexual meaning, such as the Great Rite, specific rites to the Horned God, and even some of the dark moon rites, all of which are discussed in later chapters of this book. Skyclad workings and the performance of these other rites are never conducted in public and are held only between fully aware and consenting Coven members or participants.

4. Idol worship

The God and Goddess are typically represented by the pine cone and seashell, respectively. Wiccans recognize the symbol of the God as the sun and that of the Goddess as the moon, but these items and symbols are not worshipped as divine. They are only images used to represent our Lord and Lady during our various rituals.

5. Black magic

Magic aimed at harming someone is not done at Wiccan rituals. The previous discussions in this chapter should amply clarify that statement.

We recognize, of course, that some of the actions already mentioned either are or have been practiced by other Pagan religions. We even recognize that in some cases human sacrifice may have played a part in some of the Druidic celebrations, at least as far as those celebrations are described by Julius Caesar.[6] However, those acts are or were viable parts of those religions, and they are or were meaningful and important to the practitioners, just as much so as our rites and rituals are to us. It would be hypocritical of us to comment negatively on activities or practices of other religions simply because we do not understand or agree with those practices, or because they may not fit into our particular belief system. Any practice undertaken by a path of religious pursuit must be understood to be acceptable to those who follow that path. I only wish to make it clear that these actions are not, generally speaking, practiced by Wiccans today.

Chapter Summary

As you can see, Wiccans do have a very strong code of ethics that lies at the very core of what it means to be Wiccan. Within the basics of that code of ethics is one of the concepts that may set Wicca apart from some of the more mainstream and patriarchal religions. In most of these other religions, if someone breaks a divine law, that person can either receive redress and forgiveness directly from the divinity or, more commonly, through the intercession of a priest. In most cases, the offender is simply required to acknowledge the transgression and usually do some form of penance in order to obtain complete absolution. That is all that is required. The problem is solved, and the offender is usually free to move on and probably repeat the offense, since resolving it again and again is relatively painless.

That is not the case in Wicca. As witches, we are fully and sometimes painfully aware that each act we take, be it good or bad, is totally our personal responsibility. There is no "higher authority" to grant us absolution, and no priest to say, "Do such-and-such for your penance and all will be forgiven." No, each one of us is individually responsible for all the consequences of our actions.

These thoughts about Wiccan ethics and the fact that we are each individually responsible for our own actions are not meant to intimidate or dissuade one from exploring our religion. They are, however, concepts that must be seriously considered and understood if one is to progress, to learn, and to evolve in the Old Religion. Your attention has hopefully been directed to this very important topic, because it is one that will surface again later in this book in chapter 6 on magick and spell casting.

---

1. Public records of the U.S. Court of Appeals for the Fourth District at Alexandria, VA, CA-84-1090-AM, in the case of *Dettmer v. Landon*, September 4, 1986. Richard L. Williams, District Judge.

2. The Helms Amendment, introduced in Congress on September 26, 1985, as SAMDT.705 to amend HR.3036, reads: "No funds appropriated under the Act shall be used to grant, maintain, or allow tax exemptions to any cult, organization, or other group that has any interest in the promoting of satanism or witchcraft."

3. See U.S. Government, "Religious Requirements and Practices of Certain Selected Groups," *United States Military Chaplain's Manual* (Washington, D.C.: U.S. Government Printing Office, 1988) 231–236.

4. *The American Heritage Dictionary of the English Language*, 3rd ed., s.v. "ethics."

5. *The 1991 Concise Columbia Encyclopedia*, s.v. "ethics."

6. See Julius Caesar, *The Conquest of Gaul*, trans. S. A. Handford, book VI (London: Penguin Books, Ltd., 1951) paragraph 16.

3

Getting Started

*I*n Wicca, most of our work is done within the confines of a specially purified and consecrated space known as a Sacred Circle. In that circle will be the worshippers and all the various objects, tools, and instruments used in the performance of our rituals and rites.

The first part of this chapter describes the tools and instruments that are an integral part of our ceremonies. We will discuss the items you will need in performing your own rituals and rites, how to prepare them for use, and how to protect them when not in use. The second part of the chapter discusses the basic preparations for performing the rituals and rites, such as casting the Sacred Circle, invoking the deities, and closing the circle when the ritual is ended. The actual performance of specific rituals and rites will be discussed in succeeding chapters.

You will also read references to the Goddess position and the God position relating to some rites or rituals. The Goddess position is generally taken by the High Priestess or other Priestess and is done with the legs slightly spread, arms outstretched from the shoulders with palms up, and the head up or slightly thrown back. The body in this position essentially forms a pentagram. The God position is generally taken by the High Priest or other Priest and is done with the feet together and the arms crossed at the chest. The fingers of both hands are curled into a loose fist, with the exception of the first and little fingers, which are extended to form the horned symbol of the God. If necessary, both positions can be assumed from a sitting or kneeling stance by just using the arm and hand positions. Generally speaking, holding the arms outstretched over the head in a "V" symbol is a position used by all practitioners regardless of gender during many invocations.

If you are working in a Coven environment, the High Priestess or High Priest usually takes responsibility for the tools and implements typically used by the Coven as a whole. This is the case particularly if the home of the High Priest or High Priestess is normally the location for Coven meetings, which is generally referred to as the Covenstead. These implements might include virtually anything used in the Sacred Circle, with the exception of a Covener's personal athame, Mirror Book, and personal Book of Shadows. However, practitioners may wish to perform spiritual or magickal work alone on occasion, and Solitaries obviously need to have their own set of working tools. It is quite logical, then, for all practitioners to have a complete a set of tools at their disposal.

The Mirror Book and the Book of Shadows

You will need to start keeping two books devoted to your path through the Old Religion. Whether or not these are two individual books, or just one actual volume with internal separations, is up to you. It has been my experience that the two should really be separate volumes. These books deal with two somewhat separate subjects related to your progress as a witch, and I personally found early on that trying to put both subjects into the same volume quickly made it too large and unwieldy. Your Mirror Book may rapidly grow into more than a single volume, depending, of course, on how much material you wish to record in it. The choice is yours, and you can always change the way you handle these books later on.

The Mirror Book

The Mirror Book is essentially a diary, an account of your growth as a witch. In it you should keep dated notes on the Sabbat or esbat rituals you attend, your feelings and impressions about the rituals, what you did to participate, and anything special related to your Coven or yourself. Later on, as you begin to work magickal rites, it will be a place to note the reason for a spell, how and when it was cast, your thoughts and feelings afterward, and the results. It can be as detailed as you want to make it, from a simple paragraph to multiple pages for each entry. The degree of detail is totally up to you, but it should be sufficient to enable you to recall the events surrounding what you have written months or even years later.

The Mirror Book can also contain information about the things you learn or are taught in the Coven, although I do not feel it should be used as a working textbook or notebook, since it is too personal for that purpose. If you are attending formal classes, or even taking notes during general Craft discussion sessions, you might want to consider using a separate book for that purpose and not your Mirror Book.

Your Mirror Book should not be loose-leaf or spiral-bound, but rather something with a permanent binding, such as a theme book, which can be purchased from a stationery store or any store having an office or school supplies section. You should make your entries as soon after the event as possible, in ink. The reasoning behind this is that the Mirror Book is supposed to represent your impressions, your feelings, and sometimes your very personal thoughts. As such, the writing should be done as soon as possible after the event, and it should not be altered or amended later due to "second thoughts," since your first impressions are generally the ones that will be the most accurate and significant.

I personally write in my Mirror Book on every other page. Although this is admittedly not a very conservative use of paper, it does leave me a blank page that I can go back to later in order to note some of my second thoughts about a particular incident or ritual, or to record the results of spell work. As you will learn later, magickal work does not always have an immediate and obvious result, and it may not be until much later that you realize the work was effective. There should be space in your Mirror Book on which to write the results even if they occurred weeks or even months after the work was done.

The Mirror Book is a very personal document and, next to your own Book of Shadows, it is one of the most important books in your library. As such, you should protect it accordingly. Do not leave it on your coffee table for the casual visitor to thumb through. Use it to make your entries or read what you have previously written, and then put it safely away. I keep mine in my office bookcase next to my Book of Shadows, but neither volume is marked on the outside in a way that reveals the contents.

The Book of Shadows

Your Book of Shadows is your Craft workbook containing all your ritual and spellcraft information. It is your working guide to your written invocations, rites, and spells. The Book of Shadows can also include Sabbat observance details about theology, foods, practices, and such, as well as directories and Internet links to Pagan or Wiccan sources and stores. Additionally, it may contain information relative to the Mysteries and teachings of your Tradition. Thus, given the quantity and quality of the information it contains, it must always be protected. It must never be intentionally shown to those outside of the Craft, nor should it be left out in the open where others may inadvertently have access to it. When not in use, keep it safely put away.

Some Covens maintain a Coven Book of Shadows. This Coven Book is usually under control of the High Priestess, who is responsible for any changes to the contents and for its protection. It is the workbook used in all Coven rites and rituals and sometimes for teaching the Mysteries. As part of your training into a Tradition, you may be asked to copy this Book, or at least parts of it, by hand, as the basis of beginning your own personal Book of Shadows. If you are an initiate into one of the more traditional Paths or Traditions, you may be oathbound to never reveal the contents of the Coven Book of Shadows to any person who is not initiated into that Tradition.

A Book of Shadows is a working document and, as such, is subject to changes and updates. A loose-leaf binder generally is appropriate, although some practitioners prefer to write their personal Book of Shadows in a hardbound volume. I personally feel that using a hardbound volume makes the Book too awkward to use, particularly if you are trying to repeat a spell or other magickal work that has been changed for some reason, sometimes more than once. The changes can make the text too hard to read, particularly by candlelight, which could conceivably lead to confusion or mistakes in the ritual or magickal work you are trying to accomplish.

The alternative to changing the text of a rite or spell in a hardbound book would be simply to rewrite it from scratch on the next unused page. This can be time consuming, though, and you might very soon find all your information on, say, healing spells scattered throughout the entire volume in no particular order. I have found a loose-leaf notebook to be much easier to use, since it lends itself easily to either major or minor reorganization as the user deems fitting.

That brings us to the Floppy Disk of Shadows. According to tradition, a Book of Shadows should ideally be done in ink and in the witch's own handwriting; but in this day and age of the affordable home computer, I must confess that writing a ritual or spell using a word processor has some distinct advantages, such as ease of editing for one. Although I expect that some practitioners might scream at this, I personally find nothing wrong with generating the text of a ritual or rite on a word processor and then printing the text on hard copy for inclusion in a Book of Shadows.

I personally draw the line at keeping a Book of Shadows only on computer disk and printing out the desired pages as they are needed for ritual work. In the first place, I feel that not having the actual Book available during a ritual or magickal rite detracts from the performance of that ritual or rite. Secondly, the Book of Shadows, particularly the Coven Book if you are working in a group, can be an integral implement of the Sacred Circle. It sits on or in front of your altar, it is part and parcel of your sacred tools, and it belongs in the circle just as much as the altar candles and your other tools. Lastly, it simply goes too far against tradition for me personally not to have an actual Book to work with. Having said all of that, I think that doing your rituals, rites, and spells either by hand or with a word processor is equally acceptable, though you really should have all the materials printed as pages in a physical volume and not just stored on a computer disk.

Tools and Instruments

There are many tools and implements used in witchcraft, and although I believe this part of the book is rather complete, there may be an instrument that I have inadvertently neglected to include. In that case, I apologize for any unintentional oversight. This section is meant to describe our general tools and instruments, so there may be some specialized items that are not included. The tools are listed in alphabetical order and not in any order of importance or use. Please remember that before any tool or instrument is used in the circle, it must be purified and consecrated. There is a suitable consecration rite described in chapter 5, and it, or one like it that you can devise on your own, should be used with every new tool or instrument. Once a tool has been purified and consecrated, it must only be handled by other people who have themselves been consecrated to the God and Goddess.

Altar

Your altar can be either permanent or something you set up each time it is needed, or you can have both. It should be at least large enough to hold three candles (Goddess candle, God

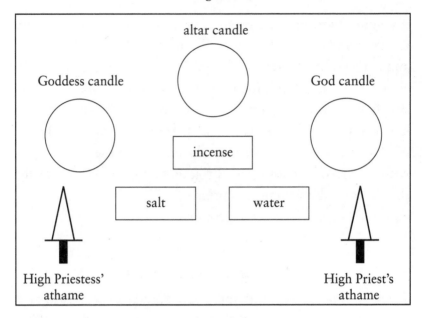

Figure 4. Placement of Altar Objects.

candle, and altar candle), as well as your salt and water dishes, the athames of High Priestess and High Priest, and the incense censor (see figure 4). Additional items, such as a small cauldron (or chalice, depending on the rite to be performed) and your Book of Shadows, can also be placed on the altar if there is sufficient room. Although we have a permanent indoor altar, I personally use a small wooden footstool our daughter made in a woodshop class at school for outdoor use. It is easily transportable and works quite well when draped with an appropriate altar cloth.

Altar Candles

There are generally three candles placed on the altar: a white Goddess candle, a red God candle, and an altar candle representative of the ritual or rite being performed. The color of altar candle for each Sabbat is suggested in the paragraphs detailing the individual Sabbats in chapter 4, and can also be found in table 2 at the end of this chapter. Various types of suitable candleholders can be found in either Craft or novelty stores. We prefer to use votive candles rather than tapers since the glass shell surrounding the votive candle gives the flame some protection from the wind when working outside.

Altar Cloth

The altar cloth is usually draped over the top and front of the altar. Its color is representative of the season, with the softer pastel colors generally used in the spring and early summer. Reds or dark greens can be used in summer into early fall, and orange or black are suitable in fall and winter. We are not quite so color-specific in our Coven, using white from Imbolc through Litha and black from Lughnassadh through Yule. The altar cloth is not to be used for any other purpose; it should be folded and put away when not in use.

Athame

The athame is generally a double-edged, dark-handled knife with a blade of about five or six inches in length. The blade edges are not sharpened. This is a tool used in many rites and rituals, and is not usually considered to be a weapon. It is used to mark the perimeter of the circle, to stir the salt and water used in consecrating the circle, and as a marking implement to carve words or symbols on candles for use in candle magick. It can also be used as a phallic representation in such things as a symbolic Great Rite. The athame is a personal tool and can be marked either on the handle or blade with your own unique glyph or sigil that is representative of your Craft name taken at initiation. Your athame should be put safely away, wrapped in a white cloth or stored in a white container.

Besom

The besom is a sacred broom used to sweep away any lingering energies around the area in which a circle is to be cast. I personally do not own a besom and have yet to find a use for one, relying on purifying an area with sage in order to cleanse it for ritual work; but this is up to you. If you feel the need to use one, then by all means do. They can usually be purchased in Craft shops, or, failing that, try novelty or home craft stores for any small broom. If necessary, you can make your own with an old broom handle or any piece of wood of a suitable length and some twisted straw or grass tied in a bundle at the end.

Boline

The boline, or herb-harvesting knife, is a small and very sharp white-handled knife with a curved blade resembling a small sickle. The blade is generally made of copper, not steel. It is used to cut herbs and for nothing else, and whether or not you need one will depend on your own requirements. The boline should be put safely away when not in use.

Cauldron

A cauldron can have many uses, from holding a small balefire on Beltain to functioning as the female counterpart to the male athame in a symbolic Great Rite. It is also used to burn any incantations used in spell work or to burn a Covener's written request to the deities during some rituals. They come in various sizes, and the size of the cauldron you acquire depends on its anticipated use. We use a small one of about a one-quart capacity that seems adequate for all our needs. Any iron pot will do for this purpose, but the old-fashioned, three-legged black cauldrons, some emblazoned with a pentagram, are usually only available from Craft shops.

Chalice

The chalice is a glass or metal drinking goblet and is another of those tools for which I personally have found very little application. It can be used in the initiation rite when drinking a toast to the Lord and Lady, and it can also be used as the vaginal representation in a symbolic Great Rite. Some Covens also use a single chalice in the Cake and Ale Rite, passing it around the circle after being blessed by the High Priest. However, the requirements for its use seem to be rather limited, and we have not found it necessary to procure one for our Coven. They can be purchased, with or without a pentagram marking, from many Craft catalog sources as well as most Craft shops.

Incense and Holder

The type of incense burned at any ritual depends on the purpose of the ritual. A table of incense types with their suggested functions can be found in table 3 at the end of this chapter, but, generally speaking, I have found that sandalwood seems to be quite effective as a generic incense for most occasions. Whether you use stick, cone, or powdered incense is up to you, but I have found that sticks burn more reliably and with less bother than cones or sprinkles of powder used with a charcoal block. A censor is necessary for use with either cones or powder, but only some form of stick holder is needed with stick incense. Incense, censors, and incense stick holders can be purchased in virtually any store. The burning incense represents the elements of both air and fire in the circle consecration process and in some initiation or dedication rites.

Pentagram Symbol

The pentagram is a basic symbol of witchcraft. It is the focal point for spell work and is generally placed on or in front of the altar. Some altar cloths are emblazoned with it, or, if you have a homemade altar cloth, you can purchase a pentagram tile or trivet to place on the altar. The altar candle can be placed on the pentagram or it can be used to hold the athames of the High Priestess and High Priest. The five points of the pentagram represent the elements of spirit, earth, air, fire, and water (see figure 5). They can also be identified in some rites or rituals as Birth, Initiation, Consummation, Repose, and Death.

Purifying Sage
Sage generally comes in small bundles and is available from most Craft shops. Once lit, it gives off a considerable amount of gray-white smoke that is a purification agent used to remove any negative or other unwanted energies from the area in which a circle is to be cast. Sage should be used the first time a circle is cast in a new area and anytime thereafter when the participants feel it is necessary.

Quarter Candles
There are four quarters used in casting a circle, sometimes called Guardians or Watch Towers, with each represented by an individually colored candle: yellow for East (air), red for South (fire), blue for West (water), and green for North (earth). These are placed at the appropriate cardinal points of the circle and form the perimeter edge of your circle that you will inscribe with your athame.

Salt Container
Salt is one of the purification agents (representing earth) used in casting a circle and is usually held in either a glass dish or seashell, the seashell being preferred. Any type of salt will do, and only enough salt is needed to give three small pinches that will be mixed with water. The salted water then represents the

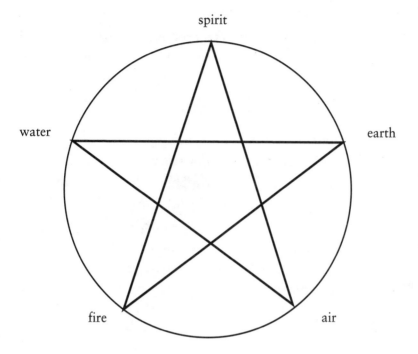

Figure 5. The Pentagram and Its Meanings.

elements of earth and water for consecration of the circle and in some initiation or dedication rites.

Sword

The sword is one more of those Coven instruments for which I personally have never found a use, although some prefer it over the athame when casting a circle. The choice is yours, but to me it seems to be an unnecessary tool since the athame works quite well.

Wand

Like the besom and sword, the wand is something I have never used. There are many written rituals that specify its use, but again I feel this is a personal choice since the athame works equally well in place of the wand. However, if you feel the need for a wand, then by all means you should have one. It is probably preferable to make your own wand from a suitable length of tree branch that can be trimmed, sanded, and marked, as you feel appropriate.

Water Container

Water is another of the circle purification agents. The water container should be any vessel capable of holding water without leaking and of sufficient size to allow you to add three pinches of salt and stir with your athame. In addition to purifying the circle, the mix of salted water is also used in some consecration and initiation rites. I have a minicauldron of about a one-cup capacity that works quite well for this purpose. If you are using an iron vessel, make sure you rinse and dry it thoroughly before putting it away in order to prevent rusting.

Clothing and Adornments

The type of clothing you elect to wear is totally up to you. If you prefer to work skyclad, that is also your choice. Working skyclad in even a small Coven environment may not always be practical, since each member must fully agree and be aware of which rituals will be performed skyclad beforehand—no surprises!

I have a hooded, floor-length robe of forest green that I wear for High Sabbats and other special occasions such as consecrations or initiations. Other than that, our Coven members normally work in street clothes that reflect the colors of the season or of the Sabbat. You can wear whatever jewelry you prefer. Our members normally wear a pentacle necklace in a circle, and I always wear my pentacle ring, regardless of where I am. Robes and cloaks can be purchased from the larger Craft stores or even through mail order. If you want to go further and really dress for the occasion, then medieval and even classical-type shirts, pants, and footwear can be purchased from any museum replica store. Several of these outlets are included in appendix D.

Preparation for Rituals and Rites

Before any ritual or rite is conducted, an appropriate area must be prepared. This is known as Casting the Circle. The circle is a sacred space, a world between the worlds and a place without time. It is a place where you and the God and Goddess will meet and communicate. It is the place of all rituals and rites, never-beginning and never-ending, symbolically eternal.

The area you select for this function should be one in which you as a Solitary, or the members in your Coven, can work easily and not be disturbed. If the area is outside, which is the best place to conduct your rituals, it must be free of unwanted observers and should be in a place where a little bit of noise on your part will not bother your neighbors. If inside, you may need to rearrange some furniture temporarily in order to get an area large enough for all the participants to fit into comfortably. If at all possible, the same area should be used for all your ritual and rite workings. If you are working as a Solitary, a space as small as three feet in diameter will probably be sufficient. If you have a Coven of up to about six people, you will need an area large enough to inscribe a sacred circle of either nine or twelve feet in diameter.

The basic tools you will need for almost any ritual include the God and Goddess candles, an altar candle, the four quarter candles, a salt and water dish, an incense burner or holder, the athame of the High Priest and High Priestess, and possibly your Book of Shadows. Each Covener will have his or her own athame, if possible, and a cauldron may be included for some of the rituals. If extensive readings are to be done, such as having someone read *The Charge of the Goddess* as part of the ritual, a reading candle would also be appropriate. The Cake and Ale Rite is typically part of each Sabbat and esbat ritual, and these materials should be prepared and placed on plates near the altar before the ritual starts, but out of the way so that they do not get stepped on or knocked over during the circle casting.

It is also a good idea for the High Priestess and High Priest to discuss the purpose of the ritual with the Coveners before it begins so that all participants understand what will be done, and individuals should be assigned to call and release each of the quarters. Your Coven will hopefully be large enough so that these functions can be shared and one person will not have to take on more than one assignment. There is nothing wrong, though, with one person doing several tasks, and if you are working as a Solitary, you will be doing it all yourself anyway.

Purifying the Area

The area of your circle should first be purified with sage in order to remove any undesirable energies or forces. Either regular sage or white sage can be used. Both types are relatively inexpensive and are usually available from any Craft shop. Sage is bound in a small bundle about six inches or so in length and, when lit, gives off a considerable amount of relatively strong smoke. If you are working inside, it may be a good idea not to light the entire sage bundle. Just light one corner of the bundle or possibly disable your smoke detector if it is in the same room as the circle since the sage smoke might activate it. I usually do not feel it necessary to purify a circle each time I cast it if the circle is being cast repeatedly in the same area, but the choice is yours and it does no harm to purify each time if you so desire.

Begin by standing in the center of your circle for a few seconds with the smoking sage bundle extended over your head as you spin slowly deosil (meaning in a clockwise direction, pronounced *day-sil* or *jay-sil*) three times. Then walk slowly in a spiral, in a deosil direction, until you spiral out and reach the perimeter of the proposed circle area, ending your spiral at the East Quarter. Each quarter of the circle should then be addressed with the smoking sage bundle, beginning with the East and again moving deosil. Pause briefly at each quarter, moving the sage bundle up and down several times, then holding it at arm's length over your head for a few seconds before moving to the next quarter. Each participant should then be purified by briefly moving the smoking sage up and down in close proximity to the body. If you are working alone, simply move the sage around your body once or twice to purify yourself. When the purification is finished, the sage bundle can be snuffed out by grinding the smoking end gently in your cauldron or in any nonflammable dish. The bundle can be relit and reused numerous times and can last for many months.

Set up your altar at the East side of the circle. On it, place the God and Goddess candles, salt and water dishes, athames of High Priestess and High Priest, and an incense holder. If you are working in a Coven environment, the High Priestess should place her athame by the Goddess candle and the High Priest should place his athame by the God candle, or both athames can be placed on the altar pentagram. Place the quarter candles on the perimeter of your circle at each cardinal point of the compass—yellow at the East, red at the South, blue at the West, and green at the North.

Casting the Circle

The actual casting of the circle is typically done by the High Priestess, but the High Priest can also perform this function, and any consecrated Covener can call the quarters (see figure 6). Light the incense and all candles, always lighting the Goddess candle first. Stand in the center of your circle, feet spread slightly, holding your athame in your right hand with arms at your sides. Take your time until you feel calm, in control, and at peace with our Lord and Lady. Then, holding your athame firmly in both hands, raise it high over your head. Hold this position for as long as needed until you feel the time is right, then lower the athame so that it is pointing at the floor (or ground) at the East point of your circle perimeter. Move to the East Quarter candle and, with your athame pointing at the circle perimeter, slowly walk deosil around the entire circumference of your circle until you are back at the East starting point. You have now inscribed the boundaries of the circle while understanding that the circle is in reality a sphere. It is a three-dimensional space and surrounds you above and below. The inscribed circle you have drawn is only the theoretical boundary line on the surface of your working area.

Move to the altar and bless the salt and water by placing the point of your athame in each individually as you recite the following words:

> *I consecrate this salt that it may be used in my*
> *Sacred Circle. I bless this water that it may be used*
> *in my Sacred Circle.*

Mix three pinches of salt in the water and stir nine times with your athame, three stirs for each pinch of salt. Briefly lift the container and hold it over the altar. Then, starting in the East and moving deosil, sprinkle the salted water around the perimeter of the circle. Replace the salted water dish on the

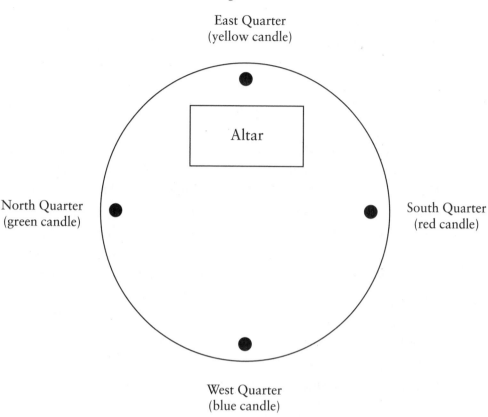

East Quarter
(yellow candle)

Altar

North Quarter
(green candle)

South Quarter
(red candle)

West Quarter
(blue candle)

Figure 6. Layout of the Sacred Circle.

altar, and pick up the smoking incense and briefly hold it over the altar. Again starting in the East, and moving deosil, carry the incense around the full perimeter of the circle. The circle has now been purified with sage, marked and consecrated with earth, water, fire, and air. It is now time to call the quarters.

I should point out that in some Traditions it is customary to have all participants already inside the space designated to be the cast circle before the casting is even begun. In others, it is customary for the High Priestess to mark the circle boundary with her athame, purify it with salted water and incense, and then admit all Coveners one by one. After all Coveners have been admitted, the quarters are called and the circle-cast is complete.

Whichever way you choose to cast your circle is really immaterial, but I recommend that you be consistent. If you elect to mark the circle first and then admit the rest of the practitioners, then stick with that technique for all rites and rituals.

If you elect to admit others after the circle has been cast, the High Priestess should first admit the High Priest. This is done by the Priestess cutting an opening in the circle boundary as described in the section "Temporarily Opening and Closing the Circle" later in this chapter. She then extends her right hand to him and brings him into the circle with a brief kiss as the two quickly execute a circular turn around each other. The Priest then brings in the next female Covener in a like manner, with that Covener then bringing in the next male, as everyone alternates between the sexes. If there is an unequal number of men and women, the High Priest or High Priestess will return to the edge of the marked circle to bring in whoever may be left. After all have entered, the High Priestess closes the circle.

Calling the Quarters

This rite has many names, depending on the Tradition. Calling the Quarters, Invoking the Guardians, Calling the Watchers or Watch Towers, Invoking the Old Ones: all mean the same thing. You are inviting into your circle the Spirits of the four elemental realms of earth, air, fire, and water. They are your protectors, your guides, your witnesses, and your guardians.

It is important when invoking or calling them to visualize the element that each represents. When calling the East, the element of air, it would be appropriate to think of gentle breezes clearing away confusion and bringing clarity. When calling the South, the element of fire, it would be appropriate to think of heat and warmth dispelling darkness and bringing light, energy, or affection. When calling the West, the element of water, it would be appropriate to think of cool streams bringing the water of life, cleansing and nurturing. When calling the North, the element of earth, it would be appropriate to think of moss-covered earth and tall trees, bringing soundness of thought and a firm grounding in your spiritual awareness. I prefer to identify this rite simply as Calling the Quarters. Appendix C lists several iterations that can be used, but the following paragraphs give a general description of the process.

Stand or kneel facing the East Quarter. Raise your right hand and, with your athame, mark a pentagram in the air in front of you and then mark a circle around the pentagram. Draw the pentagram beginning and ending at the top or the spirit point, and draw the circle in a clockwise direction. Raise the palm of your left hand outward toward the East, and lower your right hand so that your athame points at the quarter candle at the perimeter of the circle. Your raised left hand is your receiving hand and with it you are receiving the element or the Guardian; your right hand with the athame is your projecting hand and with it you are directing the element or Guardian to take a place at your circle. Recite the following words:

> *Spirit of the East, Ancient One of the Air, I ask you to join with us. Be with us and guard us in our circle. Blessed be, Spirit.*

Move deosil to the remaining points of the compass and, at each one, recite the same phrase, changing the compass point and the element name:

> *Spirit of the South, Ancient One of Fire, I ask you to join with us. Be with us and guard us in our circle. Blessed be, Spirit.*

> *Spirit of the West, Ancient One of Water, I ask you*
> *to join with us. Be with us and guard us in our circle.*
> *Blessed be, Spirit.*
>   *Spirit of the North, Ancient One of the Earth, I ask*
> *you to join with us. Be with us and guard us in our*
> *circle. Blessed be, Spirit.*

Typically, all members of the Coven stand or kneel together and all turn to face each quarter as it is called. The area has now been purified, the circle has been cast, and the quarters called. Once this rite has been completed, no one should step across the circle boundary to enter or leave the sacred space without good reason and without a proper opening and re-closing of the circle. The action to accomplish this is described in the section "Temporarily Opening and Closing the Circle" later in this chapter. You are now ready to invoke the God and Goddess and begin the ritual.

Deity Invocation

The deity you will invoke during Sabbat or esbat rituals will be dictated by the ritual itself. For esbats, it will of course be the Goddess in Her manifestation as Earth Mother, the Silver Lady of the Night. For Sabbats, the invocations will include both God and Goddess and will be driven by the ritual associations and requirements of each festival. Chapter 4 on Mysteries and rituals lists sample invocations for each Sabbat and for the esbats. The following is an example of a generic Goddess and God invocation:

> *Earth Mother, creatrix of us all and protectress of all*
> *the Wicca, by all the thousands of names by which You*
> *are known, we ask You to join with us this night. Be*
> *with Your children, bring us Your love, Your guidance,*
> *and Your protection. We bid You welcome, dear Lady.*
> *Welcome and blessed be.*

Sky Father, creator and protector of us all, consort of our Lady, by all the thousands of names by which You are known, we ask You to join with us this night. Be with Your children, bring us Your love, Your guidance, and Your protection. We bid You welcome, dear Lord. Welcome and blessed be.

Once the circle has been cast, the quarters called, and the deities invoked, it is usually appropriate to announce to all that the Sacred Circle has been completed or erected. With all members of the Coven seated or kneeling and facing inward, holding hands if so desired, the High Priestess or High Priest makes this statement:

We are between the worlds and within time, the circle surrounds us above as it does below. Let nothing but love enter here and nothing but love leave here. So mote it be.

Temporarily Opening and Closing the Circle

From time to time, it may be necessary for someone to leave the circle and reenter it, or to bring someone into the circle who may have arrived late. This is usually done by either the High Priestess or High Priest, but can also be done by anyone they so designate as the "Keeper of the Circle" or "Keeper of the Gate."

Taking the athame in the left hand and moving to the East of the circle on either side of the East Quarter candle, point at the top of the enclosing sphere of the circle. Draw a line downward, with the athame to the floor or ground where you had previously inscribed the circle boundary, then back a foot or so toward the East Quarter candle. Either side of the quarter can be used, depending on your physical space restrictions. This action effectively makes an opening in the energy field that is the physical circle. Extend your right hand to the person to bring them in or out of the circle as necessary. As the person steps in or out of the circle, they are generally kissed once as the two execute a quick pivot around each other. In order to close the circle, take your athame in your right hand and simply reverse the opening procedure. Start at the ground or floor where you have ended the opening and move the athame along the floor or ground for a foot or so, then back up toward the top of the enclosing circle. The circle has now been closed and the ritual can continue, all ritual work having been halted during the time the circle was open.

We should note one thing about animals, either pets or not. From time to time, an animal may cross the boundary of the cast circle. We recognize that animals are an intrinsic part of the natural environment and may, on occasion, actually be associated with the deity you have invoked. In the case that the animal is a Familiar, an animal with a psychic connection between the witch and his or her personal God or Goddess, it is a given that it will be associated with the deities in some way. Therefore, animals have essentially free rein in moving in or out of the sacred space. An opening or gate is not needed for them, and their movements have no impact on the integrity of the circle.

Closing the Circle

The ritual has been completed and it is now time to close the circle. Thank the deities for Their help and bid Them goodbye:

Lady of Silver Magick, protectress of all the Wicca and creatrix of us all, we thank You for being with us this night. Go in power, dear Lady. Hail and farewell. Blessed be.

Horned One of the Forest, consort of our Lady and creator of us all, we thank You for being with us this

night. Go in power, dear Lord. Hail and farewell.
Blessed be.

Release the quarters, beginning with the East and again moving deosil around to all four quarters. The pentagram is again drawn in the air over the quarter candle while you recite words similar to the following, while changing to the appropriate element at each quarter:

Spirit of the East, Ancient One of the Air, I thank
you for your presence here tonight and for protecting
us in our circle. Go in power, Spirit. Hail and farewell.
Blessed be.

Take down the circle by placing your athame in your left hand, directing it outward to where the circle was inscribed when it was cast, and move around the circle widdershins (meaning in a counterclockwise direction), starting and ending in the East. When this act is completed, stand or kneel in the middle of what was the circle and recite these words:

The circle is open but never broken. Nothing but love
has come here and nothing but love has left here, so
mote it be. Merry meet and merry part until we merry
meet again. Blessed be.

Chapter Summary

This chapter has presented some discussion on understanding the very basics of ritual work. The brief examples I have included for calling the quarters and for invoking our deities are only meant to give you a feel for the structure and idea, but not necessarily the content, of these actions. It is not my intention in writing this book to write another boilerplate dissertation, giving paragraph after paragraph of ritual text that you can simply repeat verbatim. The idea here is to encourage you to think about what our Craft is and to begin to develop your own sets of rites and rituals, to find the Lord and Lady in your own way. Whether that way is through one of the established Traditions, or if it lies in somehow developing your own relationship with the deities, is immaterial.

I believe it is important, though, that if you intend to follow your own heart and not embrace an established Tradition, that you do so with rites and rituals that are meaningful to you, and that does not mean parroting somebody else's words. Hopefully, by using the examples detailed here, in the following chapters, and in appendices B and C, you can develop your own ritual wordings; ones that will fire your own Pagan heritage, speaking to you as surely as those found in any Book of Shadows or spoken in any Coven.

Table 2
Candles

Candles can be purchased in virtually any market, bookstore, or New Age shop, as well as in Craft or candle specialty shops. Most outlets will have them in tapers of various lengths as well as votives. Be aware, though, that many colored candles sold in supermarkets are only coated on the outside and not made entirely of colored wax. Before purchasing candles, you might want to scratch the base with your fingernail to see if the color is more than just an outside coating, since candles that are made entirely of colored wax are preferred for Craft workings.

Candle Color	Meaning or Application in Ritual or Magick
Red	Love, lust, anger, courage, protection, revenge.

Orange	Adventures, innocence, new beginnings.
Yellow	Clarity, freshness, wisdom, healing.
Green	Growth, expansion, material needs.
Blue	Health, well-being, awakening.
Violet	Expanded knowledge, fame.
Pink	Affection, care, nurturing.
White	Healing, spirituality.
Black	Negativity removal, breaking bad habits or bonds.

Table 3
Incense

The following table offers several suggested types of incense that are generally considered to be related to the itemized uses. Most general or non-Craft stores, such as novelty shops or even your local supermarket, may not have all these readily available, so you may need to purchase them from Craft sources. I have found that sandalwood is an excellent all-purpose incense and can be used for virtually any rite or ritual. Sandalwood incense is usually available almost anywhere in both cone and stick forms.

Incense Type	Suggested Uses
Lavender	An air incense. Use for any ritual or spell involving clarity, any of the aspects associated with the Air Spirit, or the color yellow.
Frankincense	A fire incense. Use for any ritual or spell involving love or warmth, any of the aspects of the Fire Spirit, or the color red.

Sandalwood A water incense. Use for any ritual or spell involving cleansing, any of the aspects of the
Water Spirit, or the color blue.

Pine   An earth incense. Use for any ritual or spell involving wisdom or grounding in the basics, any
aspect of the Earth Spirit, or the color green.

4

Mysteries and Rituals

*T*he rituals and rites of Wicca can be as varied as the members of the Covens of all the myriad Traditions or Paths that perform them. Even some of the dates on which a ritual is celebrated may differ somewhat between Paths or Traditions. Each Coven or each individual may invariably work these various celebrations in their own way, with every one of us bringing something different to the practice of the Old Religion. The rituals I have described in the following pages, however, are generally those that I believe are recognized by a majority of practitioners within Wicca and are observed by most Wiccans at about the same times of the solar year or lunar month.

The rituals and rites described in this chapter are influenced by my own Tradition. Some of the concepts of the Sabbats, as well as some steps of specific rituals, will surely differ between Traditions, Paths, and practitioners. I believe, nonetheless, that most of what I have written should be generically acceptable to any follower of Wicca. As for the eclectic or Solitary practitioner, you might think of the descriptions in this chapter as a starting point. These may be the concepts from which you might develop your own philosophy of how to honor our Lord and Lady as you celebrate those rituals that define the Wheel of the Year. This information may provide you with the beginnings of your own Mysteries.

The Wiccan Mysteries

I use the word *Mysteries* in this book, and it is appropriate to have some understanding of what this word means. Wicca is understood to be a Mystery Religion; that is, a religion with much of its theology or rhetoric hidden from the general view. As the word *Mystery* is generally used in Wicca, it refers to that specific and unique teaching or philosophy inherent in each Tradition of the Craft that essentially defines and clarifies the very essence of that particular Tradition. In some Traditions, the Mysteries are indeed buried and only revealed after initiation; in others, their teachings are part of the first year-and-a-day training process. In still others, they are not really Mysteries at all, since most of the content can be discerned from open or published source materials.

Any one set of Mysteries can be comprised of many elements. To use just one single thought to give an example of something that could comprise part of a Mystery teaching, we might consider the concept of rebirth, which is a major part of the spring Sabbats. The following text is meant only to provide an example of what one might consider or encounter as part of a Mystery teaching. It is not to be inferred that this example is necessarily an integral part of a specific Tradition.

In many Wiccan Traditions, the theme of annual rebirth or regeneration is usually an integral part of the Mystery teachings and may be explained by various stories about the descent of the Goddess into the underworld in order to recover Her God-consort. In the some of these stories, She descends in the winter with the death of the God in an attempt to rescue Him from the clutches of death. She is then either trapped or coerced into staying with the underworld God-aspect, although sometimes She stays willingly. In spring, She recovers Her consort and returns with Him to the surface to begin life with Her again. This specific example thus describes how a Tradition might accept, understand, and interpret the cycles of nature and the concept of death and life everlasting and ever-renewing; how a Tradition understands the annual impregnation of the Goddess as seen in Her aspect of Earth Mother by the God in His aspect of Sky Father, thus insuring the regeneration and renewal of all life.

The Mysteries of a Tradition will by necessity go far beyond this single theme of annual death and rebirth, and they will go beyond an explanation of the Sabbat festivals as depicted on the Wheel of the Year. They involve the very theology that comprises the heart and soul of the Tradition. The Mysteries are a Tradition's basic teachings about its history and lineage, about magickal ethics, and about Summerland and reincarnation. Much of the liturgy and ceremony that make up the rites and rituals, either wholly or in part, including the names of a patron god and goddess, are also usually part of a Tradition's Mysteries.

Each Tradition has its own set of Mysteries, and many prefer to keep their unique version known only to initiated members. The British Traditionals are typical examples of Craft

Mystery Traditions. Initiates are invariably oath-bound to never reveal the teachings they have received to the uninitiated.

In any case, if you are a largely eclectic or Solitary practitioner, it is highly unlikely that you will ever have access to the details of any of the existing oath-bound Mysteries. You can build your own, though, by developing your own set of ritual rules and your own version of how to practice Paganism. This can then eventually become your own Path with its own set of Mysteries. In time and with like-minded companions, it can evolve into more than a Solitary practice, more than a small Coven or even a Path, theoretically evolving into its own form of a Mystery Tradition. The British Traditional form of Gardnerian Wicca has certainly been augmented by dozens if not hundreds of other Traditions, some similar to the original as described by Gardner and some very diverse. Each in its own way has its own teachings and its own set of Mysteries, and each one rightfully calls itself a Wiccan Tradition.

Since the Old Religion is, before anything else, a religion devoted to the worship of nature as we understand Her, it is vitally necessary that you recognize the spiritual elements within Wicca before seriously contemplating the magickal elements. It is important that the novice understand that Wicca is a religion that venerates the mysteries of nature, and that witchcraft is really the practice of specific rites of magick within that religion. The magick of witchcraft manifests itself in power raising and spellcraft. It will develop and grow within you as you learn and evolve, and it will come in due time.

First and foremost, there must be in the practitioner an awareness of the origins and deep meanings of our ritual festivals in both the secular and the spiritual realms. There must be awareness, acceptance, and love of the Lord and Lady and an understanding of how we are all bound together; how we are all part of each other and part of all things both animate and inanimate, all part of the same life force, the same cosmic energy.

Sometimes this relationship between practitioner and deity does not come quickly. Sometimes it may even come painfully as your spiritual self grows. Regardless of how much time it takes or in what form it comes, this relationship will eventually manifest itself. It is not up to you to determine on your own when that will occur; the God and Goddess will tell you when, and They will do that in Their own good time. This is something that cannot be rushed and it cannot be ignored, since recognition of how we perceive our divinities, and our relationship and interaction with Them, lies at the core of what it means to be a witch.

If you do not or cannot, in your own heart and soul, recognize and experience this spiritual relationship, then anything you do in the way of rituals or magickal rites will be nothing more than mouthing words and going through the motions. The building of this relationship may take time and hard work, but as I mentioned previously, Wicca is essentially an esoteric religion and its workings were never meant to be quickly or easily understood by reading a few books.

In chapter 2, we discussed the Wiccan Law, the Wiccan Rede, and the Rule of Three. These are vitally important concepts, but they are only tools that will be used in the shaping of your own relationship with our deities and with all Their aspects. The relationship you must develop with Them will be a personal one built on the Wiccan tenet of perfect love and perfect trust, and, once established, it will never go away. It will change your life forever.

This book, and the dozens of others like it, should really be used as a starting point on your path through Wicca. Read them all, study as much as you possibly can, go to lectures, or, better yet, attend classes sponsored by your local Pagan or occult Craft shops. Work your way through the Craft, learning as you go, and eventually, sooner for some than others, the day will come when you realize that you are indeed Pagan, that you are indeed Wiccan. The Lord and Lady will let you know when the time is right, and there will be no mistaking it when They do.

Sabbat Rituals

There are eight festivals of celebration in the Wiccan year; four major festivals and four minor festivals, referred to as Sabbats. Remember that Wicca is a preindustrial, agrarian religion, one having its base of worship originally tied to and driven by nature. Aside from the religious significance attached to these holidays relating to the everlasting themes of birth, death, and rebirth, they all had a very real and secular meaning for the Neolithic and Paleolithic cultures that originally recognized them. Practices conducted at these festivals could literally mean the difference between survival and extinction for the clan; thus, performing the associated rites and practices was both a religious (prayers and invocations to the God and Goddess) and secular (planting, harvesting, and domestic animal slaughtering) series of events.

The four major Sabbats are Imbolc, Beltain, Lughnasadh, and Samhain. Imbolc is the time of the first planting of spring. Beltain, also called May Day, represents the rebirth of all nature and signifies the time for the second planting as well as cultivation of the spring crops. Lughnasadh is the first fall harvest, while Samhain is the time of the second fall harvest and the selection of livestock for slaughter to provide meat for the winter. The four minor Sabbats are the Spring Equinox (Ostara), the Summer Solstice (Litha), the Autumn Equinox (Mabon), and the Winter Solstice (Yule).

My personal Path of the Old Religion is Eclectic-Celtic Wicca, as I understand it through extensive reading as well as instruction from others on the same Path. The wording used in the following paragraphs naturally reflects my orientation; however, if you as an individual wish to pursue other ways of worship, that is fully understandable. What I offer in this section should serve only as guideline—I certainly do not pretend to present the definitive word on our Sabbats. There are many fine works available that describe the eight rituals in great detail, which I've noted in the bibliography. I urge you to read as many of them as possible, since if you are just beginning a study of Wicca, what you may be individually seeking will most assuredly not be found in any one single reference. The eight yearly Sabbats are described in the following paragraphs in the accepted order of appearance as understood in Celtic Wicca, beginning with the birth of the God at Yule and ending with His death at Samhain.

The festivities surrounding a Sabbat can last for several days, but the actual ritual performed in honor of the God and Goddess is typically held on the evening before the day of the actual event; this is the actual Sabbat. It does not matter if you are performing the Sabbat ritual in a large Coven, a small Coven, or as a Solitary. The rituals are an integral component of what it means to be Pagan, and you do not have to be Wiccan or a witch to worship at Sabbat. All that matters is a firm realization that you are recognizing and celebrating the changes in nature that represent the eternal cycle of life, death, and rebirth.

The following sections describe each Sabbat and some of the activities associated with honoring it. I do not go into great detail about ritual content since that will, in most cases, be determined by the Tradition or Path of the practitioner. It is not my intent in this book to give the reader a word-for-word ritual description complete with a fully annotated script for the Priest or Priestess. What I have attempted to provide are some very simple and general guidelines that any small Coven or Solitary practitioner could build on in establishing their own set of rituals. For the Solitary practitioner, I suggest that you select whatever you can use from both the High Priestess and High Priest parts of the rituals, treating them essentially as gender-free. Those ritual guidelines will be found at the end of each Sabbat description, and variations on calling the quarters and deity invocations can be found in the appendices. I urge you to use this text only as a general guide and to develop your own set of ritual wordings in your own vernacular.

The Sabbat descriptions and ritual content in this chapter have been taken mostly from my Book of Shadows and represent various materials that I have incorporated into my own rites and rituals over the years. Since I have been influenced extensively by at least Buckland, Cunningham, Fitch, and McCoy, and, to some extent, by the Farrars, you may see some of those influences reflected here.

Yule

Yule is celebrated at the Winter Solstice, the shortest day of the year. This occurs on about December 21, although the actual date can vary year to year. Yule is the Celtic celebration of the Goddess becoming the Great Mother, giving birth to the God who died at Samhain of the previous year. It is celebrated as the sun returns after the longest night of the year. In actuality, the holiday of Christmas has always been more Pagan than Christian, which is why many early Christians did not recognize it. Yule/Christmas was too closely associated with preexisting stories of Pagan deities possessing histories of divine birth, death, and resurrection that predated the stories of Jesus, sometimes by thousands of years.

The wreath is a typical Yule decoration, representing the Wheel of the Year. It is usually made of holly interspersed with pine cones representing the God, and either fruit or small seashells representing the Goddess. The Celts decorated evergreen trees with nuts, fruits, coins, and occasionally candles. The evergreen tree, holly, ivy, and mistletoe were important plants of the season, each in its own way symbolizing fertility and everlasting life. The traditional Yule log is also a Celtic custom, with the log decorated with evergreen and holly strands before being lit at sunset. The Yule log is burned throughout the night until sunrise the following morning, another representation of the return of the sun and the turning of the Wheel of the Year. The altar candle for Yule can be either purple or dark green. Some Pagans prefer to change the color of the God and Goddess candles from the more traditional red and white to red and dark green for the Yule Sabbat celebration. Typical decorations include holly, mistletoe, pine branches, or pine cones.

Some events for the Yule Sabbat could include an exchange of gifts between Coveners, a turning of a physical representation of the Wheel of the Year to help our Goddess in the birth of our God, and the placing of wishes for the coming year on a Yule tree. A basic ritual for Yule might involve the following steps:

Purify the area and cast your circle.

Call the quarters and invoke the Lord and Lady. A simple format for calling the East Quarter might be something like this:

Spirit of the East, Ancient One of Air, we call upon You to clear our minds and clear our hearts. Bring us Your clarity and Your protection, Spirit. We welcome You to our circle, enter and be with us. Welcome, Ancient One of Air. Blessed be.

After all quarters have been called, the High Priest can invoke the God with words similar to these:

Lord and Father whose symbol is the sun, return again to us and to the Lady our Goddess. Death has gone and life has come. Welcome back, Father God. Blessed be.

The High Priestess can then invoke the Goddess:

Lady and Mother, our God who comes from You has returned to us all. Come and join us, dear Lady, as we bid Him welcome. Blessed be.

If in Coven, *The Charge of the God* can be read by the High Priest. The High Priestess then says:

Welcome to the end of the solar year and to a new beginning. Our Lord has returned from death and, with our Lady, He will face the world again. May the Wheel turn ever onward. All hail Yule and welcome, Lord and Lady.

Coveners can exchange gifts, and wishes for the coming year can now be written and hung on the Yule tree.

Perform the Cake and Ale Rite.

Thank the Lord and Lady for Their attendance. A typical thank you to the deities can be said by either the High Priestess or High Priest and might consist of something like the following:

We thank You, Lord and Lady. We have rejoiced in Your presence here this night, and we ask for Your blessings of peace and love. Go in power, Lord and Lady. Hail and farewell. Blessed be.

Release the quarters and take down the circle. A release of the quarters, starting with the East, might be something like this:

Spirit of the East, Ancient One of Air, we give thanks for Your presence here tonight. We thank You for Your protection. Go in power, Spirit. Hail and farewell. Blessed be.

Imbolc

Imbolc occurs on February 2 and is the time of year when the God steps aside in favor of the Goddess and the first plantings of spring crops occur. This is the time for the Earth Goddess to prepare for the return of Her consort, the Sun God. Extensive lighting of ritual fires occurs at Imbolc, symbolizing birth, healing, and inspiration, and a lighted candle is carried through each room of the house. These rites are done to banish darkness and encourage the return of the sun's light and the warmth of spring. This holiday is also called Brigit's Day or Bride Day, in honor of the Celtic Goddess Brigit, also known as Bride or Brede. She is considered a goddess of fire and is the patroness of smithcraft, poetry, and healing. She bestows her special patronage on any woman about to be married or handfasted, with the woman being called a bride in Bride's honor.

A major symbol of Imbolc is the Candle Wheel, a small circular frame of lighted candles that can be either carried into the ritual circle or worn as a headdress by the High Priestess. The Grain Dolly is another symbol of Imbolc and is made from last year's grain sheaves twisted or woven to represent a symbolic figure of the Goddess. The figure is then laid in a small bed on Imbolc night to wait for the appearance of Her Sun God consort. Another custom of the holiday is the weaving of a "Brigit's Cross" from straw to hang around the house for protection. Imbolc is commonly recognized today by non-Pagans as Valentine's Day, with its associated romantic pursuits and the red heart that symbolizes those relationships.

Imbolc is traditionally the time for spiritual cleansing, purification, and initiations, and for retaking your own vows of dedication or consecration to the Goddess. The full text of *The Charge of the Goddess* is read at ritual, and this is the time for new initiates to take their Craft names. Evergreen and willow are traditional plants of Imbolc, and the typical colors for the altar candle are pink or pale green. Altar displays could include seeds and nuts. A basic ritual might involve the following steps:

Purify the area and cast your circle.

Call the quarters and invoke the Lord and Lady. A simple format for calling the South Quarter might be something like this:

> *Spirit of the South, Ancient One of Fire, we call upon*
> *You to warm our minds and hearts. Bring us the pure*
> *and cleansing heat of Your protection, Spirit. We wel-*
> *come You to our circle, enter and be with us. Welcome,*
> *Ancient One of Fire. Blessed be.*

A suitable invocation to the God might consist of the following words, as spoken by the High Priest, with the ubiquitous

Lord in the last sentence possibly being replaced by either the generic Sky Father or any specific name of the God:

> *Lord of death and resurrection, You who bring the gift of life, plant within us the seeds of Your own resurrection. As we are part of You, so are You part of us. Join with us, Lord. Blessed be.*

The High Priestess can then invoke the Goddess, either by specific name or with the generic Earth Mother or Great Mother title:

> *We behold You, Mother, our Earth Mother who teaches us that without spring there can be no summer, without summer no winter, and without winter no spring. Through the Lord and Lady we banish winter and welcome spring. Blessed be.*

If in Coven, the High Priestess then usually reads the long version of *The Charge of the Goddess*. If desired, Coveners can be led by the High Priestess in the following God and Goddess chant:

> *We all come from the Goddess, and to Her we shall return as water flowing to the ocean. We all come from the God, and to Him we shall return as sparks rising to the skies.*
>
> *Fruit and grain must wither to rise again,*
> *Both animal and we must die to be reborn.*
> *The God and Goddess live in each and every one.*

Perform any desired purification, consecration, or dedication rites.

Perform the Cake and Ale Rite.

Thank the Lord and Lady for Their attendance. A typical thank you to the deities can be said by either the High Priestess or High Priest and might consist of something like the following:

> *We thank You for Your presence, Lord and Lady, and we ask for Your blessing. May we all go forth in peace and love. All power is Yours. Hail and farewell, Lord and Lady. Blessed be.*

Release the quarters and take down the circle. A release of the quarters, starting with the East and moving now to the South, might be something like this:

> *Spirit of the South, Ancient One of Fire, we give thanks for Your presence here tonight. We thank You for Your protection. Go in power, Spirit. Hail and farewell. Blessed be.*

Coveners now adjourn for a ritual feast, if desired.

Ostara

Ostara celebrates the Spring Equinox, around March 21, but the actual date can vary year to year. It represents a new beginning, a rebirth of life as the first new plants emerge, and is celebrated with feasting. This is the time of balance between day and night, the time when light overtakes the darkness. It is one of the times of sexual union between God and Goddess, symbolizing the fertility of the year to come. Ostara is only one of the Sabbats that some Traditions accept as the time when the virgin Goddess first consummates her love with the Sun God and becomes impregnated with the new God, who will be born at Yule. Beltain, described later on in this chapter, is the other Sabbat sometimes revered as the time of mating between the God and Goddess. In this instance, I am using the word *virgin* in its original connotation, that of being unmarried, not of being chaste. Ostara or Beltain, depending on the Mysteries of your Tradition, represent the time of sexual union, marriage, or handfasting between God and Goddess.

This Pagan festival is symbolized by eggs as the meaning of new life and was appropriated by the Christian Church as Easter. The decorations for Ostara should be any of the spring flowers, and the altar candle is light green. This is a time to contemplate new beginnings or fresh ideas. A basic ritual might involve the following steps:

Purify the area and cast your circle.

Call the quarters and invoke the Lord and Lady. A simple format for calling the West Quarter might be something like this:

> *Spirit of the West, Ancient One of Water, we call upon You to refresh and clean our minds and hearts. Bring us Your purity and Your protection, Spirit. We welcome You to our circle, enter and be with us. Welcome, Ancient One of Water. Blessed be.*

The High Priest can open the invocations with something like the following. The name of the God can be changed as needed, or the generic names *Lord* or *Father God* can be used:

> *In the presence of the Ancient Ones, we invoke Thee, Father God. Be the warmth of spring within us and the flame of love that ignites us all. Blessed be, Lord.*

The High Priestess then can invoke the Goddess, either by the specific name or any of Her generic names:

> *Beginner of life, Mother of us all, You who are the womb of all creation, we invoke You by all Your thousands of names. We call upon You to join with us and join with our Lord. Blessed be, Mother Goddess.*

After the invocations, the High Priestess can say:

Merry meet to all at this rite of spring. Lord and Lady, we are here to welcome You and to welcome spring. Blessed be.

This is a time for serious meditation on your hopes and dreams for the coming year. The altar candle is moved to the center of the circle to act as a focal point as Coveners either vocalize their thoughts or keep them private. If your meditation is to be nonvocal, some signal must be decided upon in advance as to when to end the meditation session.

Perform the Cake and Ale Rite.

Thank the Lord and Lady for Their attendance. A typical thank you to the deities can be said by either the High Priestess or High Priest and might consist of something like the following:

We thank You, Lord and Lady. We have rejoiced in Your presence here this night and we ask for Your blessings as You depart. May we all go forth in peace and love. All power is Yours, Lord and Lady. Hail and farewell. Blessed be.

Release the quarters and take down the circle. A release of the quarters, starting with the East and moving now to the West, might be something like this:

Spirit of the West, Ancient One of Water, we give thanks for Your presence here tonight. We thank You for Your protection. Go in power, Spirit. Hail and farewell. Blessed be.

Beltain

Beltain, also sometimes spelled Beltane or Beltaine, occurs on May 1. It is typically presided over by the Goddess and represents the end of the spring planting season, the final change from hunting as a prime source of food to planting. Harvesting, both of crops and domestic animals, now occurs.

This and the Ostara festival of the Spring Equinox are both fertility festivals of the Wiccan year wherein the Church-levied charges of promiscuity and rampant sexual activity among Pagans may actually have some merit. Beltain in particular is a holiday of rejoicing and merriment and is quite typically celebrated with sexual abandon and gusto. Most of us readily acknowledge the phallic symbolism of the May Pole and the May Pole dance, which intertwines colored ribbons around the shaft, representing sexual union.

Long after the Christian form of marriage, with its sexual monogamy, had replaced Pagan handfasting, the rules of strict fidelity were still generally relaxed for May Eve, with some May Day customs being identical to the old Roman feast of flowers, the Floriala. This was three days of unrestrained and uninhibited sexuality beginning at sundown on April 28 and reaching a peak on May 1. There are other even older associations with May 1 in Celtic mythology. According to the ancient Irish *Book of Invasions*, the first settlers of Ireland arrived on May 1, and it was on May 1 that the plague came, which destroyed those people. Years later, the Tuatha De Danann, who in their turn had conquered Ireland, were themselves conquered by the Milesians on May Day.

Beltain is derived from a Celtic word meaning "balefire." The British royal family supposedly still lights the first balefire on May Eve, and it was a tradition for Pagans to take home some of the smoldering brands or embers from the village balefire to start their own cooking fires. Jumping over the smoldering balefire was thought to insure protection for the individual, and even livestock were occasionally driven through the smoke clouds for the same reason. Likewise, any ritual tools or clothing you may wish to protect or purify may be passed through the smoke of the Beltain fire.

All types of bells are rung on Beltain morning, and dancers around the May Pole traditionally wear bells on their clothing. The ringing bells are meant to scare away any bad spirits and bring protection to the ringers. The bells are typically hung over the entrances to homes after the Beltain celebrations, where they remain until the following year.

Any spring flower, and in particular the rose, is a symbol of Beltain. The altar candle is usually white, although red, symbolizing love, or pink, symbolizing deep affection, are also used. Beltain is the time to appreciate and accept the love and affection in your life given by a partner or even by the Lord and Lady. Like Ostara, it may even be considered a time to dwell on new beginnings, new concepts, or new ideas that have just been impregnated. A basic ritual might involve the following steps:

Purify the area and cast your circle.

Call the quarters and invoke the Lord and Lady. A simple format for calling the North Quarter might be something like this:

> *Spirit of the North, Ancient One of Earth, we call upon You to ground and strengthen our minds and hearts. Bring us Your strength and Your protection, Spirit. We welcome You to our circle, enter and be with us. Welcome, Ancient One of the Earth. Blessed be.*

The High Priestess can invoke the Goddess with something like the following, again substituting the name of the Lady as appropriate:

> *Dear Lady of mysteries, Queen of the Gods, we invoke Thee. We call upon Thee to join with us and to join with our Lord.*

The High Priest can then do the God invocation, such as something similar to this:

> *Dear Lord of all that is wild and free, King of the Gods, we invoke Thee. We call upon Thee to join with us and to join with our Lady.*

If in Coven, both the High Priestess and High Priest use tapers to light the altar candle simultaneously after the invocations. At this time, the Great Rite is usually performed, but it must be decided in advance and agreed on by all members of the Coven if the Rite is to be purely symbolic or if it is to be more explicit in nature. After completion of the Great Rite, the altar candle is moved to the center of the circle, and each Covener can express his or her feelings about the meaning of this Sabbat.

Perform the Cake and Ale Rite.

Thank the Lord and Lady for Their attendance. A typical thank you to the deities can be said by either the High Priestess or High Priest and might consist of something like the following:

> *We thank You, Lord and Lady. We have rejoiced in Your presence here this night and we ask for Your blessings as You depart. May we all go forth in peace and love. All power is Yours, Lord and Lady. Hail and farewell. Blessed be.*

Release the quarters and take down the circle. A release of the quarters, starting with the East and moving now to the North, might be something like this:

> *Spirit of the North, Ancient One of Earth, we give thanks for Your presence here tonight. We thank You for Your protection. Go in power, Spirit. Hail and farewell. Blessed be.*

Coveners now adjourn for the ritual feast.

Litha

Litha is the Midsummer festival occurring at the Summer Solstice, about June 21, but the actual date varies year to year. It is the longest day of the year and represents the peak of the God's strength. Both the Goddess and the Earth have been impregnated, and midsummer rituals are performed in order to protect and continue these pregnancies. Litha represents the midpoint of the year, and Pagans understand that the winter months will soon follow. Since it is the year's midpoint, it is also common in some Traditions for the High Priest to begin taking more of a dominant role in Sabbat rituals. The Pagan celebration of Litha was eventually adopted by the Christian Church as the Feast of John the Baptist.

It was the custom on this night to light large bonfires after sundown, which served the purpose of providing light to the revelers and warding off evil spirits. Other customs included decking the house with birch, St. John's wort, and white lilies. The two chief icons of the holiday are the spear, as the symbol of the Sun God in his glory, and the summer cauldron, as the symbol of the Goddess in her bounty. The Litha Sabbat is also a time for family gatherings or reunions, parties, and entertainment, with tribal or clan gatherings at Litha including various athletic games. The Sabbat is also typically known for the blessing of animals of all types, from farm animals to Familiars. Decorations for Litha are any of the summer flowers, and the altar candle is usually white or pale yellow.

This may be a time to reflect on the year thus far, to recognize the special strength of this Sabbat as a peak of magickal powers, and to realize that all things are cyclic and that nothing lasts forever. A basic ritual might involve the following steps:

Purify and cast your circle.

Call the quarters and invoke the Lord and Lady. A simple format for calling the East Quarter might be something like this:

Spirit of the East, Ancient One of the Air, we call upon You to clear our minds and clear our hearts. Bring us Your clarity and Your protection, Spirit. We welcome You to our circle, enter and be with us. Welcome, Ancient One of the Air. Blessed be.

The High Priestess can do an invocation to the Goddess similar to the following:

We call upon You, the ruler of the seas, of dreams, and of destiny. The tides of all belong to You, for You are the eternal woman everlasting, and we call to You.

The High Priest can then do an invocation to the God with something like the following words:

Hail Lord, You who are the warmth of the sun. We call and invoke You as our Lord of Light. We call to You to join with us. Come, Lord of the Greenwood, come to Your children.

If in Coven, the High Priest says:

All hail the Lord of the Greenwood, the Lord of light. As there must be pain in order to know joy, there must be darkness in order to know light. We thank our Lord for His spark of light and life, and for that love and trust that binds us all together.

The High Priest then usually reads *The Charge of the God.* The white altar candle can be moved to the center of the Coven circle, and all can take turns voicing their thanks or even their disappointment over events that occurred during the first half of the year, as well as their hopes and dreams for the second half.

Perform the Cake and Ale Rite.

Thank the Lord and Lady for Their attendance. A typical thank you to the deities can be said by either the High Priestess or High Priest and might consist of something like the following:

> *We thank You, Lord and Lady. We have rejoiced in Your presence here this night, and we ask for Your blessings as You depart. May we all go forth in peace and love. All power is Yours, Lord and Lady. Hail and farewell. Blessed be.*

Release the quarters and take down the circle. A release of the quarters, starting with the East, might be something like this:

> *Spirit of the East, Ancient One of the Air, we give thanks for Your presence here tonight. We thank You for Your protection. Go in power, Spirit. Hail and farewell. Blessed be.*

Litha is typically the night of maximum solar or god power and the longest day of the year. It is also a time of ease and enjoyment, a time to relax and to enjoy each other's company after the ritual, if the Coven so chooses.

Lughnasadh

Lughnasadh (also sometimes spelled Lughnasad or Lugnassad, pronounced *lew-nassa*) occurs on August 1. This is the time when the Goddess yields to the God as winter approaches and is essentially the first grain harvest festival. In his Celtic form, the god Lugh (as god of harvest, fire, and light) is honored, which gives this Sabbat its name. The Goddess is also honored for Her part in bringing forth the first yields of the winter harvest.

In Celtic Ireland, a feast was held at this time and was referred to as Lughnasadh, the feast to commemorate the funeral games of the Irish sun god Lugh, and was also the traditional time of year for craft festivals. The medieval guilds would create elaborate displays of their wares, decorating their shops and themselves in bright colors and ribbons and performing ceremonial plays or dances. A highlight of such festivals was a large wagon wheel that was taken to the top of a nearby hill, covered with tar, set on fire, and ceremoniously rolled down the hill. This is a Pagan rite symbolizing the end of summer, with the flaming disk representing the Sun God in his decline.

Lammas was the medieval Christian name for this holiday, meaning "loaf mass." This was the day on which loaves of bread were baked from the first grain harvest and placed on the church altars as offerings. It was a day representative of first fruits of the early harvest, and nothing the Church did could totally remove the Pagan connotations associated with this holiday.

Portions of the harvest are usually plowed back into the fields as a sacrifice to ensure that the remaining crops thrive until their time for harvest. Since this Sabbat is one of feasting, it is customary to eat samples of each of the grains, melons, and fruits harvested at this time, including the consumption of various breads, particularly corn bread, and drinks of ale or mead. This feast is typically dedicated to our Earth Mother, even though it is the god Lugh who is really being honored. Nuts and grains, as well as late summer flowers, are typical decorations for the Sabbat, and the altar candle is usually either gold or bright yellow.

A piece of fruit symbolizing the perfect fruit of the harvest is served at ritual, and a loaf of cornbread can also be consumed as part of the Cake and Ale Rite. This is a time of change and transformation when we reflect again on the events of the past year. A basic ritual might involve the following steps:

Purify and cast your circle.

Call the quarters and invoke the Lord and Lady. A simple format for calling the South Quarter might be something like this:

> *Spirit of the South, Ancient One of Fire, we call upon You to warm our minds and hearts. Bring us the pure and cleansing heat of Your protection, Spirit. We welcome You to our circle, enter and be with us. Welcome, Ancient One of Fire. Blessed be.*

An invocation to the God can be done by the High Priest, such as the following:

> *Blessed be the power of the Ancient Ones. Blessed be our Lord as the Wheel turns ever onward.*

The High Priestess can invoke the Goddess with words like this:

> *Blessed be the power of the Ancient Ones, blessed be the Lady, and blessed be Her Lord as the Wheel turns ever onward.*

If in Coven, the High Priest says:

> *Great is the power of our Lord through our Goddess. Blessed be our Lord and blessed be our Lady. May the fruits of Their union sustain us and the land. We thank the Lord and Lady for Their unending bounty.*

The High Priest and High Priestess can lead Coveners in the God and Goddess chant:

We all come from the Goddess and to Her we shall return as water flowing to the ocean. We all come from the God and to Him we shall return as sparks rising to the skies.

> *Fruit and grain must wither to rise again,*
> *Both animal and we must die to be reborn.*
> *The God and Goddess live in each and every one.*

The altar candle is moved to the center of the circle, and each Covener comments or discusses his or her views on events of the past year.

Perform the Cake and Ale Rite.

Thank the Lord and Lady for Their attendance. A typical thank you to the deities can be said by either the High Priestess or High Priest and might consist of something like the following:

We thank You, Lord and Lady. We have rejoiced in Your presence here this night, and we ask for Your blessings as You depart. May we all go forth in peace and love. All power is Yours, Lord and Lady. Hail and farewell. Blessed be.

Release the quarters and take down the circle. A release of the quarters, starting with the East and moving now to the South, might be something like this:

Spirit of the South, Ancient One of Fire, we give thanks for Your presence here tonight. We thank You for Your protection. Go in power, Spirit. Hail and farewell. Blessed be.

Coveners now adjourn for the ritual feast.

Mabon

Mabon, also known as the Autumn Equinox or Harvest Home, occurs on about September 21, with the actual date varying somewhat year to year. It represents another day of balance between light and dark, but is the time of year when darkness overtakes the light. This is the holiday of rest from harvesting and is a celebration of thanks for the crops and herds of the previous year.

This is the Pagan day of thanksgiving. Any festival of Thanksgiving that may have first been celebrated in the New World's Plymouth Colony quite possibly grew out of this original Pagan observance, as the Pilgrims gave thanks for the success of their previous year's crops. As Pagans, we thank the Goddess for Her abundance of the year and for Her blessings, with part of the Mabon ritual feast typically dedicated to the Goddess as sacrifice. Harvest Home, or Mabon, involves a concept of sacrifice that is purely symbolic. The sacrifice is the spirit of vegetation, sometimes understood to be personified by John Barleycorn.

Mabon decorations could include any of the harvest foods, particularly wheat, corn, apples, grapes, or peaches. The altar candles are usually either dark brown or red. This is the time to be thankful for the blessings of the previous year and to accept those things that have been given to you. A basic ritual might involve the following steps:

Purify and cast your circle.

Call the quarters and invoke the Lord and Lady. A simple format for calling the West Quarter might be something like this:

> *Spirit of the West, Ancient One of Water, we call*
> *upon You to refresh and clean our minds and hearts.*
> *Bring us Your purity and Your protection, Spirit. We*

welcome You to our circle, enter and be with us. Welcome, Ancient One of Water. Blessed be.

The High Priest can do an invocation such as the following:

Lord of us all who will soon depart this cycle of the Wheel. We welcome You tonight in the knowledge that though You must leave us, You will return. Blessed be, Lord. Welcome and blessed be.

The High Priestess can then invoke the Goddess with phrases such as the following:

As our Lady prepares to escort Her son and lover to the door of death, we welcome Her. We welcome Her in the knowledge that She will return Him safely to us as the Wheel turns yet again. Blessed be, Lady. Welcome and blessed be.

If in Coven, the High Priest says:

Now we enjoy the fruit of our harvest, the fruit of our year's work, as our Lord begins His journey into night. To our Lord and Lady we give and ask blessings of love and abundance.

The altar candle is moved to the center of the circle, and Coveners are given the opportunity to describe what they have been thankful for during the past year.

Perform the Cake and Ale Rite.

Thank the Lord and Lady for Their attendance. A typical thank you to the deities can be said by either the High Priestess or High Priest and might consist of something like the following:

We thank You, Lord and Lady. We have rejoiced in Your presence here this night, and we ask for Your blessings as You depart. May we all go forth in peace and

love. All power is Yours, Lord and Lady. Hail and
farewell. Blessed be.

Release the quarters and take down the circle. A release of the quarters, starting with the East and moving to the West, might be something like this:

Spirit of the West, Ancient One of Water, we give
thanks for Your presence here tonight. We thank You
for Your protection. Go in power, Spirit. Hail and
farewell. Blessed be.

Samhain

Samhain (pronounced *sow-en*) occurs on October 31 and means "summer's end" in Celtic. This is the end of autumn and the beginning of winter. In the ancient dual division of the year, summer ran from Beltain to Samhain, and winter ran from Samhain to Beltain. Samhain is thus the Celtic New Year Sabbat and is a God-dominated holiday. Now is the time for possible travel and communication between the worlds of the living and the dead, and between those who are here now and those who have gone into Summerland. The two themes of celebrating the dead and attempting to see into the future are intermixed at Samhain just as they are in many modern New Year's Eve celebrations. As a feast of the dead, it was believed the dead could, if they wished, return to the land of the living for this one night to celebrate with their family, tribe, or clan. Extra places are set at the table and food is set out for anybody who died that year.

It is also traditional to leave an offering of food or drink at the doorstep on this night to refresh those souls who may wander between the two worlds. This is the origin of our Western holiday of Halloween, with its attendant offerings of treats to young "ghosts and goblins" going door to door. Carved turnips were the original jack-o'-lanterns and were carried by Celtic travelers going from feast to feast on Samhain night to dissuade any wondering spirits from interfering. This symbol continues today in our use of carved and illuminated pumpkins.

The Samhain Sabbat celebrates the eternal cycle of reincarnation and marks the beginning of the Celtic winter. The old God dies tonight to be reborn at Yule, and the Wheel of the Year will continue. Samhain is not totally a somber Sabbat; it is also a time of games and frivolity. Harmless and mischievous pranks can be performed and blamed on the spirits of fun, while feasting from the fall harvest and final slaughter of the herds for meat can result in lavish Samhain ritual meals.

With such an important holiday, Pagans might hold two distinct celebrations—a large Halloween party for non-Craft friends, often held on the previous weekend, and a Coven ritual held on Halloween night itself, which is done late enough so as not to be interrupted by trick-or-treaters. If the rituals are performed properly, there is often a feeling of invisible friends taking part in the rites.

Fall fruits such as apples, harvest foods of gourds and melons, and fall grains or nuts are typical Samhain decorations. The altar candle is usually either orange or brown. A basic ritual might involve the following steps:

Purify and cast your circle.

Call the quarters and invoke the Lord and Lady. A simple format for calling the North Quarter might be something like this:

Spirit of the North, Ancient One of Earth, we call upon You to ground and strengthen our minds and hearts. Bring us Your strength and Your protection, Spirit. We welcome You to our circle, enter and be with us. Welcome, Ancient One of the Earth. Blessed be.

An invocation to the God is spoken by the High Priest, such as this:

> *Lord of life and Lord of death, we both welcome You and bid You farewell this night. We urge You swiftly through the gates of death so that You may return to bless us with Your strength, love, and guidance. Blessed be, dear Lord, blessed be.*

The High Priestess can then do an invocation to the Goddess, such as this:

> *Mother of us all, be with us this night. Bless us with Your strength, love, and guidance as our Lord enters the darkness of death. Be with Your children, Mother. Guide us and comfort us. So mote it be.*

If in Coven, both the High Priestess and High Priest use tapers to light the altar candle simultaneously. The High Priestess says:

> *Gracious Goddess, we thank You for the joy and bounty of this year. Walk with our Lord into the darkness to bring Him safely again into the light, He who is with us at the beginning and end of time, the darkness of death and the spark of life. We give thanks to You, Lady, who shall see His safe return.*

The High Priest and High Priestess can lead Coveners in a Samhain chant:

> *'Tis the time of death that will have an end, let life return, life without end. Open body and spirit wide, for tonight is the change of the tide. As we have welcomed death with all our hearts, now we embrace life as death departs.*

The altar candle can be moved to the center of the circle, giving each Covener a chance to talk about the loss of any loved one, friend, pet, or Familiar during the year.

Perform the Cake and Ale Rite.

Thank the Lord and Lady for Their attendance. A typical thank you to the deities can be said by either the High Priestess or High Priest and might consist of something like the following:

> *We thank You, Lord and Lady. We have rejoiced in Your presence here this night and we ask for Your blessings as You depart. May we all go forth in peace and love. All power is Yours, Lord and Lady. Hail and farewell. Blessed be.*

Release the quarters and take down the circle. A release of the quarters, starting with the East, might be something like this:

> *Spirit of the North, Ancient One of the Earth, we give thanks for Your presence here tonight. We thank You for Your protection. Go in power, Spirit. Hail and farewell. Blessed be.*

Coveners now adjourn for the ritual feast.

Esbat Rituals

Both the major and minor Sabbats are festivals of rejoicing or celebration, and no magickal work is done at these rituals. The Sabbats are solar-driven, representing celebrations directed at fertility, life, death, and rebirth of both animal and plant life. Esbats, however, are rituals held at specific phases of the lunar cycle in order to acknowledge the Lady in Her aspect of the Lady of the night sky, or to do work in the form of spellcraft or other magick. The esbats are typically held at the full moon, if worshipping the Lady in Her nurturing or mother aspect; at the dark moon, if some of our stronger more basic emotions such as anger or passion are to be involved; or at the appropriate lunar phase, if specific magickal work such as growth, healing, or banishing is to be done. The full moon and dark moon esbat rituals are discussed in the following paragraphs, but the magickal workings of spellcraft will be discussed in detail in chapter 6.

I have included three tables at the end of this chapter. Table 4 is a full moon table, and table 5 is a dark moon table, both listing full and dark moon dates through the year 2004. Table 6 is a lunar correspondence table that gives the Craft name of each full moon by month as well as a brief summary of each month's lunar meaning. Additional lunar phase information can also be obtained online from any of the many moon phase calendar websites, one of which is listed in the bibliography, as well as from *The Old Farmer's Almanac* or *The American Ephemeris and Nautical Almanac*.

Full Moon

The full moon esbat is a recognition and acceptance of the Goddess, an understanding of Her eternal presence and Her influence over all aspects of fertility in the reproduction of both plant and animal. It is the time to acknowledge Her as the creatrix and protectress of us all and to give thanks for Her guidance and love. The full moon esbat is typically done in a cast circle, but there is nothing wrong with simply taking a few minutes and just connecting with Her. I have spent more than one esbat pausing for five or ten minutes at our indoor altar and just contemplating what She has given me and thanking Her. Sometimes I have spent the night sitting outside under the moon with only a white Goddess candle, meditating on what it means to me to recognize Her divinity, to be a Pagan, and to follow the path She has set me on. The important thing is to acknowledge Her and to recognize Her; this is the essence of the full moon esbat.

This ritual does not necessarily need to be done on the exact night of the full moon, but it should be performed no more than one night on either side of the full moon night. It should be done outside fairly soon after moonrise when the moon is in view and can shine on the worshipper, if at all possible and weather permitting. The moon shining through tree branches is perfectly acceptable, but buildings or other structures should not obscure the lunar disk.

Since this is a lunar ritual in praise of the Lady, it is not always necessary to use a God candle unless you personally feel it necessary. You will need the nominal circle-casting tools as well as at least the white Goddess candle. Arrange the quarter candles, and place the Goddess candle at the East side of your circle so that you can sit while facing it and the rising moon. Cast the circle, call the quarters, and, either standing or kneeling in front of the Goddess candle, open your arms wide to Her and recite an invocation to the Lady. The following is one I have used many times that seems to have an especially comforting effect, making me feel quite close to the Lady. This invocation is a somewhat modified version of one of Scott Cunningham's full moon rites, the complete text of which can be found in appendix B. You can easily modify this one or develop one of your own that may be more suitable to your personal feelings.

Wondrous Lady of the Moon, Silver Lady of the night sky, Mistress of the night and of all magick. You who reveal all mysteries past and present. You who are ruler of the tides of seas and the tides of woman. All-wise lunar Mother, queen of the night sky, I greet You with a rite in Your honor. My Lady of Silver Magick, I ask that Your gracious presence be with me here this night to guide and strengthen me. May all magick and power be Yours. Blessed be, dear Lady, blessed be.

When the invocation is completed, it is traditional to have the High Priestess, or some other appointed Priestess, read the full text of *The Charge of the Goddess*. Additionally, the rite known as Drawing Down the Moon can also be performed, although Drawing Down the Moon requires multiple participants and is therefore not a viable rite for Solitaries.

After completing all invocations and rites, sit comfortably with your arms either outstretched to Her or even folded in your lap. Close your eyes and envision Her as you believe Her to be in Her form as our Mother. Talk to Her about what is in your heart, your innermost thoughts and feelings, and give Her a chance to answer you. Do not be surprised if some sign appears; tree branches may rustle when there is no wind, small animals may sniff at the edge of your circle, or you may actually hear Her voice in your ears. Know that She hears you and that She is there. The very stillness of the night may represent Her presence. Now is the time to sit and meditate on what our Lady means to you personally, on what it means to be Pagan, and to express your love to Her. If several practitioners are present, this would be a good time for each to vocalize some of these feelings. Take as much time as you need because She will be there in some form—you can count on it.

This is also the time when some witches like to do a short rededication or a thank you to the Lady for whatever She may have helped with during the past month, or maybe just to say thank you for Her love and guidance. If you are working in a

Coven environment, the Cake and Ale Rite can be included, if desired. When you feel the time is right, thank the Lady for Her attendance and bid Her good night:

> *Gracious Lady, we give thanks for Your presence here tonight. We give thanks for Your love and guidance, and for Your attendance in our circle. May all strength and magickal power be Yours. Hail and farewell, dear Lady. Blessed be.*[1]

Release the quarters and take down your circle. The ritual is ended.

Dark Moon

While the full moon represents the Goddess in all Her loving and nurturing aspects of the mother, there is also a dark side to Her that is addressed at the new moon or what is usually called the dark moon. In this aspect, She can be chaotic, angry, petulant, and even wantonly sexy, the temptress. Some workings will also place heavy emphasis on the potential sexual or even martial components that may manifest. It is not uncommon for the High Priest to take a dominant role in this rite, even though the moon is always a Goddess symbol, as opposed to the High Priestess, who usually leads most rites and rituals.

This is a time when very strong protection or defensive work can be done. It is also the time to look deep inside one's self, to get in touch with the darker and baser elements of the psyche, and the time to recognize and deal with aggression, anger, or fear. The Dark Lady is all these things, and if you are working in a Coven environment, that particular aspect of Her that you call upon during a dark moon rite must be fully understood by all participants. It will do absolutely no good for anyone if even a single member of your group is focusing on fear when the rest are all focused on anger.

The following rite is one used by our Coven to channel and vent anger. It seems to have worked fairly well for us in the past, but I suggest that you use this structure only as a guideline for developing your own wording of the ritual. Since this is a ritual aimed at anger, a volatile expression with significant martial overtones, we typically use a red altar candle. The size of the candle depends on the number of participants, since each person must inscribe a single word on the candle body that is representative of the anger he or she wishes to face and release. For our Coven, a taper of six or seven inches usually works quite nicely.

Cast your circle as you normally do, but, because of the nature of the work, I suggest that the area be purified both before and after this ritual. If you cannot purify afterward, at least be sure to do so before any other workings are done in the same place at a later time. After the circle has been cast and the quarters called, the High Priestess takes the Goddess position and invokes the Goddess:

> *Dark Lady, Queen of the Underworld, creatrix of us all and protectress of all the Wicca. We call upon You to join us this night. Be with us, accept our place in Your realm, assist and protect us in this rite. So mote it be.*

The High Priest then assumes the God position and invokes the God:

> *Dear Lord, consort of our Lady, creator of us all and protector of all the Wicca. We call upon You to join us this night. Be with us, accept our place in Your realm, assist and protect us in this rite. So mote it be.*

The High Priest then takes up the red altar candle and holds it aloft in both hands as the High Priestess recites *The Call to the Goddess*. Please note that this *Call* is not the same thing as *The Charge of the Goddess* that was referenced and quoted earlier. The entire *Call* from appendix B can be read, if desired, or a somewhat shortened and modified form that is more directed to the work at hand can be used, such as this:

> *You who are the Great Mother, worshipped by all. You who are the primal female force, boundless and eternal. Goddess of the moon, Lady of all magic, the winds and moving leaves sing Your name. Tonight we worship You as the channel of our anger, we seek the wisdom of the Crone and the passion of the Dark Lady. Goddess of the Moon, the Earth, the Seas, Your names and strengths are manifold. You pour forth magick and power. You are the eternal Maiden, Mother of all and Crone of darkness, and we ask Your blessings of limitless understanding at this rite.*[2]

The High Priest then takes his athame and inscribes the word most representative of his anger on the candle body. He passes it to the Covener on his right, typically the High Priestess, so that it moves around the circle widdershins. Each member of the Coven similarly inscribes the candle until it has come full circle back to the High Priest. The High Priest then again holds the candle overhead in both hands as he recites *The Call to the God*. Please note that this *Call* is not the same thing as *The Charge of the God* that was referenced and quoted earlier. The entire *Call* from appendix B can be read, if desired, or a somewhat shortened and modified form that is more directed to the work at hand can be used, such as this:

You who are the radiant King of the Heavens, who lifts Your shining spear to light the lives of all beings and daily pour forth Your gold upon the Earth, You who are the master of the beasts wild and free. We worship You as the thousand-named protector of all the Wicca, as the great hunter and warrior. We worship You as the consort of the Dark Lady, and we ask You to send Your rays of blessings to guide and strengthen the minds of us all in this rite.[3]

The High Priest lights the red candle from the altar Goddess candle and places it in the center of the Coven circle, usually on a pentagram tile or pentagram drawing. All Coveners, either sitting or standing, hold hands and channel their thoughts into the candle—all their thoughts surrounding the words they have inscribed on the candle body describing their anger. As everyone does so, the High Priest leads the Coveners in a power-raising chant, gradually increasing the pitch and volume over several minutes until the energy is felt to peak. The Witches Rune chant, as described in the section "Power Raising" in the following chapter, is an excellent choice here. Then the High Priest rapidly lifts his hands skyward along with those on either side of him, so that everyone in the circle has their linked hands upraised and all release the energy in a loud yell or scream. Sometimes the exclamation "By the Power of Three Times Three, So Shall It Be!" is used to release the energy. The vocal release is usually said three times, with maximum emphasis on the last utterance. Afterward, everybody must ground themselves thoroughly, which may take several minutes, in order to release any residual energy.

If the participants have elected to stand during this rite rather than sit or kneel, all should begin moving widdershins at the same time the High Priest begins the chant. The move-

ment increases in speed as the chant builds, with the buildup
and release of energy being done as described above. After
grounding, the Cake and Ale Rite is observed while the red
candle is left either to burn itself out in the middle of the
Coven circle, or it can be moved to the altar after the circle is
opened at the end of the rite.

In order to close the rite, the High Priestess thanks the
Goddess:

> *Dark Lady of the night, we give thanks for Your*
> *presence here with us and for allowing us this release*
> *of our anger. Hail and farewell, dear Lady. Go in*
> *power. Blessed be.*

The High Priest then thanks the God:

> *Dear Lord, we give thanks for Your presence here*
> *with us and for allowing us this release of our anger.*
> *Hail and farewell, Lord. Go in power. Blessed be.*

The quarters are then released, and the circle is taken down in
the usual way.

It is common during the grounding process or during the
Cake and Ale Rite for Coveners to embrace and hold onto
one another, either in pairs or as a group while still in circle,
in order to put a closure to the ritual. Some very basic emotions and feelings may have been tapped into and released
during a performance of a dark moon ritual, so do not be surprised if spontaneous reactions surface almost immediately.
These reactions could possibly manifest in tears, intimate
hugging, or other physical contact between Coveners. There
is nothing to be alarmed at or to feel guilty about if this does
occur. It is a normal response to the stirring and releasing of
some very primal urges.

It is also one reason why the dark moon ritual is seldom, if ever, done in public, and is never done without consenting participants who are all fully aware of these possible reactions. It is, to a great extent, the responsibility of the High Priest to keep everything under control and be sure the emphasis is first and foremost on grounding the excess energy, not solely on physical contact with your immediate partner or partners. Remember from chapter 3 on the ethics of the Inviolate Circle that you have an obligation to protect your fellow Coveners. Assume some responsibility of control for yourself while recalling that whatever is said and done by anybody within the confines of the circle must remain within the circle —there are no exceptions.

This rite, as I have described it above, is aimed at the anger component. You will need to make suitable modifications if other emotions are to be addressed, including changing the text of *The Call to the God* and *The Call to the Goddess* as necessary in order to fit your own requirements.

Not all rites done during the dark moon need to be aimed at our more basic or volatile urges, instincts, and desires. This time of the Lady's persona can also be devoted simply to getting more in touch with your inner feelings or thoughts, particularly as they may relate to the Lady as the all-wise and loving grandmother, Her Crone aspect. It is also the ideal time for divination, particularly with the scrying mirror. The arts of divination are discussed in detail in chapter 7, as is a suitable Crone ritual, but the following dark moon working will give you a reference point in addition to the more volatile working just described. This part of the rite can begin with the same form of invocation that was used in the preceding rite.

After the circle has been cast and the quarters called, the High Priestess takes the Goddess position and invokes the Goddess:

Dark Lady, Queen of the Underworld, creatrix of us all and protectress of all the Wicca. We call upon You to join us this night. Be with us, accept our place in Your realm, assist and protect us in this Rite. So mote it be.

Coveners can then link hands and chant, usually three times in succession, several of the various Goddess names together, each time ending with the phrase "and by all the thousands of names by which You are known." Here is an example:

Isis, Astarte, Kali, Demeter, Cerridwen, Bridget, Dana, Diana . . . and by all the thousands of names by which You are known.

Insert as many of Her other names as you see fit, but keep in mind that this passage will be recited by all Coveners; thus, the number of names should probably be kept to a minimum. The High Priestess then raises her hands from the kneeling Goddess position and recites the following:

We welcome the Dark Lady to our circle. We welcome our maiden, our mother, and our grandmother. She who shows us the cycle of our own lives, the beginning, the middle, and the ending. She who is youthful spirit, She who is nurturing, and She who is all-wise. We open our arms and embrace Her in all Her many aspects, for in all of these She is we and we are Her. We bid You welcome to our circle, Lady, and ask Your blessing and guidance. Join us, Lady, join us now. Welcome and blessed be.

Now is the time to pass and use the scrying mirror, or to just sit while each Covener either meditates or vocalizes on what this aspect of the Goddess means to him or her. When this part of the ritual is completed, it is appropriate to do the Cake and Ale Rite. Then release the Circle with words similar to the following:

> *Dark Lady of the night, we give thanks for Your presence here with us this night. Hail and farewell, dear Lady. Go in power. Blessed be.*

Note that the God element has not been represented in this ritual. It is up to each individual as to whether the God should be invoked or otherwise included, but many tend to feel that this particular ritual is devoted to the Goddess only, since it is Her in Her Crone aspect that is being addressed. However, if you feel the necessity to include the God, as well, then by all means do so.

Grounding

It is essential that after power has been raised or spell work has been done, that any and all residual energies in your body be allowed to flow back into the earth. Since your body has been the conduit for the movement and shaping of energy, it will by necessity retain some of that very energy even after you have launched or directed it. In order to properly ground yourself, you should be sitting on the floor or ground with both hands placed firmly on the same surface, palms down. If necessary, you can even lower your forearms and head so that they, too, come in contact with the grounding surface. Remain in this position for several minutes until you feel that the excess energy has all drained away.

Chapter Summary

The purpose of this chapter on our basic Sabbat and esbat rituals is to give you a brief and very basic introduction to these activities. You have hopefully found enough information here to whet your appetite for more, and will now make the effort to delve deeper into our rites and rituals by examining the books listed in the bibliography. For the novice, I believe you would be best served by reading almost anything by either Buckland or Cunningham as a starting point.

I think it bears repeating here that it is imperative that you not settle on any one work or on any one author as the absolute and final source of your information. Our Craft is simply too rich and too complex for that. Read as much as you can get your hands on. If you cannot accept an existing Path or Tradition from the information obtained in your readings, then develop your own sets of rituals and Mysteries and your own Path. Whether you approach the Craft of the Wise from within a structured Tradition or as a Solitary on an eclectic Path, the choice is yours and the rewards to be reaped are also yours.

Table 4
Full Moon Dates Through 2004

	1999	2000	2001	2002	2003	2004
January	1, 31	20	9	28	18	7
February	—	19	8	27	6	6
March	2, 31	19	9	28	18	6
April	30	18	7	26	16	5
May	30	18	7	26	15	4
June	28	16	5	24	14	3
July	28	16	5	24	13	2, 31
August	26	15	4	22	12	29
September	25	13	2	21	10	28
October	24	13	2	21	10	27
November	23	11	1, 30	19	8	26
December	22	11	30	19	8	26

The instances in this table where there are two dates for each month, such as January 1999 showing "1, 31," indicates that there are two full moons in that month—one on January 1 and another on January 31—a so-called "blue moon" month.

Table 5
Dark Moon Dates Through 2004
(extrapolated from table 4)

	1999	2000	2001	2002	2003	2004
January	17	5	25	13	3	22
February	16	4	23	12	2	21
March	17	4	24	13	3	21
April	15	3	22	11	1	20
May	15	3	22	11	30	19
June	13	1	20	9	29	18
July	12	1	20	9	28	17
August	11	30	19	7	27	15
September	9	29	17	6	25	14
October	9	29	17	6	25	13
November	7	27	16	4	23	12
December	7	27	15	4	23	12

Table 6
Lunar Correspondence Table

Month   **Name**
Correspondence

January   *Wolf Moon*
A time of new beginnings, protection, and reversing spells. Release the past and accept the events of the coming year. Let go of unwanted or unneeded things.

February   *Storm Moon*
A time of growth and healing as well as self-forgiveness and acceptance of past actions. Discover the new potential within yourself.

March   *Seed Moon*
Nurture new desires and new beginnings. See the truth in your life and determine the spiritual needs you wish to expand. Reverse poverty in the spiritual as well as the material worlds.

April   *Hare Moon*
Instill self-confidence and reliance. Work spells to control or enhance your spiritual and emotional well-being.

May   *Dyad Moon*
Improve your intuition and creativity through contact with the spirit worlds. This is a time of cleaning and purification, and a time to see the interacting harmony in all things.

June   *Mead Moon*
Take responsibility for present happenings and reward yourself for positive actions and accomplishments. Seek inspiration and guidance from the deities through meditation.

July   Wort Moon

Plan and meditate on achieving your goals spiritually, emotionally, and physically. Prepare yourself for success.

August   Corn Moon

Preserve what you have attained and prepare to reap the rewards of your efforts. This is a time of harvest and of appreciation of all things, both spiritual and material.

September   Harvest Moon

Realize your goals and rejoice in attaining them. Clean out any emotional, spiritual, mental, or physical clutter in your life. Now is the time to harvest and accept your rewards.

October   Blood Moon

This is a time of thanks and of letting go of the past. Honor those things in all realms, particularly the animals, that have given their lives to sustain and maintain yours, and ask their understanding in that sacrifice.

November   Snow Moon

Remove all negativity, and strengthen your communications with your patron deities.

December   Oak Moon

Maintain your principles and convictions. Extend your warmth to friends and family, and welcome new beginnings.

1. See Scott Cunningham, *Wicca: A Guide for the Solitary Practitioner* (Saint Paul, Minn.: Llewellyn Publishing, 1988) 125.
2. Ibid, 114.
3. Ibid, 115.

5

Other Rites

*T*he *1999 World Book Encyclopedia* defines *ritual* as "a form or system of rites,"[1] and *rite* as "a solemn ceremony, formal procedure, or act in a religious or other observance."[2] We can thus consider a rite to be something usually performed within the broader definition of a ritual. The Sabbat festivals or esbat ceremonies are times when special rituals are done, and, as part of those rituals, we may also perform specific rites. The rededication rite typically done during the ritual of the Imbolc Sabbat is an example.

There are many rites within Paganism and within Wicca that are done in conjunction with other rites or rituals, and many that can be done independent of a supporting ritual. Your Tradition or Path will generally dictate what rites will be performed and if they will or will not be done inside the framework of a larger ritual. There are, however, several rites that I believe are more or less common to most of the major

Wiccan Traditions. These include the Consecration, Dedication, or Initiation Rites, the rites used for the consecration of tools, raising power, Drawing Down the Moon, the Great Rite, as well as Handfasting and Passing into the Summerland. There are many others, but these are several of the major ones.

Some of these rites, because of the very nature of our religion, have, either totally or in part, an overt or rather explicit sexual overtone. These could include parts of the Initiation or Dedication Rite as well as the Great Rite. Do not lose sight of the fact that Wicca is firstly a religion dedicated to the worship of nature, or more directly to the worship of the rejuvenation of nature through rebirth. This concept must by necessity involve a sexual element or component at some level, either physically between Coven members or symbolically. It is up to you as the practitioner to decide which parts of any of these rites, or possibly even the entire rite, may not be suitable for your Coven and to make the necessary modifications to the ritual that you feel are necessary. Going back to our discussion in chapter 2 about the Inviolate Circle, it is absolutely essential in building the trust between your Coven members that each and every one of you are fully aware of how these rites are to be performed and the meanings behind them.

There is nothing wrong with later changing your approach to some of the rites. You may elect for now to eliminate something like the Fivefold Kiss from your practice, yet possibly decide to reinstate it at a future time when all participants are more comfortable with the internal relationships and dynamics of your group. It's important to recognize that parts of the various rites might better be left undone or possibly modified and that each member of the Coven must be totally aware of and totally in agreement about how the rites will be handled.

As in working skyclad or not, once you set the precedent, stick with it until such time that all can agree to make a change—there must not be any surprises.

While the rite descriptions are in my own words, they may reflect the influence of various teachers as well as suggestions from friends and members of my own Coven

The Consecration Rite

This is one variation on the Consecration Rite drawn from my own interpretation of the rite and inspired by the works of Scott Cunningham and Raymond Buckland. There are many other variants of greater and lesser complexity, with some having a more sexual connotation than this one.

If in Coven, the Consecration Rite is normally done by the High Priestess if the consecratee is male, and by the High Priest if the consecratee is female. The person to be consecrated is led to the center of the circle, turned to face the altar, and asked to assume the Goddess position. The High Priest/ess then says:

> *(Consecratee's name), do you wish to consecrate yourself to our Earth Mother, by whatever name you choose to call Her, and by all the thousands of names She is known?*

The consecratee answers in the affirmative, and the High Priest/ess then recites the words of the Consecration Rite as the consecratee repeats them:

> *Earth Mother (or deity name if desired), I stand before You as Your child. I stand before You in full realization of Your love and acceptance. May that love grow and flourish in me as it has in the countless numbers of*

*my brothers and sisters who have stood before You
throughout all time. Mother, as the creatrix of us all, I
return as Your child to be reborn yet again. Blessed be.*

The High Priest/ess circles deosil three times around the consecratee while sprinkling him or her with salted water, saying:

*Earth Mother, this is Your child (given name), newly
consecrated by earth and water in Your name and in
Your service.*

The High Priest/ess circles deosil three times around the consecratee with an incense sensor, saying:

*Earth Mother, this is Your child (given name), newly
consecrated by fire and air in Your name and in Your
service.*

The High Priest/ess then assists the consecratee to sit or kneel
in front of the altar to allow him or her to meditate for a few
minutes on what the Consecration Rite means. When the consecratee signals to the High Priest/ess that the meditation has
been completed, the High Priest/ess assists the consecratee to
stand, embraces him or her briefly, then introduces the newly
consecrated individual to the rest of the Coven:

*My friends, this is your brother/sister, newly conse-
crated to our Earth Mother. I charge you to welcome
him/her, to guide him/her in the Mysteries of our Craft,
and to love and trust him/her as you love and trust each
other. So mote it be.*

If the Consecration Rite is to be done by a Solitary, it can be
considerably shortened. Sit or kneel in front of your altar and
repeat the following:

*Earth Mother (or deity name if desired), I stand be-
fore You as Your child. I stand before You in full realiza-*

tion of Your love and acceptance. May that love grow and flourish in me as it has in the countless numbers of my brothers and sisters who have stood before You throughout all time. Mother, as the creatrix of us all, I return as Your child to be reborn yet again. Blessed be.

After the rite is done, sprinkle yourself with salted water and wave the smoking incense around your body, saying:

Earth Mother, I am Your child (given name), now consecrated by earth, air, fire, and water in Your name and in Your service.

Remain sitting or kneeling in front of the altar for a few minutes in order to meditate on what the Consecration Rite means to you.

The Dedication or Initiation Rite

Most of the steps in this description have been strongly influenced by Raymond Buckland, Ed Fitch, and the Farrars, which will be obvious to those who have read their works. The Dedication or Initiation Rite is typically performed in Coven only in front of those who have been similarly dedicated or initiated. If you are performing this rite in a Coven environment, any Covener who has yet to be dedicated or initiated should be asked to leave the circle until the rite is completed. As in the Consecration Rite, a Dedication is performed by the High Priest if the dedicant is female, and by the High Priestess if the dedicant is male. If it is not specified in your Tradition's Mysteries, it is up to the discretion of the Coveners and of the dedicant if the rite is to be done skyclad or clothed, although this is one of the rites where working skyclad is typically considered the norm. This is also the time a dedicant will be introduced to the God and Goddess for the first time by using his or her Craft or witch name.

In order to perform this rite in Coven, the High Priest/ess leads the dedicant into the center of the circle, and the dedicant assumes the Goddess position. The steps of the Consecration Rite are first performed with the following changes. The High Priest/ess dips his or her finger into the salted water and draws a pentagram over the dedicant's body—forehead to left thigh, to right shoulder, to left shoulder, to right thigh, and back to forehead.

Depending on the preferences of your Coven, a ritual kiss, referred to as the Fivefold Kiss, may also be used at this time. The Fivefold Kiss is applied once on the tops of each foot, once on each knee, once on the lower abdomen or pubic area, once on the breast over the heart, and once on the mouth. As each kiss is applied, the appropriate line from the following text is uttered by the High Priest/ess:

> *Blessed be thy feet that that will walk the sacred path.*
> *Blessed be thy knees that shall kneel before Her.*
> *Blessed be thy loins that are the source of all life.*
> *Blessed be thy heart that rejoices in Her.*
> *Blessed be thy mouth that shall utter Her sacred names.*

The use of the Fivefold Kiss is part of the rite that must be agreeable to all participants, and there should be no changes without the full consent of all. If any participant is even remotely uneasy with this act, it must be omitted.

Upon completion of the Consecration Rite, the High Priest/ess faces the dedicant, saying, and having the dedicant repeat:

Earth Mother, creatrix of us all, protectress of us all.
You who gave us life and who will welcome us to Sum-
merland. I am before You to be reborn in Your service
and in Your love. With You as my witness, I swear to
honor and follow the Wiccan Law. I swear to honor and
defend You and all those who love You throughout this
life and all those lives yet to come. I am part of You as
You are part of me. I am newly born as Your child. I ask
You to accept me now as (witch name), dedicated to
You now and forever more. So mote it be.

The dedicant now sits for a few minutes in front of the altar
and meditates on what this Dedication means and how his or
her life may be forever changed by this step, and then thanks
the Goddess for Her acceptance of this Dedication.

This rite can easily be accommodated to the Solitary with
only a few changes. Ideally it should be done skyclad. The
Dedication or Initiation Rite is also the time you will introduce
yourself to the God and Goddess using your new witch or
Craft name. In order to complete this rite as a Solitary, dip the
fingers of your right hand in the container of salted water used
to cast your circle. While standing, draw the pentagram symbol over your body—forehead to left thigh, to right shoulder,
to left shoulder, to right thigh, and back to forehead. Sit down
facing your altar and open your arms wide to embrace Her.
Meditate for a few minutes on the step you are about to take
and what this Dedication means to you. When your meditation is complete, repeat the steps of the Consecration Rite,
then open your arms wide to embrace Her and say:

Earth Mother, creatrix of us all, protectress of us all.
You who gave us life and who will welcome us to Sum-
merland. I am before You to be reborn in Your service
and in Your love. With You as my witness, I swear to

*honor and follow the Wiccan Law. I swear to honor and
defend You and all those who love You throughout this
life and all those lives yet to come. I am part of You as
You are part of me. I am newly born as Your child. I ask
You to accept me now as (witch name), dedicated to
You now and forever more. So mote it be.*

Sit for a few minutes longer, as long as you desire, and meditate again on what this Dedication means to you and how
your life may be forever changed by this step. When you feel
the time is right, thank the Goddess for Her attendance and
Her acceptance of your Dedication.

The Cake and Ale Rite

Virtually any food or drink item can be used in the Cake and
Ale Rite, and whatever you choose may be dictated by the requirements of your Coveners. This might include nonalcoholic
drinks, fat-free cakes, or any other limitations. Since some of
our Coveners have either nonalcoholic requirements or dietary
restrictions, we typically use salt-free crackers and water in
this rite. The Cake and Ale Rite is not a ritual feast, it is simply
a way of connecting with the God and Goddess and with the
abundance of this Earth provided by Them. This rite is similar
to the communion rites of other religious denominations and
probably was the original rite behind those similar Christian
observances.

A plate of cakes and a plate containing cups of ale, enough
for each Covener, is prepared while the circle is being set up
and is placed near the altar. When the rite is ready to be conducted, the High Priestess picks up the plate of ale cups and
offers it to the High Priest. The High Priest takes his athame
and draws a pentagram in the air over the plate, saying:

> *I infuse these drinks with the love of Mother Goddess and Father God, may we all never thirst.*

The plate is then passed deosil around the circle to each Covener with the words "May you never thirst" uttered each time the plate changes hands. The High Priest then picks up the plate of cakes and offers it to the High Priestess, who takes her athame and draws a pentagram in the air over the cakes, saying:

> *I infuse these cakes with the love of Mother Goddess and Father God, may we all never hunger.*

The plate is then passed deosil around the circle to each Covener with the words "May you never hunger" uttered each time the plate changes hands. When both the ale and cake plate have made a full circuit of the Coveners, they are placed in the middle of the circle so that any remaining cakes can be consumed, if desired. Coveners now take a few minutes to discuss the Sabbat or esbat ritual and talk about what it meant to each of them.

Consecration of Tools

This rite must be done before any tool is brought into the circle to be used in ritual or magickal acts. It is usually done by the owner of the tool, but can be done by either the High Priest or High Priestess if the tool is to be for general Coven use. Kneel in front of the altar, take the tool in both hands, hold it over your head, and say:

> *God and Goddess, Lord and Lady, Father and Mother of all life. I present this (item or tool name) for Your approval and ask that it be used in Your service.*

Place the item on the altar and kneel for a few minutes, thinking of how it will be used. Dip your fingers in the salted water
and sprinkle all sides of the item. Wave it through the smoke
from the incense, turning it so that all sides are cleansed, and
then say:

> *May the essence of earth, air, fire, and water cleanse
> and purify this (item name) so that it may be used in
> Your service. So mote it be.*

Hold the (item name) in the palms of both hands for a few
minutes, consecrating all your thoughts and energies into it,
and say:

> *I charge this (item name) by the thousands of names
> of our Lord and Lady and ask that They accept it in
> Their service. So mote it be.*

Raising Power

This is one rite that may be somewhat less effective when
done by Solitaries since it involves the generation of energy.
While a Solitary practitioner can obviously accomplish this,
and does so when casting a spell, the power raising as described here can generally be more effective when done by an
entire Coven.

All participants first decide upon a focal point for the rite.
This could be a healing energy for a sick Covener or friend,
energy raised for protection, or almost any other purpose. In
this rite, you will be channeling and directing energy or power
that is drawn through the collective bodies of the Coveners
from the Earth itself. This rite comes very close to spellcraft,
but I feel it does not quite qualify to be placed in the chapter
devoted to spell work. Be aware, however, that you are still

directing energy to do a specific task, and the ramifications of that must be considered in light of the Wiccan Law.

Typically, the rite is led by the High Priestess, who may either stand in the center of the circle or join the circle itself. Coveners all stand and hold hands while slowly walking around the circle deosil. As they do so, the High Priestess leads the Coveners in a chant that slowly builds in intensity with each completed circuit around the circle. The chant can be anything that everyone can do easily from memory and is meant to help each person focus their portion of the energy toward the center of the circle. The chant could be simply a slowly rising moan, or it could be words that are meaningful to the participants. One chant that is frequently used is called the Witches Rune wherein the last two lines usually reflect the names of the Tradition's patron god and goddess:

> *Eko, Eko, Azarak,*
> *Eko, Eko, Zomelak,*
> *Eko, Eko, Cernunnos,*
> *Eko, Eko, Aradia.*

With each circuit around the circle, the Coveners move faster and the chant increases in intensity. By the time three full circuits of the circle have been completed, the Coveners are almost running and the chant has become a shout. When she feels the peak energy has been reached, the High Priestess vocally stops the movement and leads all Coveners in yelling the following:

> *By the hand of our Mother, so shall it be!*

At this point, everyone drops their hands and lifts their arms skyward, repeating the yell three times. All Coveners and the High Priestess then drop to the floor or ground, thoroughly grounding themselves and allowing any residual energy to flow back into the Earth. This grounding process can take several minutes, and it is not uncommon for everyone to feel weak or almost exhausted for a few minutes after the power raising.

Drawing Down the Moon

Drawing Down the Moon is a rite wherein the High Priestess functions as the Goddess incarnate, actually speaking and acting for Her. The Triple Goddess is invoked either by the High Priest into the High Priestess, or, in some cases, the High Priestess will evoke that entity into herself. If the rite is performed properly, it is quite common to have the High Priestess suddenly speaking with accents or voice inflections that are obviously not her own. This rite is actually of great antiquity, since graphical representations of its performance can be seen in wall paintings from both Greek and Roman civilizations. The companion rite, Drawing Down the Sun, is similar, but in that rite the God is invoked into the body of the High Priest.

Drawing Down the Moon is one of those rites that is really not applicable to the Solitary, since it requires two people, but I have included it since this book is also written for use by small Covens. Drawing Down the Moon is generally associated with the full moon esbat, but is certainly not limited to that time, and it can be done in conjunction with any lunar rite or ritual. It is not, however, a rite that is part of the Sabbat rituals. It is also another one of those rites where working skyclad is virtually a requirement, and, as such, it must be up to the discretion of your Coven if Drawing Down the Moon is to be part of your repertoire of rites and rituals. Many parts of this ritual have been strongly influenced by Raymond Buckland, Ed Fitch, and the Farrars, which will be obvious to those who have read their works.

The High Priest and High Priestess stand facing each other at the altar. The High Priest assumes the God position and the High Priestess the Goddess position. The High Priestess then invokes the God by saying:

I invoke Thee, Father God, consort of Mother Goddess. Father of us all, live now within the body of Your Priest.

The High Priestess then changes somewhat from the Goddess position to place her arms folded on her chest. The High Priest kneels in front of the High Priestess and gives her the Fivefold Kiss, starting with kissing the tops of her feet, then moving to her knees, lower abdomen, breasts, and mouth, saying as he does so:

Blessed be thy feet that will walk the sacred path.
Blessed be thy knees that shall kneel before Her.
Blessed be thy loins that are the source of all life.

The High Priestess now removes her arms from her chest and again assumes the full Goddess position, as the High Priest continues:

Blessed be thy heart that rejoices in Her.
Blessed be thy mouth that shall utter the sacred names.

The High Priest now invokes the Goddess:

I invoke Thee, our Mother, creatrix of us all. I invoke Thee to descend upon the body of Your Priestess. Now hear the words of the Great Mother, She who is also called Artemis, Astarte, Athena, Diana, Aphrodite, Cerridwen, Dana, Arianrhod, Bridgit, and by all Her thousands of names. Hear the words of the Star Goddess, She in the dust of whose feet are the hosts of heaven and whose body encircles the universe.

Now is the time when it is sometimes possible for the Goddess to speak through the High Priestess; her voice my change, lilt, adopt an accent, or assume a phraseology not her own. The Goddess is speaking to Her children; this is the essence of the rite, its real purpose. When, and if, this event occurs and is concluded, the High Priestess then reads the full text of *The Charge of the Goddess*. At the completion of this reading, the High Priest and High Priestess say in unison:

As it is above it is below, so within and so without.

Drawing Down the Moon has been concluded and the rite is now over.

The Great Rite

The Great Rite is typically done at the Beltain Sabbat. It represents sexual union between the God and Goddess, impregnating the Goddess in Her form as Mother Earth to bring forth the harvest bounty, as well as in Her form as Mother of the God giving birth to Him at Yule. This rite can take many forms, ranging from the purely symbolic to the more graphic, and each member of the Coven must be in full agreement as to what form will be used. Generally speaking, if the rite is to be more than symbolic, it is done in private between the High Priestess and High Priest, with the remaining members of the Coven having left the circle. Upon their return, they are not permitted to know what actually transpired between the High Priest and High Priestess, leaving the details of the rite up to their collective imaginations.

A symbolic Great Rite can be performed between the Coven High Priestess and High Priest using a cauldron or chalice (a vaginal representation) to be held by the High Priestess, and either an athame or wand (a phallic representation) to be held by the High Priest. The cauldron or chalice should be of about the half-quart size, easy enough to be held by either participant but large enough to contain the athame or wand. The rite is conducted by our Coven as follows:

The High Priestess kneels at the Goddess side of the altar, picks up the cauldron, and faces the High Priest, who is kneeling at the God side of the altar. The High Priest picks up his athame and faces the High Priestess, who says:

> *Young Sun King, Horned One of the Greenwood.*
> *Come dance and sing with the Maid of Spring.*
> *Come, our King, to the Beltain fire.*
> *Come share our joy this night.*

The High Priest then says:

> *Lovely Maiden, Mother, Wise One, Threefold*
>   *Goddess.*
> *Be a flame within our hearts tonight.*
> *Come, our Queen, to the Beltain fire.*
> *Come share our joy this night.*

Both the High Priestess and High Priest then recite the following together as the High Priest slowly lowers his athame into the cauldron:

> *For I am the secret door that opens onto the land of*
> *youth, and I am the cup of the wine of life, the Cauldron*
> *of Cerridwen.*

The High Priest then takes the cauldron with the athame still inside it from the High Priestess and, holding it over his head with both hands, proclaims:

> *This rite symbolizes the union of our God and Goddess in perfect love, perfect trust, and perfect pleasure.*

May we draw from it the same love, trust, and pleasure.
So mote it be.

Handfasting

A handfast represents one of the earliest forms of a marriage ceremony. By taking each other's hands, usually the left hand, which is still symbolized today by the wearing of wedding rings on that hand, the two lovers were pledged to live together in mutual love and support for at least one year. Originally, the handfast ceremony was renewed each year at Beltain, but current usage tends to equate this rite with the more conventional civil or mainstream religious marriage ceremony in that it is either enforced until death do they part, or the relationship is dissolved by mutual consent.

In most states, the handfast ceremony has the same legality as any civil or other religious wedding. This is generally true as long as the service is performed and the marriage documentation signed by a certified or licensed member of clergy. This can be either a member of the Wiccan clergy as sanctioned by the Covenant of the Goddess, a minister of the Church of all Worlds, or any individual who can obtain ministerial credentials of virtually any type. This legality, however, may not extend to other Priests or Priestesses, be they High Priest/ess or not, and may not be legally binding or valid in all states. This is of particular concern if you desire to obtain spousal medical insurance from your employer, or to list your mate as a beneficiary in a will where she or he is identified as "spouse."

The bottom line here is that I am not sure about the legality of any marriage license that may be signed by Gary Cantrell, Priest of Wicca, since I am not recognized by the Covenant of the Goddess or the Church of All Worlds as a certified member of clergy; nor do I hold any ministerial credentials recognized by the state of California. It would be advisable for you to investigate the legality of any proposed handfast you may be considering, probably through the Covenant of the Goddess as a starting point, before allowing just any High Priestess or High Priest to perform the ceremony.

The Crone Rite

The Crone Rite is done in recognition of the more mature aspect of the Goddess and, correspondingly, with the more mature aspects of the female practitioner. As such, this is one of those rites that is more identified with women's Mysteries and is normally not done by a male practitioner. In reality, though, there is neither a gender nor an age requirement for performing this rite, so it could be done by anyone.

The Crone is an aspect of the Goddess to be venerated and admired, since it represents that stage in life where the Goddess, and Her female followers, have reached that stage of wisdom and maturity akin to what one might consider a beloved grandmother to possess; they are willing to share and pass on what they have learned. It is this aspect of the Goddess that is summoned when a woman feels the need to laugh at her age, to admire her own success in this life, to examine her own store of spiritual and worldly wisdom, or even to question that wisdom if she feels the need.

The following rite of invitation to the Goddess in Her Crone aspect is inspired by the book *In Praise of the Crone* by Dorothy Morrison and will give you some idea of how this rite is structured. My wife has read *In Praise of the Crone* and uses many of the concepts therein for her own Crone rituals. She is of the opinion that it is indeed a worthwhile addition to any

Pagan's library, particularly those who have reached those later stages in life.

Use sage incense to purify your circle, and cast it three times using a raven's feather or any black feather. As you cast the circle, recite the following incantation:

I cast the circle thrice about,
bringing goodness in, keeping badness out.
Crone of darkness, crone of light,
Be with me again, be with me tonight.
Crone of wisdom, strength, and power,
Come in the circle now, join with me this hour.

Now is the time to sit and meditate, to listen to what the Crone may wish to say to you. The thoughts may come swiftly or they may take some time, but be assured that She will speak to you in some form. When the meditation is completed, close the circle and complete the Crone Rite with something like the following words:

We end this rite, myself and Crone,
For now we act as one.
We have joined and spoken together,
This sacred rite is done.

Passage to Summerland

As Pagans, we are all aware of the balance that must exist in nature, and we are all aware that life and death (as we know them) are only two aspects of our existence in this present physical realm and on this place we call Earth. Our belief in the philosophy of the Old Religion tells us that our present lives are only a phase we must all pass through as we explore our various incarnations. We know and understand that death, as we may perceive it in the physical sense, is only the demise of the shell of our physical bodies. We know that our spirits are eternal and everlasting, that our physical death simply releases that spirit through the door into Summerland to begin yet another reincarnation.

Even though we know this with every fiber of our being, we still grieve for loved ones who have died. We miss and grieve for the lover, family member, friend, Familiar, or pet who has left this incarnation. This process of grieving is a necessity because it give us closure; it lets us have a time and place to remember the ones who have crossed over and to understand that they have moved on to a new place and a new beginning. There have been countless books written about the grieving process and there are professional counselors who are able to help us through this process; thus, it is not my intention to write a lengthy discourse on the subject. What I will attempt to present are some brief workings that can be done by either Solitaries or Covens in order to help those who may have lost a loved one. The Passing Rite, as I describe, is not designed to replace the work of professional grief counselors who may sometimes be needed. The rites and workings are presented here only in the hope that they may be of some small help in providing at least a modicum of closure to the loss of someone you have held dear.

In many cases, the loved one who is passing on may not be a Pagan, and the funeral service may therefore be held in a non-Pagan environment. If you wish to honor this loved one in a later Pagan ceremony as well, you might consider the following ritual or one like it that you can devise on your own. The same ritual can be used for the passing of a Pagan friend, as well. This ritual for Passage into Summerland can be performed on the night of the funeral, or it can be done later at any time between the full and new moon. On the altar, place a white and red candle surrounded by one candle for each of the four quarters, as well as a picture of the deceased, if that is practical. It is not necessary to cast a circle, and all in attendance can simply sit either clustered around the altar in a circular pattern or grouped in front of it. If the deceased is male, the High Priestess should officiate; if female, the High Priest should take charge.

The High Priest/ess lights the four quarter candles, saying:

> *Ancient Ones of earth, air, fire, and water. Please release from pain and suffering all those who remain in this physical realm. Escort the spirit of our loved one through the gates of Summerland and bring peace to all.*

The High Priest/ess then lights the center white candle, saying:

> *Earth Mother, creatrix of us all, we ask You to receive the spirit of our loved one into Your heart. (Name of deceased) has returned to You as water flows to the ocean.*

The High Priest/ess then lights the center red candle, saying:

> *Sky Father, Creator of us all, we ask You to receive the spirit of our loved one into Your heart. (Name of deceased) has returned to You as sparks rise to the skies. Lord and Lady, we give You thanks for accepting our loved one into the glory and beauty of the Summerland. So mote it be.*

At this time, the High Priest/ess (if desired) can now lead a power-raising chant, which is designed to aid the deceased spiritually in passage to Summerland and to release any energies that have been built up during the performance of the rite. The Cake and Ale Rite is almost mandatory at closing because it is then that all participants can sit, relax, and talk about the one who has gone over, to remember the good times had by all, and to comfort each other. All the candles should be left to burn themselves out.

Many Pagans elect to be cremated rather than buried, since many of us feel it is more appropriate to return our physical selves to the Earth, or to the sea, in this form. If this is the case, then it would be appropriate to have the cremation urn placed on the altar along with a picture of the deceased. If the ashes are to be scattered as part of this ceremony, the time to do this could be either before or after any power raising but before the Cake and Ale Rite. All can adjourn to wherever the scattering is to take place, returning to the altar site later to complete the passage rites and to put closure to the ritual. A simple rite to be recited as the ashes are spread might be as follows:

Mother Goddess, Father God. Here we bring to You the corporeal remains of Your child and our (spouse, friend, lover, Familiar, pet) (name of deceased). May he/she be embraced by Your light and love. Blessed be.

Meditation

One of the things that has come up several times in this book, and something that most of us are probably at least a little familiar with, is the term *meditation*. What exactly is meditation, and how does it fit with the practice of witchcraft?

The 1991 Concise Columbia Encyclopedia defines *meditation* as "a religious discipline in which the mind is led to focus on a single point of reference. It may be a means of invoking divine grace as in the contemplation by mystics of a spiritual theme, question, or problem. Or it may be a means of attaining conscious union with the divine through visualization of a deity or inward repetition of a prayer or mantra. Employed since ancient times in various forms by all religions, the practice of meditation gained popular interest in the United States in the twentieth century when Zen Buddhism rose in the West after World War II. In the 1960s and 1970s, the Indian Maharishi Mahesh Yogi taught a mantra system called Transcendental Meditation (TM), which is now also used by many nonreligious adherents as a method for achieving a relaxed physical and mental state."[3] *The American Heritage Dictionary of the English Language* defines *meditation* as "a devotional exercise leading to contemplation, or a contemplative discourse usually on a religious or philosophical subject."[4]

Meditation, then, is the relaxed and inward state of mind we enter, sometimes as part of our rituals and sometimes as a practice unto itself, when we feel it necessary or prudent to communicate with our deities or even to get in touch with our own inner thoughts. There are several levels of meditation one can go into, ranging from the alpha state, which is somewhat similar to deep daydreaming, to the theta state, in which virtually all awareness of conscious thought and of the physical surroundings are eliminated. I must admit that I am not personally a practitioner of meditation on a daily basis and I have never gone into anything deeper than the alpha state; but I have found that even going into the alpha state can be quite relaxing and spiritually uplifting.

One certainly does not have to meditate within a cast circle unless your meditation is part of some other ritual or rite such as an esbat. Like almost everything else we do, it is essential that you have a quiet and private place in which to do this. I like to sit in my backyard, either on a bench or even on the ground, and close my eyes or just let my vision drift over the valley and mountains across from me. If I am meditating in circle I usually watch the incense smoke or candle flame, not actually focusing directly on them, but seeing them almost as defocused, or again I just close my eyes.

There are some general guidelines or techniques necessary in meditation in order to get both your mind and body into a receptive condition. You should be relaxed and comfortable, and I recommend sitting with your legs either crossed or folded under you, with your hands folded in your lap. If you are in a position or location where you can use something for a backrest and you feel you need that support, then by all means use it. Take several deep and cleansing breaths, and let your body relax.

Once you are comfortable, you can begin to place yourself into the meditational state. In order to accomplish this, some practitioners use a countdown method by slowly counting backward from ten to one, and others use a color method by visualizing colors changing from bright yellow to soft reds or pinks and finally to cool greens or blues. Still others mentally focus on the Third Eye, that special spot in your forehead inside your skull, above and between your two eyes. Whatever method you use should have essentially the same end result. All or most conscious thought and awareness of your physical surroundings should fade into the background, and you should enter a state of mind very similar to deep daydreaming.

Let your mind drift where it will, and allow images to come of their own volition. You have entered a state of mind that will allow you to sense your own inner thoughts and feelings. It is a state of deep contemplation and peace, one that will allow you to maybe resolve some issues or concerns in your life, and one that may also bring you a closer awareness of the God and Goddess. I find that when meditation is done at full moon esbat, I almost always recognize the presence of the Lady in that meditation, even if She has already manifested in some other physical form around me. The moon may have already grown brighter, the tree branches may have softly moved without any perceptible wind, or I may have sensed Her physical presence in some other way. When I am in the alpha state, I can almost see Her and I know full well that She is there beside us in our circle at that time. Meditation can indeed be a very powerful and spiritually fulfilling experience.

While there are techniques used to enter a meditational state, there are also techniques that you should use in order to leave that state and bring your conscious mind back to the reality of the present time and place. When you feel the meditation is or should be ended, lift your hands from their folded position in your lap, and slowly bring them up toward your chest. Turn your hands palms outward as you bring them toward the chest, gently pushing the air away as you move your hands out and down so that you end with your palms flat on the floor beside you. Take several deep breaths to return your senses completely to the here and now. The meditation is over.

Chapter Summary

This chapter has attempted to present several rather common or generic Wiccan rites. Some are generally used within the framework of other rituals, while some can stand alone. Although it is not a complete lexicon of those rites, the material presented here will hopefully give you some indication and feeling of the depth of our rites and rituals.

Many of the invocations and other ritual words in this chapter have been influenced by other writers. Since it is important that you develop your own relationship with our deities, I feel that these words, as you read them here, should be used only as a starting point in your own development. Read all the books you can, talk to others in the Craft, and develop your own rites and rituals as you go. Those rituals performed with your own wordings will be much more effective and meaningful to you those done using someone else's words.

1. *The 1999 World Book Encyclopedia*, s.v. "ritual."
2. *The 1999 World Book Encyclopedia*, s.v. "rite."
3. *The 1991 Concise Columbia Encyclopedia,* s.v. "meditation."
4. *The American Heritage Dictionary of the English Language*, 3rd ed., s.v. "meditation."

6

Spellcraft and Magick

What Is Spellcraft?

*T*he Old Religion is first and foremost an acceptance of the divinity that we realize is personified by that thing we call Nature, and our practice of the various rites and rituals we use to recognize and communicate with that divinity in all its glorious aspects and manifestations. It is an awareness of the Old Ones, the gods and goddesses, elements, and spirits who have been with us from the beginning of time. It is a belief in Them and in that inexplicable force that binds us to Them and Them to us. It is our connection to our ancestors and our heritage and to that very thing that speaks to us from the mists of antiquity. This is, after all, what the Old Religion is really about. Only after all of this is Wicca concerned with the special arts of divination and magick, also known as spellcraft.

The material presented in this chapter has been derived from my own experience and learning, reflecting both what I have been taught and what I have amassed on my own. I in no way present it as the only way to do spellcraft, nor do I imply that it is by any stretch of the imagination even the best way. It is simply a description of the concepts and methods that have worked for me. I am sure there are many other approaches to spell work that may be equally effective. As in all things related to understanding the Craft, I urge you to learn as much as possible from as many sources as you can so that you can make the choices that work best for you.

The art of working a spell, casting a spell, or working magick is serious work. It is not something that can be approached lightly, casually, or flippantly. Spellcraft must be approached with a serious attitude and a realization that, as a witch, you are responsible for all the consequences and ramifications that may arise from whatever actions you take. You will be bending and shaping energies that will, without question, have an impact on the world around you, and it is vitally important that you realize and remember this. Your responsibilities are clearly spelled out in the Wiccan Law with the attendant Wiccan Rede and Rule of Three, all of which were discussed in detail in chapter 2; never forget the old axiom of spellcraft, "Be careful what you ask for because you most assuredly will receive it." How you understand and apply these concepts and how you address or approach your own personal attitudes and feelings on spellcraft will, to a large extent, define your persona as a witch.

All this is not meant to dissuade you from undertaking spell work or to raise any unwarranted fears, but rather to make you readily aware of the significance of the forces and energies that will manifest during the spell-casting process.

Done properly and with sufficient preparation, and with a full awareness of your own powers as a witch, working magick can be both an exhilarating and powerful experience. Do not be afraid of taking this step, but do be aware.

In some Traditions or Paths, the training in spellcraft begins only after an initiation; in others, it is a basic part of your training as a novice. Many practitioners firmly believe that only an initiated witch should be working magick, but I personally feel that education and information is infinitely better than ignorance. If one approaches spellcraft with sufficient training and preparation, then responsible work can be done regardless if one has been formally initiated or not. Obviously, for a Solitary, the decision as to when to begin spell work will be totally up to you, based on your own presumed level of Craft competence and on your own personal feelings.

Some practitioners may opt to avoid working magick altogether, deciding that worshipping our deities by performing the Sabbat or esbat rituals is enough. They may decide that these are the acts that bring them personally into contact with the deities and that the solar and lunar rituals are all that is really significant and meaningful as far as they are concerned. There is absolutely nothing wrong with working the Craft in this way, since in many cases the majority of our Pagan ancestors did exactly the same thing. They took full part in all the ritual celebrations of the Sabbats and esbats, while leaving the magickal workings up to just one person in the clan or village. That one person was the clan spiritual leader and officiated at all the rituals; the shaman, druid, wizard, or witch who communicated with the gods and goddesses, who was knowledgeable of herbs and spell incantations, and knew the proper times to harvest the herbs or work the magick in order to achieve the desired result and to make the result both powerful and effective.

In many instances, you may have already been exposed to a degree of spell work if you have taken part in a power raising. While power raising is obviously not the same as casting a spell, the basic components are still there. The work is done in a purified space, in a cast circle with the four quarters or Guardians called, and some aspect of one of our deities present. Finally, energy is tapped into and manipulated with the aid of probably a chant or other rhythmic act, then released to do a specific task.

What differentiates power raising from spell casting is the use of an incantation with the spell. The incantation is at the heart of the spell or magickal work and specifically invokes an aspect of the God or Goddess, requesting that a specific or direct action be taken on your behalf. Some physical object is usually used to act as the spell's focal point, such as an appropriately colored candle or possibly a knotted string. The physical object can then be manipulated during the reading of the incantation so that it becomes charged with the spell energy. How the built-up energy is directed or released will, in many cases, depend on the type of magickal work being done. The spell may determine if the energy is to be released simply by burning a candle, or possibly more aggressively by launching it toward a specific target.

There are no guarantees, either in power raising or spell casting, that our efforts will always be totally successful. We all realize that there are forces beyond our comprehension that can sometimes have an impact on the outcome of any of our attempts to manipulate that universal energy or force that continually flows through us all and through all matter. All we can do during the casting of a spell is to get in touch with that force, to try and focus it, to maybe bend it or manipulate it just a bit in such a way that results in some positive change.

There is no guarantee that our efforts will have an immediate effect in precisely the way we had hoped, although being as specific as possible and keeping the spell action as simple as possible can certainly help in obtaining the desired result. The results of spellcraft may not be immediately apparent or even obvious. It may only be in hindsight that we are able to realize that our actions did indeed have an impact, and that it was pretty much what we had hoped to achieve.

Just how one can go about tapping into this universal energy, to manipulate it in order to bring about positive change, sometimes differs between practitioners. Some methods imply that because of the inherent balance in all things that Wicca embodies, one must replace any positive energy sent out by drawing in søme equal amount of negative energy. An example of this concept might be in the use of both a black and white candle in a healing spell. In this case, let us assume that you are attempting to generate healing energy for someone by sending that person positive energy using an appropriate incantation and a white candle. You then must also counter the loss of this "white" energy with a black candle that takes in and absorbs an equal amount of negative or "black" energy.

Personally, my learning and the teachings of my own Tradition tell me that even though this concept addresses the issue of balance, it may not necessarily be germane to how I would do spell work. My philosophy tells me that energy is neither positive nor negative; it is neutral. It is only in how we address and manipulate that energy that gives it the positive or negative connotation. In spell casting, or in power raising, we do not actually create or change energy. All energies from everything are always present, in all aspects and all complexities, and we draw that energy from the Earth using our bodies and minds as the conduit. All we are doing, when casting a spell, is defining that specific energy aspect we wish to use, and then acting as a lens to focus or bend that energy component toward a defined goal. We draw it up through ourselves, tweak it just a bit, and then launch it in order to derive the positive change we desire.

You have acted as the conduit for this movement of energy, and the act of grounding yourself afterward allows any residual energies to flow back into to the Earth; thus, in that sense, completing or balancing your actions. You have not added nor have you subtracted any energy from anything. You have simply focused and redirected just a little bit of what was already there.

As in most acts of witchcraft, be it ritual work at Sabbats or magickal work at esbats, there is a time for everything. As I already mentioned, the festivals of our Sabbat celebrations are not for magick or spell work. That work is generally reserved for the times of the esbats, the lunar rites. The moon as the symbol of the Goddess, our Lady, exhibits three phases that represent Her three aspects of Maiden, Mother, and Crone. This is the Triple Goddess image that is represented in most Pagan religions as the first quarter moon, full moon, and last quarter moon. Many High Priestesses wear this symbol as a headband during ritual to indicate their special relationship with the Lady.

The Maiden is presumed to represent both innocence and a bit of mischievous sexuality. This is the aspect of the Goddess that is young, playful, and fertile, and full of life and laughter. The Mother represents the Goddess at midlife. This is Her aspect that has just given birth, all-loving, nurturing, and settled. In this aspect, She is love personified. The Crone is the Goddess in her twilight years, all wisdom and caring, all-knowing and wise, willing and able to pass on what She has learned. There is another aspect of the Goddess that is not always mentioned in texts on our religion—Her aspect during the dark moon where some Traditions portray Her as the temptress or vixen. In this aspect, She can be petulant and the worker of magick that is special and unique to what might be considered Her darker side, one that may even involve anger or chaos, one that is in diametric opposition to Her full moon Mother aspect.

These various aspects of the Lady are generally specific to the type of spell work to be done. The times of the waxing moon, those times when She is growing from the new moon to the first quarter, are the times for working magick aimed at new beginnings or new endeavors. From the first quarter to the full moon are the times for working any spells involving growth in some existing situation. These could include improvements in personal attitudes or emotions, advances in career, additional finances, or spells seeking clarity of vision or inspiration—virtually anything that might be considered growing, adding, or generally improving on something. Spells related to increased fertility would also be done under either of these lunar aspects.

The time of the full moon is typically the time of the main monthly esbat, which is held regardless if magick is to be done or not. This is the ritual of recognition to the Goddess as creatrix and protectress of us all. This is the time to thank Her for Her bounty and for all that She has given of Her guidance and love that has led us down this path. This may also be the time for ritual dedication or consecration of new working tools, and of yourself, as well. While consecration of one's self is typically done at the Imbolc Sabbat, it is not uncommon for a witch to feel the need to rededicate or reconsecrate to the Lady at other times during the year, and the full moon esbat is the time to do that rite. This is also the time for working any magick involving divination or prophecy, or anything needing extra power such as the healing of a serious ailment or affliction.

The times of the waning moon, those times when She is shrinking from full to the last quarter, are the times for working spells involving anything related to removal. These are times to do binding or banishing work, healing spells aimed at removing an illness or a negative attitude, or spells designed to remove an obstacle or some obstruction in your emotional, financial, career, or physical path. Anything that can be construed as being taken away, reduced, or removed could be the subject of spellcraft done under this lunar aspect.

The times of the dark moon, that time beginning a few nights after the last quarter until the time when She is hidden from view, are the times of dealing with darker aspects, including frustration and anger. Here one would do work to repel attackers or seek justice for obvious wrongs. This is also the time to be very careful in your understanding of exactly what you are trying to accomplish. Whatever magick is done during the dark moon must always follow the tenets of the Wiccan Rede and the Rule of Three. Remember that once a spell is cast, it may not be easy to totally undo, so you must know and fully understand what you are doing and why you are doing it before you act. Be very aware of the possible ramifications of your actions and always consider them in light of the ethics of our Craft.

The actual words of a spell are typically written in rhyme, and the spell is also generally quite short. The purpose of the rhyming is to lend a cadence or rhythm to the incantation as it is recited and also to make it easier to remember. The brevity of length also aids in remembrance and tends to keep the work specific and focused.

Some authors have theorized that the rhyming of spells grew out of a necessity to commit everything in a Book of Shadows to memory, since a Coven could not afford to have a physical book fall into the hands of the Inquisition. This seems somewhat plausible, but I also suspect that in many cases the literacy rate of many of the medieval practitioners may have been such that maintaining a detailed written record was simply beyond them. Going back even earlier than the Dark Ages, back before the appearance of the Romans, neither the Celts nor the Britons had a real written language in 1000 B.C. Clan histories and other lore were handed down verbally. In the case of at least the Celts, this eventually became the responsibility of the bards, who comprised one class of the Druidic Priesthood. This lends credence to the concept that ease of remembrance may have been at least one of the necessities for rhyming. In any event, spells have probably always been written in rhyme, and it is traditional to do so today. For those who may find themselves somewhat poetically challenged, as I am, I have included an online rhyming dictionary as one of the listings in appendix D.

Since successful spell work depends on being very exact in what you are asking for, it is generally necessary to keep the incantation short. This forces the practitioner to stay focused on the issue at hand and to be specific. It does absolutely no good to give the deity you have invoked a dozen lines of background information as to why you are casting the spell, so keep the spell short and to the point. If you feel the need to clarify what you are trying to accomplish, then it is best to do this directly with the deity before casting the spell; but do not make it part of the spell and thus let extraneous words interfere with the actual spell work.

Most of my spells generally consist of no more then four stanzas, with either two or four lines per stanza, so there are usually no more than sixteen lines of rhyme. Of these sixteen lines, the first four are the deity invocation and the last four are a self-protection caveat, which leaves me eight lines for the actual spell words. In my personal experience, I have seldom found it necessary to write a spell using more than eight lines of magick. Typically, a spell is ended with some form of a charge to the deity you have invoked, such as "so mote it be" or "so shall it be" or other words to that effect, giving a formal ending to the magickal words.

Preparation is a large part of spellcraft. In addition to preparing the written words and identifying the time of month for the work, there is always the necessity of preparing yourself. Cleansing baths or showers, while not necessarily mandatory, do aid in performing the rite, as does the proper attire. Unless you prefer to work skyclad, you should wear loose and comfortable clothing or robes and remove anything that will detract from your focus on the business at hand. Cleanse your mind as well as your body, and focus on your inner self in all aspects—emotionally, mentally, and spiritually. This is an important requirement in successful spell work. Such things as binding or uncomfortable clothing or superfluous dangling jewelry will only detract from that focus.

Obviously, such potential interruptions as ringing telephones, television or radio sounds, and noisy neighbors should also be eliminated as much as possible. Achieving the solitude needed for spellwork can sometimes be a problem, particularly if you live in an apartment or condominium complex. It may be best simply to wait until very late at night before beginning, when most human-made noises or other interruptions should be minimized.

It is generally preferable to do most of this work outside unless, of course, the weather conditions are such that working outside is simply not possible. Regardless of whether the work is to be done outside or inside, you should choose your area so that you have the maximum likelihood of privacy and a sufficient degree of physical comfort. You should choose a place where you will not be interrupted or disturbed for at least an hour or more.

Set up all the required physical properties for purifying and casting the circle, such as the various candles, purification or consecration items, all of your spell materials and working tools, and a reading candle, if appropriate. Everything you will need during the performance of the rite should be identified and made ready for use. It is important that all your tools and implements are ready at hand; you should not interrupt your work by leaving the circle to collect something you have forgotten.

The incense used to purify your circle can be the generic sandalwood, which is usable for virtually any rite or ritual, or it can be one of the specific incense types designed to add impetus to the work at hand. Some basic types of incense for spell work include rosemary or sandalwood for protection and healing, frankincense or myrrh for romance or affection, pine for grounding or introspection, and lavender or mint for clarity or growth.

The appropriate spell candle color for the request or problem at hand is also important. Some general candle colors for basic spells include white or light blue for healing, yellow for clarity, green for growth, red for love or power, and black for absorption of negativity or removal. These are usually small thin taper candles of four to six inches or so in length. They will be used as the focal point to receive the directed energy when doing candle magick.

Table 2 at the end of this chapter lists various candle colors that are appropriate for specific charms and spells, and table 3 lists some suggested incense types for several specific uses.

Performing Magick

The actual magickal work is led by one person, either by the High Priestess or High Priest, if in Coven, or, obviously, done by yourself, if Solitary. Spellcraft can be equally effective in either environment; both have their strong points. As a Solitary, you and you alone are responsible for meeting the requirements of the Wiccan Law, and you alone decide on the wording of the spell, the deity to be called, and exactly how and when the spell is to be cast. The power in such an act can be considerable, particularly so if you are doing the work for yourself, but is still considerable when doing it for others who have asked for your help.

If the work is to be done in Coven, it becomes necessary that all participants agree on all aspects of the spell. The deity to be invoked, the wording of the spell, the spell's purpose, and the time to do the work must be acceptable to all participants. All Coveners must stay totally focused during the performance of the rite, because it will only detract from the energy if someone is distracted and thinking of something totally irrelevant to the spell. This can sometimes be difficult, but the upside to having multiple participants instead of doing the work alone is the increase in energy that can be directed in order to accomplish the desired end.

As you have probably realized from reading the earlier chapters, I am a proponent of keeping things as simple as possible. I firmly believe that extraneous or unneeded tools, as important as some of them may be to other work, can only get in the way and detract from what you are trying to accomplish. There is no need to clutter up your circle with tools or materials that will not be used, particularly if you are working inside in possibly limited space.

The materials you will need are all the standard tools for purifying and consecrating a Sacred Circle and the necessary spell materials that will probably vary depending on what your are trying to accomplish. It is vitally important that all spell work be done in a properly cast Sacred Circle. You will be manipulating and directing very powerful energies. The circle will aid you in focusing those energies and also provide protection for yourself and any others who may be present at the spell work. Once all participants are in the circle and it has been cast, no one should enter or leave until the work has been completed.

The smaller the circle, the better confined and easily directed the energy of your spell will be. The circle you intend to cast should be as small as possible, while still containing all participants and materials, and possibly giving you enough room to move and change your position, if you desire. Generally speaking, a three-foot diameter circle is used for Solitary work, and a circle of either nine or twelve feet in diameter is used for Coven work.

Purify the Area

The area of your circle, and all participants, should first be completely and thoroughly purified with sage, as was described in chapter 3. I feel that for spell work it is important to purify the area each time a spell is cast, regardless of whether other ritual work has previously been done in the same physical space or not. Spell work, like the dark moon rite, can manifest some very strong deities or elements, and it is necessary that these influences be allowed to focus only on the task at hand. Purifying the area after the spell work will also ensure that no residual energies remain that might interfere with rites or rituals you may hold in the future. I generally prefer to use white sage for this purification, but the choice is yours.

Casting the Circle

Set up your altar at the East side of the circle. On it should be the God and Goddess candles, salt and water dishes, athame, and incense holder. If you are working in a Coven environment, the High Priestess should place her athame by the Goddess candle, and the High Priest should place his athame by the God candle. Any special magickal tool to be used in the spell, such as a specially colored candle for candle magick or a string for knot magick, should also be on the altar. The Book of Shadows, or a single sheet of paper from the Book of Shadows with the spell written on it, can be either on the altar or in front of it. A small cauldron may be placed either in front of or beside the altar if it is your intention to burn the spell after the work is completed.

Place the quarter candles on the perimeter of your circle at each cardinal point of the compass and light the incense and all candles, except for any candle that might be selected for candle magick, always lighting the Goddess candle first. Using your athame, salted water, and incense, cast your circle and call the quarters in the manner described in chapter 3. The circle has now been purified with sage, marked, and consecrated with earth, water, fire, and air as represented by the salted water and burning incense. The elemental spirits have been called for your protection, and it is now usually appropriate to announce to all that the Sacred Circle has been completed or erected:

We are between the worlds and within time, the
circle surrounds us above as it does below. Let nothing

but love enter here and nothing but love leave here.
So mote it be.

You are now ready to invoke the aspect of the God and Goddess that you have previously identified as the one most closely associated with the type of spell or issue at hand.

Deity Invocation

In the case of spellcraft, you will not be invoking our generic Earth Mother or Sky Father entity in Their appropriate lunar or solar manifestations, as is typically done at Sabbat rituals, nor are you invoking the Lady in Her lunar manifestation, as is done in an esbat ritual. In spell work, you will be invoking a specific aspect of the God or Goddess uniquely suited to a specific task, and it is imperative that you identify the aspect that is appropriate for what you are attempting to accomplish. While calling or invoking the deity by the correct name is certainly a step in the right direction, in many cases your intentions, more than your vocalization, may determine who shows up.

I have heard of practitioners invoking a specific deity expressly by name, but who got a bit of a shock when they received the definite sense that someone other than who they had invoked actually manifested. In hindsight, it usually turned out that even if the name was vocalized, it was what the practitioner had in heart or mind that really made the connection. In short, be honest with yourself about what you are trying to accomplish and carefully identify the deity aspect most suited to that work.

There are many fine books available that do a good job describing our deities and identifying Their various aspects, some of which are included in the bibliography. I suggest obtaining a copy of these volumes and referring to them regularly in order to identify the deity aspect most appropriate to what you are attempting to accomplish. As I have said before, it is not wise to assume that only one text or volume has all the correct answers. Sometimes even the most carefully re-searched materials contain inadvertent errors, so it is always a good idea to crosscheck the names and functions of our deities in several works. As a starting point, you will find a short tabulation of Celtic deities along with Their associated spheres of influence in appendix G. Be aware that this partic-ular appendix lists relatively few deity names and identifica-tions. Far more detailed listings can be found in *Celtic Myth & Magick* by Edain McCoy, as well as *The Witches' God* and *The Witches' Goddess,* both by Stewart and Janet Farrar.

The deity you have identified as the one germane to what you are trying to accomplish can be invoked initially with a simple request to join your circle in order to offer help or guid-ance. You first invite Her or Him into the circle with a basic invocation, and then, through your spell incantation, you ask that deity to take a specific action on your behalf. The initial invocation can be done as follows:

Face the altar if you are working as a Solitary, or, if in Coven, continue facing inward with the rest of the Coven-ers. I personally prefer to do the invocation from the kneel-ing position as opposed to standing, but do what is more comfortable and meaningful for you. Extend your arms out and upward to embrace Her/Him, as the case may be, and invoke Him/Her with phrases such as this sample invocation to Cerridwen:

Cerridwen, Lady of Silver Magick, Keeper of the Cauldron of Knowledge, please hear me and be with me. Lend me Your guidance, Your love, and Your strength, dear Lady. Join with me. Be with me. Blessed be, Cerridwen.

After giving the invocation, it is necessary to sit back and relax. Fold your hands in your lap and breathe deeply. You can either close your eyes or focus your attention on the burning God or Goddess candle, as appropriate, or on the smoke from the incense. In this example, you would open yourself up to Cerridwen and give yourself time to feel Her presence. This could happen almost instantly, or it could take some time. How strongly you feel Her will depend to a great extent on your own preparations, as we discussed in the earlier part of this chapter. Once She has made Her presence known, you are ready to move ahead with the actual spell work.

Sample Spells of Candle and Knot Magick

The two examples I have included below are spells that I have used with some degree of success. The first example is one of candle magick and was a protection spell done at the request of a friend. The second example is one of knot magick and was designed to ease some bad habits our pet dog had acquired. I offer these only as a general guide. You will need to rewrite them in your own words to fit your own requirements.

I personally have had better success using candle magick over any of the others, although I have had some limited success with knot magick. I suggest you read as much additional material on spellcraft as possible in order to form your own opinions and use those methods that work best for you. This will probably be a period of experimentation; any one method should not be discarded too quickly, although, if you have kept detailed notes in your Mirror Book, it may become quite obvious to you within a few months if one particular method seems to be more effective than others.

As part of your preparation, you will have already identified the deity you will invoke for help and will have already selected the appropriate-colored candle. The size of the candle does not really matter. Generally, the small, four-inch or six-inch tapers are ideal for this work.

Candle Magick

The sample of spell work I present here was one that seemed to work rather well for me, or at least it accomplished the desired result. My words to this protection spell are as follows:

> *Beloved Goddess Ariadne, please hear my call,*
> *I ask for this within the greater good of all.*
> *May the powers great indeed,*
> *Surround and protect (name) in this time of need.*
>
> *Shield her from anguish and fear this night,*
> *Surround and protect her as best You might.*
> *Anxiety and fear have entered her life,*
> *Protect her now and remove this strife.*
>
> *And one last thing I ask of Thee,*
> *Let this spell bring no harm to mine or me.*
> *By my hand this spell is cast,*
> *And by the will of Ariadne it will come to pass.*
>
> *So mote it be.*

Since this sample spell involves an act of protection, and the Goddess in Her aspect of Ariadne is invoked, a white taper candle is used. In order to begin the spell, take your athame and with its point inscribe a single word most appropriate or meaningful to what is desired on the body of the candle. In this case, it may just be the word *protect* followed by the person's name. Hold the candle in your left hand and, while reciting the lines of the spell, gently stroke the candle with your athame from base to tip, one stroke with each stanza of the spell. Repeat the spell three complete times, while stroking the candle.

When the incantation has been completed, light the spell candle from either the Goddess or God altar candle, depending on the gender of the invoked deity. In this case, the spell candle would have been lit from the white Goddess candle. Place the burning spell candle on the altar if this is a Solitary rite or in the middle of your Coven circle if done in a group.

Now that you have spoken the wording, it is necessary to build the energy and release it in order to launch the spell to do its work. Sit facing the altar if you are working alone, or face inward with the rest of your Coveners if working in a group. If you are working with a Coven, you should all link hands and either chant, sing, or hum together as the energy is focused and you meditate on its purpose. If you are doing this work as a Solitary, close your eyes and chant, sing, or hum to yourself as you begin to feel the energy building.

Either in Coven or as a Solitary, you will now begin to feel the energy swirling around you. You may even mentally "see" it in some form, possibly as flashing lights or as a moving mass of color. You may feel your arms almost lifting by themselves or your whole body getting lighter and beginning to sway with the circling energy. You will probably feel warmth surrounding your body on all sides. The cadence and volume of the chant or humming should increase as the energy increases, finally reaching a peak after several minutes. It is at this time that the energy is launched to do the work. Exactly how long it will take to focus and launch the spell energy will vary from spell to spell and among practitioners. On occasion, I have had it happen quite quickly, in less than a minute, and at other times it has taken much longer, possibly as long as ten minutes. No two spell castings will be the same, neither in duration nor intensity.

When you feel the time is right to release the energy, you can either send it out to do the work or you can direct it into the candle, whichever action has been previously agreed upon. Either way is equally effective, and which one is chosen will probably be dictated either by the wording or the intent of the spell. If you desire to direct it outward and upward, quickly thrust your right hand skyward with your fingers extended, or launch it through your athame in the right hand. If you desire to direct the energy into the candle, you can thrust your extended fingers at the candle, or release it from your athame. This is an easy decision to reach if you are working as a Solitary since you and you alone will make that choice.

If you are working in a Coven environment, it should be the responsibility of either the High Priestess or High Priest to determine when and how the energy is to be released, as was done in the power-raising rite discussed earlier. It is imperative that, before the spell work is begun, all participants are fully aware of who will be leading the spell work, who will be releasing the energy, and how it will be released.

The spell candle should be left burning until there is nothing left but a stub. It can remain in your circle if there is sufficient time, or you can move it to your indoor altar after the circle is opened. After the candle has burned down, take it outside and bury it for at least one full lunar cycle. The paper on which you had written the spell can, if you desire, be burned in a small cauldron after the spell has been cast and the ash buried with the candle. I prefer to do this myself since it adds a firm act of closure to the spell work, but the option is yours.

Knot Magick

Knot magick is typically done to either bind something by tying the knots, or to break or open something by untying them. In this case, I was attempting to banish the desire of our dog, Kramer, to bark at other animals while on his leash. For this work, I had decided to invoke the help of Turrean, the Welsh Celtic goddess of small animals:

> *Kramer's bad habits are bound in knots of three,*
> *Banish them all as I untie thee.*
> *Aggression to other dogs will cease,*
> *Confrontation is gone, bringing only peace.*
>
> *By the knot of one, bad habits are undone.*
> *By the knot of two, good things start anew.*
> *By the knot of three, peace and contentment are*
> *   won.*
>
> *Three knots are undone.*
> *Bad habits are gone.*
> *Only good things now are done.*
>
> *And one last thing I ask of Thee,*
> *Let this work bring no harm to mine or me.*
> *By my hand this spell is cast,*
> *By the will of the Turrean let it come to pass.*
>
> *So mote it be.*

In this example, you would use a piece of string or twine of sufficient length to allow you to tie three knots easily. Tie them loose, because each knot will be untied as you finish reading each stanza of the spell. At the finish of the last reading and last knot, place the knotted string on the altar or in the middle of your Coven circle. Begin the chant or humming as you did with the candle magick example, allowing it to build of its own accord. Again, you will begin to feel the energy swirling around you, and the cadence and volume of the chant or humming should increase as the energy increases to its peak. When you feel the time is right to release the energy, you can either send it out to do the work or you can direct it into the knotted string. If you desire to direct it outward and upward, quickly thrust your right hand skyward with your fingers extended, or launch it through your athame in your right hand. If you desire to direct the energy into the string, you can thrust your extended fingers at the string or release it from your athame.

After the circle has been opened, take the string outside and bury it for at least one full lunar cycle. As before, the paper on which you had written the spell can be burned after the work has been done and the ash buried with the string.

Ending the Spell

Once the words have been spoken, the candle has been lit, or the knots worked and the energy released, the spell has been cast and the work is done. Sit quietly, and thoroughly ground yourself by placing both hands and your forearms, if necessary, firmly on the floor or ground. Feel any surplus energy (there will always be something left over from the spell) draining from your body back into the Earth, and release any feelings of the spell that are left. This act of grounding may take several minutes to complete, and, if necessary, any Covener sitting next to you can help by placing his or her hands over yours and absorbing some of the remaining energy through his or her body. Now that the spell has been cast and the energy projected or sent on its way, let go of the act that prompted the spell. You have placed the energy in the hands of someone much larger and more powerful than yourself and asked Them to handle this problem or issue. Do not take it back; let it go completely and totally.

Closing the Circle

The spell work has been completed, and it is now time to close the circle. Thank the deity for His or Her help with the problem or issue and bid goodbye, such as in this example with Cerridwen:

> *Cerridwen, Lady of Silver Magick, Keeper of the Cauldron of Knowledge, I thank You for being with me this night, and I thank You for Your guidance and help. Go in power, dear Lady. Hail and farewell. Blessed be, Cerridwen.*

Release the quarters, beginning with the East and again moving deosil around to all four quarters, as was described in chapter 3. Take down the circle by walking it widdershins, starting and ending in the East. After completing this act, stand or kneel in the middle of what was the circle and recite the following:

> *The circle is open but never broken. Nothing but love has come here and nothing but love has left here. So mote it be. Merry meet and merry part until we merry meet again.*

The magickal work has been completed. Now is the time, particularly if you have not performed the Cake and Ale Rite as part of the ritual, to eat and drink something. Your body and mind have experienced a significant and profound mental, spiritual, and physical level of exertion. The energy your have personally expended must be replaced by both nourishment and sleep. You may feel physically and mentally exhausted, and, if you have properly grounded yourself after the work, you will probably sleep quite deeply.

Herbs

I have mentioned the use of herbs or herbal remedies several times in this book. While it is not my intention to devote much effort to the subject, it is probably necessary to at least touch upon it. There are many fine herbal reference works available on the identification of the appropriate herb to address a specific ailment, including preparation and application instructions; however, just to give you a starting or reference point, the following herbs are those that you will most likely find to be the most useful for cooking, bathing, or magickal workings. They can be purchased from most New Age or health stores, and most certainly from Craft shops or sources. An ounce or two of each prepared herb should more than suffice for most applications.

Common herbs include, in no specific order, sage, basil, anise, parsley, catnip, geranium, angelica, jasmine, rose, rosemary, lavender, chamomile, verbena, yarrow, vervain, mint, hyssop, fennel, thyme, coriander, saffron, violet, valerian, rue, vertivert, and sweet woodruff.

Be careful about potentially poisonous herbs; in fact, it's probably better to stay away from such things as wormwood, foxglove, nightshade, absinth, oleander honeysuckle, and mugwort. Any of these should be used with extreme caution and only after you have established a full knowledge of their possible effects. Most reputable sources will not provide most of these, in any case.

Chapter Summary

In this chapter, I have only scratched the surface in my presentation of spellcraft or spell work. I have attempted to give you enough information to get started on the right foot, but how you work the magick, and any ramifications you may reap as a result of your magickal efforts, will be your responsibility and yours alone. There is no substitute for preparation in your magickal work, and believe me when I say there is no substitute for following the Wiccan Rede. You will get what you ask for, in one form or another, and at some time or other. You can count on it.

Magickal acts must at all times be approached with care and a full understanding of the forces you will be manipulating. The Gods and Goddesses of the Old Religion will help you if you ask Them, but understand that your interaction with Them is real. That interaction is not a figment of your imagination, nor is it a Hollywood movie that can be reshot or edited if something goes wrong. Before you begin, be sure that the work to be done is performed exactly as needed so that there is no mistaking what you are asking for, and be sure that your intentions follow the Wiccan Law. If you keep this credo firmly in mind, you shouldn't have any problems; instead, you will quite possibly experience a new awakening and a new belief in yourself when you look back on events and realize that your magick actually did work.

7

Divination

The Concise Columbia Encyclopedia defines *divination* as "the art or act of foretelling future events or revealing occult knowledge through divine sources, omens, or oracles."[1] Divination is thus an art that can sometimes give us a glimpse into the future or even clarify things in our past. No book on witchcraft would probably be complete without some discussion of divination and how you as a witch can apply that art in your own practice of the Craft.

The tools used for divination are many and varied, ranging from the mundane to the exotic. Tea leaves, palmistry, astrology, animal entrails, smoke, dreams, cards, runes, water, crystals, mirrors, fire—all these and more have been and are used as aids to divination. For the purposes of this book, I intend to keep the discussion relatively short and describe only three of these methods: the pendulum, the scrying mirror, and the runes. I have selected these three simply because they are the ones I have come to rely upon myself and are thus the ones about which I can talk with some degree of personal knowledge.

This is not meant to imply, however, that any other method of divination is somehow less effective or less meaningful. I have friends who will not consider taking any really significant action without first consulting a Tarot deck or astrological chart; for them, these are the tools that work. I suggest that you investigate several methods I have mentioned, or any others that may sound interesting to you, and pick the one or ones that best fit your personal needs and taste. Each tool will obviously require some study before attempting its use if you expect to achieve any real success, some more so than others, but each is also (with the probable exception of the animal entrails) rather easy to obtain and use.

The Pendulum

One of the simplest tools for divination is the pendulum. Although it is not viable for answers beyond the basic *yes*, *no*, and *maybe* types of questions, it works quite well for this specific purpose. The pendulum is made from any small weight that can be attached to the end of a string or light cord of about eight or ten inches in length. Any weight will do, and either a small crystal or stone is typically used, which is simply tied to one end of the cord. In order to use the pendulum in a divination process, you will need a flat surface, such as a desk or table, and a small piece of paper marked with about a six-inch-diameter circle containing two lines. One line is drawn across the circle from side to side and the other line is drawn down the circle from top to bottom so that both lines intersect at the center of the circle. Mark the letter Y at either end of the circle's horizontal line, and the letter *N* at either end of the circle's vertical line. There is no need to work in a cast circle when using the pendulum, nor is there any requirement about time of day or night. Literally any place at any time will do.

Sit at the desk or table with the paper containing the drawn circle and its two lines in front of you. Lean forward and hold the end of the pendulum string against your forehead using the middle fingers of both hands. Place your thumbs on the sides of your head and your elbows on the table on either side of the circle paper so that your head is supported comfortably. The pendulum should hang unmoving over the center of the circle paper and about an inch or so above the surface.

Now concentrate on and vocalize a question that requires a yes or no answer. The pendulum will gradually begin to move. If the movement is side-to-side, the answer is yes; if the movement is top-to-bottom, the answer is no; and if the pendulum swings in a circular pattern around the circle perimeter, the answer is maybe. You might experiment first with several questions to which you know the answer, just to verify that the pendulum does indeed seem to be working as expected.

Some people attribute the movement of the pendulum to the practitioner, who knows which way he or she wants the pendulum to swing, and is therefore forcing the motion by minuscule movements of either the finger tips or even of the head. I personally find this explanation ludicrous since I have seen a pendulum swinging through six or seven inches or arc, and any physical movement of the practitioner that would have caused this much of a swing would have been obvious to even the casual observer. Others find the experiment interesting, but put as much faith in the pendulum as in a Ouija board as a divination aid. Still others acknowledge the possibility of unknown forces driving the pendulum and accept it as just as viable a tool as Tarot cards, runes, or scrying mirrors.

My personal feeling after using the pendulum off and on for several years is that it does seem to give generally good results. The only way to be sure if this is a tool you can depend on for your own purposes is to use it while making notes in your Mirror Book as to when and what was asked. It may be only in hindsight, after rereading your notes, that the worth or lack of worth of the pendulum as a divination tool for you can be determined.

The Scrying Mirror

To *scry* basically means to see or predict the future with the aid of a crystal or glass ball, or other crystal or glass surfaces. A scrying mirror can be made of any material in which you can easily see a reflection. Generally, any flat reflective surface will do, but it should usually be a dark surface. A relatively good scrying mirror can be made by filling a dark-colored bowl with water so that your reflection is easily discernible when looking into it. The problem with this is that you must hunch over the bowl in order to use it. I personally find it easier to use a mirror by placing it upright so that I can gaze into it from a more comfortable sitting position.

The mirror should be backed in black, if possible, not silvered, and have a relatively simple dark-colored and nondecorative wooden frame, so as to minimize any distractions for the eye. It should be about six or eight inches long on a side. If it does not have its own stand, you can either make one or just prop the mirror in a position that makes for easy viewing. Most secondhand stores or pawnshops usually have a plethora of silvered mirrors that can do in a pinch, but mirrors backed in black are usually found only in Craft shops. It is only a matter of finding the one that seems to best fit your personal requirements, or the one that may just feel right to you.

Although you can use a scrying mirror virtually anywhere, I have usually obtained the best results when I use mine at night with candlelight, and sometimes with incense to set the mood. There is no need to cast a circle or make any other preparations before using the mirror. All you have to do is select a time and place where you can work alone without being disturbed. A scrying session is one of those things best done by yourself, since having others around will only be a distraction and probably make the session fruitless.

Sit comfortably on the ground or floor in front of your mirror, with a candle placed off to each side of the mirror so the flame does not interfere, but close enough so that you can see your face in the mirror from the candlelight. Take several deep breaths in order to relax and cleanse yourself, and then try to clear your mind of all mundane or daily thoughts. Sit quietly, without moving, and watch your reflection in the mirror. Allow your eyes to go out of focus somewhat. Do not stare intently at yourself, but rather try to look beyond or behind your reflection into the mirror.

It may take some time, but you should eventually begin to see shapes or other images forming in the glass. Do not attempt to focus your eyes on them; let the images do what they will. Try to understand what the image is—a human form, an animal, a room, a scene? Try to identify as many details as possible about the image, such as clothing if it is a person, or maybe even something in the background. The image may fade quickly, and nothing else may appear. This is the time to end the scrying session. Do not try to force the image to reappear. Contemplate what you have witnessed. You might close your eyes to relax and consider the image in light of some recent event or in regard to what you had been thinking just before the scrying session started. Don't be surprised if there isn't any obvious connection; the image may actually have been something from a past life. This is where scrying can get really interesting, because it is possible to catch glimpses of yourself as you existed in the past.

As soon as you have a chance, it would be appropriate to note in your Mirror Book all the details you remember about the image, and also note your initial reactions or thoughts on what it might have meant. This is very important since the same or similar image may appear at some other time you use the scrying mirror, and, by connecting more than one event, it may be easier to identify what the image is trying to tell you. This is particularly important if you have been fortunate enough to catch a glimpse of a past-life image, since it is quite likely that it, or another like it, may reappear. Each appearance may give you a different look and a little more insight into events in your past. By being able to connect several such sessions, you may actually begin to develop a picture of one of your past lives.

The Runes

Runes are symbols that comprised an alphabet used by Celtic tribes throughout northern and western Europe, apparently coming into use beginning quite late in the first millennium B.C. and continuing well into the sixteenth or even early seventeenth centuries. Many linguists maintain that the runic alphabet was most likely derived from either early Latin or even possibly the Etruscan alphabet, since many of the characters share a similar structure.

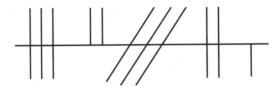

Figure 7. An Example of the Ogham Alphabet (taken from finds on the coast of Newfoundland that date to approximately A.D. 900).

In addition to runes, the Celts of the British Isles, most notably in Ireland between the fifth and seventh centuries A.D., also used another form of symbology called the ogham (or ogam) alphabet (see figure 7). This method of writing used notches to represent vowels and lines to represent consonants, with its name probably derived from the Celtic god Ogma, who was associated with the Irish Celtic pantheon. In one of Ogma's personifications, he is known as the patron god of poets or writing and in Celtic myth it was Ogma who gave the alphabet that bears his name to the Druids. Both the ogham and the runic alphabets were always written using only straight lines, which made them ideal for easily inscribing on stone or carving into wood.

While the ogham alphabet conveyed information to some degree in words or letters of the Old Celtic dialect, the runic alphabet was considerably more complex. The runic symbols were meant to convey entire concepts or thoughts as opposed to literal text. However, the oghamic and runic alphabets were not the only methods of writing used by the Celts in general, and also by the Druidic priesthood.[2] In 53 B.C., Julius Caesar wrote that "it is unlawful to commit the Druid doctrines to writing, although in other public and private accounts they use the Greek characters in many cases."[3] It would thus seem that by the time Roman armies reached western Europe and the

British Isles, the use of runes and oghams may have been relegated to only the non-Druid general populace, with the more learned Druids preferring to write in Greek.

There are several variants of the runic alphabet. The earliest is called the Elder Futhark and is comprised of twenty-four symbols (see figure 8). The Elder Futhark was widely used from the first century B.C. until approximately the eighth century A.D., when it was replaced to a certain extent by the Younger Futhark, which was comprised of only sixteen symbols. The Younger Futhark, and to a limited extent the Elder Futhark, continued in use throughout northern and western Europe until about the sixteenth or seventeenth centuries A.D.

Two additional runic forms called Futhorks were sporadically used between about the fifth and thirteenth centuries A.D. These included the Anglo-Frisian Futhork, with between twenty-nine and thirty-three symbols, and the Armanic Futhork, with eighteen symbols. Some historians maintain that the Armanic Futhork may have appeared much later, possibly not even until the nineteenth century, when it formed a considerable base of the Germanic occultism philosophies that began during this time period and extended into the early decades of the twentieth century.

The runic alphabets are not case-sensitive and there is no provision for upper or lowercase representations. It is not my intention in this book, however, to write a detailed interpretation of each runic symbol of the various Futharks or to teach a class on the use of runes. That would require a book unto itself, and there are already several very good ones available by Rune Master Edred Thorsson, such as *Rune Might* and *Futhark: A Handbook of Rune Magick*. There are also several good rune descriptions available on various Internet websites. One of the best I have found is titled *Runes—The Viking Oracle*, and the resource locator for this website is included in

FEHU—The first rune of the Elder Futhark. The exoteric meaning of this rune can be money, and the esoteric meaning can be dynamic power.

URUZ—The second rune of the Elder Futhark. The exoteric meaning of this rune can represent something wild and usually horned, and the esoteric meaning involves your formative essence, your internal being.

THURISAZ—The third rune of the Elder Futhark. The exoteric meaning of this rune is strength, and the esoteric meaning is a breaker of resistance.

ANSUZ—The fourth rune of the Elder Futhark. The exoteric meaning of this rune is the God force, and the esoteric meaning relates to sovereign or ancestral forces.

Figure 8. The First Four Runes of the Elder Futhark Runic Alphabet.

the bibliography. This website gives a brief description of each rune's base meaning and a short paragraph about its more esoteric properties.

In this chapter, I am going to discuss two relatively simple ways to use a set of runes as a divination aid, methods I have used successfully many, many times myself with the Elder Futhark. I urge you to read the two books by Thorsson I mentioned if you desire a more detailed examination of the meanings and histories behind the runic alphabets. *Futhark: A Handbook of Rune Magick*, in particular, has a very detailed description and interpretive discussion of each symbol comprising the Elder Futhark. I have found this work quite valuable in aiding my own interpretations during rune casts.

There is no reason to cast the runes in a Sacred Circle, and there is no requirement on time of day or night when a rune cast is supposedly more effective. When we do rune casts in our Coven, it is generally after the ritual has been completed and everybody is relaxing with drinks or finishing any food leftover from a ritual feast.

Types of Rune Casts

There are many forms of rune casts, usually called Renumals, that one can use, with each type requiring a different number of runes. They range from the simplest cast, called *The Candle*, which uses only one rune, up to *The Runic Circle*, which uses all twenty-four runes, or even twenty-five runes if the blank symbol for "rune of no meaning" is used. There are two types or methods for casting the runes that I typically use, *The Candle* and *Thor's Trinity*. In most cases I have found that they can yield sufficient information to choose a course of action or to verify a supposition. I personally have seldom found it necessary to go beyond the complexity of *Thor's Trinity*, but do what you feel you need to do in order to acquire your de-

Figure 9. Rune Configuration for *The Candle.*

sired level of information. If you feel you need to do *The Runic Circle* with all twenty-five symbols, then by all means do so. It is totally up to you.

Generally, runes are not used for interpretations requiring a straight yes or no answer, because their meanings are generally too complex for this. How the meaning of any rune cast is interpreted will, to a great extent, depend on your own experience and skills at reading the rune and understanding what it is trying to tell you. In most cases, the interpretation of your rune cast must also be considered in light of the history, attitudes, and emotional state of the person who has asked the question. Although I have used *The Candle* on occasion, I prefer the broader and more in-depth interpretations that can be achieved with *Thor's Trinity.*

The Candle is the simplest of rune casts (see figure 9). It uses only one rune stone and is used to clarify or define an existing condition or situation. In this case, I have the person asking a question draw one rune from the rune pouch. If you wish, you can note the symbol drawn and the interpretation of that symbol as taken from one of the runic guides previously mentioned. The information can be recorded in a Mirror Book so that it can be referred to later in order to determine how valid the interpretation was.

Thor's Trinity is a rune cast typically used in order to shed light on a current state of affairs (see figure 10). If we are

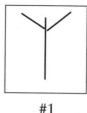

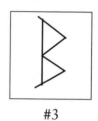

Figure 10. Rune Configuration for *Thor's Trinity*.

doing *Thor's Trinity*, I have the person who is asking the question select one rune from the rune pouch, sight unseen. I note what the selected runic symbol is on a piece of paper, and then have the person replace it in the rune pouch before drawing the second stone. This process is repeated until all three runes have been drawn. Then the interpretation can begin. The first rune drawn is noted in the middle of the sheet of paper and represents the questioner's current situation. The second rune drawn is noted to the left of the first rune and represents the factors that are working in the questioner's favor. The third rune is noted to the right of the first rune and represents the factors that are working against the questioner. As in *The Candle*, you should note the runic symbols as well as your interpretation of them in your Mirror Book so that the validity of the rune cast can later be determined.

1. *The 1991 Concise Columbia Encyclopedia,* s.v. "divination."

2. See T. W. Rolleston, *Celtic Myths and Legends* (1897; reprint, Mineola, NY: Dover Publications, 1990).

3. See Julius Caesar, *The Conquest of Gaul,* trans. S. A. Handford, book VI (London: Penguin Books, Ltd., 1951) paragraph 14.

8

The Physically Challenged Witch

$\mathcal{S}$ome readers may consider this a strange topic to include in a book on the practice of witchcraft; however, there are those who wish to practice our Craft and feel they are not capable of doing so in the most suitable or "proper" way because of some physical impairment or disability. First of all, think back to chapter 3 and remember that there is really no single or proper way to worship the old gods and goddesses. Whatever speaks to you in your innermost self will be, by definition, the right way for you, and that is all that really matters. Your own spirituality, your personal recognition of the deities in your own honest way, is what will bring you together with Them and make you part of the Old Religion. It is your intent more than anything else that will make this happen.

Having said all that, let us consider what having some kind of physical disability may mean to a person who is trying to master the aspects of Wicca and to grow in our religion. I think it is important to recognize that disabilities can come in many forms, not all of which are readily recognizable to others. The *American Heritage Dictionary* defines *disable* as "to deprive of capability or effectiveness, especially to impair the physical abilities of"; and *disability* as "the chief misery of the decline of the faculties, the lack of customary appreciation and influence, which only the rarest tact and thoughtfulness on the part of others can alleviate."[1]

Disabilities can be permanent or temporary. They can be the result of an accident or injury, or even inherited. They can be life-threatening or not, and many of these disabilities have an adverse impact on individuals attempting to follow the dictates of our Craft. Some disabilities impact the Solitary more than a witch working in a Coven environment, while some have more of an impact on a Coven practitioner.

For example, a person may have severely restricted limb movement that makes kneeling at an altar virtually impossible without help. This is not a real problem for someone in a Coven, who can be assisted by fellow Coveners, but it most assuredly could be a problem for a Solitary. A person may be confined to a wheelchair and thus unable to stand in order to address a quarter or fully assume the God or Goddess position for an invocation or dedication. This could possibly make a person feel uncomfortable in Coven or even unwilling to take part in Coven rituals to the point where he or she is forced to work the rites and rituals as a Solitary. Someone else may have such a severe hearing loss that he or she is unable to hear and follow all the ritual words. This is not a real problem for a Solitary, but it could be for someone working in a Coven.

Have you ever tried to lip-read across a nine or twelve-foot diameter circle at night, by candlelight or moonlight?

The following sections in this chapter discuss specific problems faced by people I personally know to be working the Craft under some form of physical handicap. The methods or techniques they use to circumvent their disabilities will hopefully guide others who may be similarly affected, or will at least offer some ideas for the consideration of others.

When all is said and done, regardless of how you work or do not work the rituals and rites, the ultimate connection will be between each one of you and our deities. Do not let anyone try to tell you that you cannot worship the Lord and Lady and practice the Old Religion simply because you are unable to kneel at an altar or because you are unable to cast a circle for each and every ritual or rite. The God and Goddess will recognize your intent, regardless of how you are required to conduct your observances.

Acute Hearing Loss

I would like to start this chapter with the story of a person very dear to me who suffers from a disability; not a life-threatening disability, fortunately, but nonetheless one that has made some of her Craftwork more difficult for her than for others. This person is my wife, who suffers from acute hearing loss. She is not deaf but suffers from tinnitus, a constant high-pitched ringing in the ears, as well as a severe loss of hearing in the middle frequency ranges. Even under ideal conditions of limited extraneous background noises, she still must use assistive hearing devices coupled with lip-reading skills, and even then sometimes has a hard time understanding everything that is said to her.

In my wife's situation, she typically receives as much information from lip-reading as from the use of hearing aids or other amplification devices. As such, you can readily understand that it is difficult for her to take part in all aspects of our rituals since lip-reading can be virtually impossible at night with only moonlight or candlelight to work with. In order to help alleviate this problem, she has begun to use a miniature radio transmitter coupled with a receiving loop around her neck. With the transmitter placed in or near the center of the circle, most sounds can be coupled through the receiving loop to her hearing aids so that she can hear at least the majority of what is said in the circle.

All members of our Coven are aware of the fact that this device is a radio transmitter, and that anyone with the appropriate receiving equipment could essentially eavesdrop on our activities. Fortunately, the equipment operates at an extremely low power level and at a frequency that puts it beyond the range of such mundane things as portable telephones and baby monitors. We are quite comfortable knowing that the probability of having our rituals monitored by someone outside of our home, while not totally impossible, is nonetheless quite low.

In any event, because she depends on lip-reading for a great deal of information, even this transmitter/receiver does not meet all her needs. This becomes a problem particularly when someone is calling a quarter and has his or her back turned to my wife. It is extremely difficult if not impossible for her to hear the invocation since the electronics hardware is in the center of the circle, maybe six feet or more from the person doing the talking. With the person's back turned, lip-reading is out of the question; so, unfortunately, she misses some of the quarter invocations.

She also has a problem understanding several of our Coveners who have quite low or soft voices. Even when they are directly in front of the assistive-listening hardware microphone, it is still very difficult for her to hear and follow everything that is being said. My wife misses as much as one-fourth of the verbalizations that occur in the circle. On the upside, she is sufficiently conversant with ritual, and generally with any power or spell work that we may undertake, that she can still feel comfortable taking part as much as she can right along with the rest of us.

Does she consider this a handicap? Most assuredly, yes. At the same time, she and the rest of our Coven have come to accept it as simply something that we all have to work with. This disability does not make her any less a Pagan than the rest of us, simply because she misses some things said at ritual. Her intent to follow the God and Goddess is just as strong as yours or mine, and if she has to ask twice about some part of a rite, that is perfectly acceptable to our Coven. We all believe it is also perfectly acceptable to the deities we serve. We all do the best we can, and the God and Goddess accept us with all our frailties that make us human beings. We are no less Pagans and no less witches simply because we may have some disability that sets us apart from others.

Severe Back Problems

Another one of my friends also suffers from a very real physical handicap. She has a severe back problem, one that has already required one surgery, that prevents her from kneeling in circle or at the altar, forcing her to sit on a low foot stool instead of on the floor or ground. She considers herself fortunate if she is limber enough on any given night to get one knee all the way down in order to ground herself after a spell or other power work. Because it is extremely difficult, if not impossible, for her to get up and down quickly and easily, any power raising she wants to take part in must exclude the rest of her Coven from walking the circle. The power raising in those cases is only done with all of them sitting immobile while the chant or other vocalization is conducted until the High Priestess finally releases the energy.

This does not make her any less a Pagan or less a follower of the Goddess, nor does it have any negative impact on her Coven at all. All her Coveners are fully aware of her limitations, and they all act accordingly. To them, there is absolutely no difference in the success of the work if power raising must be done immobile or not; as far as they are concerned, it still works. As far as the Lord and Lady are concerned, I would venture to guess that They understand fully why some of this particular Coven's rites or rituals may have to be done a little differently in order to accommodate my friend. After all, it is that special word *intent* again that still drives how we work the Craft and how the deities accept our workings. Their power-raising rites are just as strong to them as power raising done in any other way.

Immobile and Dependent

Another friend of mine suffers from severe medical problems. As a result of her disability, as well as the effects of prolonged treatments, she has been forced to quit her job in the medical profession and live with one of her parents in order to receive the daily care she needs. In the following paragraphs, she describes some of the issues she faces when trying to do even a simple thing like casting a circle. As for her privacy during rites, well, her statements speak for themselves.

"I am permanently physically challenged, with serious limitations on my physical abilities. There is little I can do for myself, and I have to live at home with my mother in only one very small room that I can call my own. I do not have enough physical space to really even cast a small circle or do much of anything in the way of ritual work, and my privacy is virtually nonexistent. My mother almost had a heart attack when she saw my altar, candle holders, runes, and oils at the foot of my bed.

"I don't have room inside and cannot easily get outside to do rituals since I need her help to get in and out of the house. We also have a nosy set of neighbors who would probably go ballistic if they saw me outside at night burning candles and chanting. I need and want to do a self-consecration or dedication rite, but what can I do? How can I do my other rituals or even consider working any magick? Will the Goddess understand if I can't do rituals or rites the way they're supposed to be done?"

What can a person who is emotionally and spiritually dedicated to the Craft and to the gods and goddesses do in such a situation? How do you go about doing a ritual if you cannot even cast a small circle? I think it all comes back to that single and most important word—*intent*.

Given my friend's situation, since a Solitary's circle is generally only three feet in diameter, it would be possible to cast a circle from the middle of a bed if there is no room on the floor on which to stand or sit. While the athame, salt, water, and incense are important implements used in the circle-cast, it is also necessary to remember that those physical tools are simply things that are extensions of our own minds and wills. We mark the circle with the athame and consecrate it with the salted water and incense, but our minds, wills, desires, and intentions are what really accomplish the goal of making our circle what it is. It is a place we have built for ourselves and for our deities; a place between the worlds and without time; and a place that is pure and consecrated in our own thoughts, and in the eyes of the God and Goddess.

As far as the Goddess understanding my friend's desires and intentions or not, why wouldn't She? Our God and Goddess are loving and nurturing to Their children. If we sincerely call to Them and invoke Them in perfect trust and perfect love, then They will respond to us in kind. All that is needed is sincerity and honesty in what we are trying to accomplish. We have to trust ourselves, examine what it is we want to do, focus our will and believe in what we are doing, and it will happen. If we are sincere in our beliefs about the Lord and Lady, They will understand our situation. What is in our hearts and in our spiritual awareness, what is inside us, is what really matters, and They know that.

We all follow our spiritual paths to the best of our abilities and in our own way. Our rituals can be as simple or as complex as we care to make them, but, in the eyes of our deities, it's all the same as long as our intent and commitment are there. Even in captivity, people have found ways to honor our deities by improvising, and this is perfectly acceptable as long as the honest intent to honor Them is present. After all, one does not need a cast circle to just talk to the Lady.

If we need to do a rite or ritual but feel we cannot perform it from someone else's written text for whatever reason, then we can alter that text to better fit our own needs. There are probably thousands of versions on various God and Goddess invocations, each and every one written by equally knowledgeable and dedicated authors. Although the words may differ from one version to the other, the intent is always the same. We can work our own rituals that are meaningful to us by sticking to the basics. We can talk to the deities with a single candle, or we can just use simple visualization that lets us communicate with the God and Goddess. We can even raise energy by chanting, which can be done in a whisper, if necessary.

Regarding my friend's question about her self-dedication, there is absolutely no reason why the Goddess would not recognize the intention to dedicate. I think the main thoughts here again involve that keyword *intention*, and as long as those intentions are directed openly and honestly, the Lady would probably accept any type of dedication that could be done. I believe She would accept that dedication as readily as one done in any formal ritual conducted by any High Priest or High Priestess.

The sincerity of our feelings and emotions is what drives the connection between us and the Goddess. For those of us who cannot do something like a dedication in a full ritual ceremony, well, we can only do it in the best way we can. She will understand the reasons and the problems, and She will understand our limitations. After all, one line from *The Charge of the Goddess* says:

> *If thou find it not within thee, thou shalt never find it without thee.*

This certainly implies that the main ingredient here is our own inner motivation and spirituality, the things that define our intentions. Our deities are fully understanding and aware of our problems, our difficulties, and our limitations. We are, after all, part of Them, as They are part of us; and, even more importantly, we are Their children.

Chapter Summary

I think the spiritual or ritual concerns that have been raised in this chapter can be addressed by repeating a theme that has permeated this book. The Old Religion, the Craft of the Wise, Wicca, the practice of witchcraft, is what identifies us. Our understanding and interpretation of these things define who and what we are, and that definition is inherently intertwined and linked with honoring the deities of our religion, which we accomplish by working our rites and rituals. As long as we do our workings to the best of our abilities, skills, and limitations, they will be acceptable and meaningful to Them.

Many of us have problems or issues that may make it impractical or even impossible to follow the rituals that have been spelled out in this book fully, or in any other Craft book. This inability must not be construed as somehow making a person less a Pagan, less a Wiccan, or less a witch. I have said time and time again throughout this book that your own individual practice of the Craft of the Wise must be predicated upon your own interpretation and understanding of the Old Religion and its deities, and how you interact with that religion and with Them.

That is the thing that will define you as a practitioner of the Craft, rather than the fact that you may need to cast a circle mentally from the confines of your bed, that you are physically unable to kneel at an altar, or that you need to use hearing aids or other assistive devices in circle. These things are all unfortunate, because from time to time they may indeed rob you of some of the connection the rest of us may feel to the

Lord and Lady, but they do not by any stretch of the imagination make you any less a witch than the rest of us; not in the eyes of any real witch who embraces our ethical laws, and for sure not in the eyes of our Lord and Lady.

1. *The American Heritage Dictionary of the English Language*, 3rd ed., s.v. "disable," "disability."

9

The Humorous Side

*N*ow that you have been introduced to the basic Sabbat and esbat rituals as well as some of the basic rites of the Craft, you may have the impression that witches are a very serious lot who take little joy out of life. Well, let me assure you that this is not the case by any stretch of the imagination. While our rituals are indeed serious, simply because they are so meaningful to us, this does not mean that we cannot or do not have fun at those rituals. Many of our Sabbats are celebrations, and they can be replete with games, fun, and entertainment that may exist in and around the actual Sabbat rituals. *The Charge of the Goddess* states, in part:

> *Let My worship be in the heart that rejoices, for behold—all acts of love and pleasure are My rituals. Let*

there be beauty and strength, power and compassion,
honor and humility, mirth and reverence within you.

Our rites and rituals are not bound up in total solemnity, because the Lady tells us to have fun and laugh. There are times
when something just becomes so hysterically funny that we,
and our deities, have no choice but to laugh. We are, after all,
human beings, and we do make mistakes. We do blunder and
inadvertently screw things up, sometimes even in the middle
of the most solemn rituals.

I think there are many of us who have tripped over another
Covener while walking the circle to cast it, or have kicked over
a quarter candle, dumping wax onto the carpet. There may
even be a few of us who have set off a smoke alarm when purifying an indoor circle—now there is a way to start a ritual! I
am sure there are those of us who have gotten tongue-tied or
verbally tripped over an incantation or two. There are also
probably more than just a few of us who, when releasing a
quarter, have twisted the words from "Go if you must, stay if
you will" into "Go if you will, stay if you must."

What follows here is a brief compilation from several of
my friends, as well as some personal anecdotes, on the more
humorous or even the stranger side of practicing the Craft.
Enjoy, and when you make your own mistakes or experience
your own wild or unusual ritual events, as I am sure you all
will at some time or other, try not to worry about it. We have
all done similar things, and our deities have laughed right
along with us.

A Stranger Knocks

Most of the members of our immediate family, with the exception of our son and his wife, are well aware of our Pagan

religion and that we practice the Craft. They are also aware that we have evening or nighttime Coven get-togethers at Sabbat and esbat ritual times. We have never been interrupted during our rituals, since they are generally held late at night when the chance of visitors is remote, and we take the precaution to advise friends and family beforehand that we will be indisposed that evening. Although there are several cars usually parked in and around our driveway, the interior house lights are always turned off, and it is not obvious that any activity is going on, either inside or outside. Still, we have always taken the time to lock all our doors just in case some friend, neighbor, or relative stops by for one reason or another.

We usually start off our rituals by spending a short time talking and socializing, usually discussing what we will be doing during ritual and who will be responsible for what action, such as calling the quarters. By the end of an hour or less, everybody has arrived, the ritual tools have been brought out and placed in the circle, and we are ready to begin.

On one particular night, several of our Coveners were running late, so the rest of us killed time with general chitchat until the latecomers arrived. By then, it was quite late in the evening and, being in a bit of a hurry to set up the circle and get the ritual started, I inadvertently forgot to lock the front door.

All the house lights were eventually turned off, so the only light now came from our circle and altar candles. The entire front of the house smelled of sage and incense, and we were all sitting in the center of our dining room floor in the middle of the Ostara Sabbat Ritual. There came a momentary time of quiet in the circle, for one reason or another, and then we all heard the front door knob rattle as someone began to open it. Everyone in our Coven looked immediately at me with expressions that said unmistakably, "All right, Mr. High Priest, now what?"

My first thought was a worst-case scenario in that the person coming in the door was either our son or daughter-in-law. The problem with this, the reason we have not yet taken them into our confidence about our witchcraft association, is the fact that they are both born-again Christians. In actuality, this may not be as big a problem as we currently perceive it. They are both reasonably intelligent individuals, they have seen our indoor altar with all the various decorations, and they are aware of what we have euphemistically called our late night "meditation sessions" with friends. In any case, we have elected not to open up to either of them with any in-depth revelations about our religious pursuits, at least not yet.

Having said all this as background, I am sure you will believe me when I say that a ritual never came to a halt so suddenly, a circle never got opened so quickly, and yours truly hadn't moved with such speed and dexterity in a long time. I was on my feet, out of that circle, and across the room to the door before it had opened more than just a few inches, all with moves that a professional dancer would probably envy.

Since the doorway is recessed several feet into a short entry alcove, it was impossible for anyone at the door to see into the room, and also impossible for any of us to see who might be coming in. As I grabbed the door jam and stuck my head out of the still-opening door, I was totally relieved to find not our son or daughter-in-law, but our daughter, who is fully aware and knowledgeable of our witchcraft practices. There she was, standing at the open door with hand on mouth, saying, "Jeez, Dad, the minute I smelled the incense I knew I was interrupting something." At this point we both broke into hysterical laughter, she with embarrassment and me with relief, as she slowly backed off the porch while apologizing profusely for interrupting our ritual.

I finally locked the door and returned to the circle, the rest of our group having heard all the laughter and discussion, and we finished without further incident. I can just imagine how the deities must have laughed over that one, because we sure did later in the evening.

A Unique Invocation to the Spirit of Water

A friend of mine has related this tale of how not to conduct a ritual. He and his significant companion, along with several others, occasionally work some informal rituals together. They do not really consider themselves a Coven, since there is no one designated as High Priestess or High Priest and they do not always observe all the Sabbat or esbats rituals. Nonetheless, the four of them do come together for mutual appreciation of the Lord and Lady whenever the mood strikes them.

One night last summer, they had decided to do an impromptu rite, following a barbecue dinner, in order to thank the deities for the benefits of the previous year. As my friend relates it, this dinner had taken longer than usual to prepare and cook, and they had all partaken rather extensively of various alcoholic beverages. As a result, by the time dinner was served and eaten, everybody was at least somewhat inebriated. It was then that they decided to hold the impromptu ritual.

It was late at night and quite dark when they all moved to an area in the backyard, adjacent to a swimming pool, which they had used many times before. Placing his box of candles and other implements on the ground, my friend began to cast a circle, but in his somewhat impaired condition, the circle became more of an elliptical wandering that took him quite close to the edge of the pool. It was then that one of the ladies began to giggle uncontrollably, apparently at the prospect of an impending unplanned immersion. You all probably know that when somebody in a group begins to giggle, the mood becomes infectious, particularly if the whole group is somewhat intoxicated. With my friend now laughing out loud and teetering on the edge of the pool, the giggling from the others became unrestrained laughter as he lost his balance, began to fall, and, at the last minute, jumped backward into the water.

It was then that all restraint disappeared and everybody jumped into the swimming pool after him, still laughing hysterically. After they had all finished sputtering and wiping the water from their hair and eyes, they actually did the ritual in the water. All four of them stood in a circle in the pool's shallow end, holding on to each other, looking up at the moon and taking turns vocalizing a heartfelt and personal thank you to the gods. There was no cast circle, there were no quarters called, and no real invocations were done; but, according to my friend, that very unstructured and totally nonstandard appreciation ritual was one of the most meaningful and moving the four of them had ever done together.

Candles and Small Spaces

I suppose, since we do work with candles and open flames, it was inevitable that at one time or another there would be an incident involving fire. Fortunately, in this case, there were no injuries sustained and no real damage done other than some superficial stains and burns on the carpeting. This story was related by a Pagan acquaintance of mine who thought it interesting enough for inclusion in this book.

Apparently, his Coven had assembled for a Sabbat celebration for Imbolc in the apartment of one of the Coven members, since the home of the High Priestess and High Priest where they normally met was under a fumigation tent for some infestation at the time. About twenty people had assembled for the ritual. The apartment was quite spacious, but even with the furniture moved back against the walls it became quickly obvious that they would be packed into a rather tight group in the living room.

In any event, the High Priestess set up the circle, cast it, and began to bring each Covener into the sacred space one at a time. Sure enough, by the time all had entered the circle and sat down on the floor, there was barely enough room for the High Priest and High Priestess to open the Coven Book of Shadows in front of the altar. The quarters were called, the invocations were begun, and the ritual was proceeding quite smoothly when a woman sitting near the North Quarter let out a yell and jumped to her feet. She had apparently taken off her sweater, since the number of people in the small space had made the room quite warm, and had been sitting on it during the early part of the ritual. Her sweater was also quite close to the North Quarter candle, close enough so that the sleeve caught fire. She grabbed the smoldering sweater and began to beat it against the carpet in order to extinguish the fire, only to kick over the still-burning quarter candle. The votive candle popped out of its glass holder and bounced, still burning, a foot or so across the floor where it came to rest under the floor-to-ceiling window drapes.

By this time, everybody was on their feet and the integrity of the circle had been totally destroyed as people tried to help with the burning sweater and also grab the errant votive candle before it set fire to the drapes. The High Priest grabbed a pitcher of wine that had been set aside for the Cake and Ale Rite and used it to douse the still-smoldering sweater, soaking the sweater and carpet alike with red wine. By this time, the wandering votive candle had been recovered and extinguished before the drapes had a chance to catch fire.

The entire episode had taken only a few minutes, but in that short time a fairly expensive sweater had been ruined, a light-gray colored carpet now had a two-foot diameter wine stain on it along with some small burn marks, and the ritual had been totally abandoned. The consensus of opinion for that night was to forget the ritual until the following night and, regardless of the weather, to hold it outside. Fortunately, there was no damage done to the drapes from the bouncing votive candle, and some judicious placement of furniture hid the damage to the carpet. The sweater, however, was a lost cause.

A Critter Enters the Circle

As you grow in your abilities and your confidence as a witch, you will gradually become aware that you have crossed an invisible and hitherto unknown boundary involving your relationship with nature. You will begin to become more aware of the living and growing things around you, such as the plants or trees in your own garden or yard, and especially of animals.

If you have a pet, it may be that you start to perceive your pet in a different light. Even though you may have loved the animal before now, that relationship may begin to take on a new and deeper meaning, with your pet now assuming the role of Familiar. Your pet now becomes a link between you and a specific spirit or spirits, possibly even becoming the earthly manifestation of a spirit entity. You and your animal may establish a bond that goes far beyond that of any previous owner-pet relationship. It is also not uncommon for your new awareness to extend to living creatures beyond your own pet or Familiar.

This strange awareness was brought home to me in a rather startling way several years ago. I was doing a full-moon esbat, late at night, and the moon was pretty much at zenith. It was extremely bright, the light was almost bright enough to read by since there was no cloud or haze in the sky, and the moon was well above the branches of my backyard pine trees. I had just invoked the Lady and was quietly beginning a meditation in order to resolve some troubling issues, my eyes semifocused on the Goddess candle flame, when my peripheral vision detected movement off to the right. At first, I could not see much. The moonlight coupled with the candlelight had essentially blinded me to anything in the shadows, but as I shaded my eyes from the moon and candle lights, they quickly adjusted. I realized that a rather large bobcat had approached my circle and was standing there, staring at me from beside the trunk of a pine tree at a distance of about twelve feet.

Since we live in the foothills above Los Angeles, it is not uncommon for all sorts of animals to visit our yard on occasion. We have seen raccoon, possum, coyote, and even a small deer from time to time, but never a wild cat. The animal and I stared at each other for several seconds, then it very slowly walked into the full moonlight toward my East Quarter candle, which was about three feet or so from me. The bobcat stopped maybe two or three feet from the candle and sniffed the air several times, never taking its eyes off me. Then, with complete and utter disdain for my presence, it slowly turned its back on me and strutted away into the night.

My first thought was something like, "Well, okay, now what the heck do I do?" But then all I could say to myself was, "Wow, what an experience." I began to chuckle because I knew then that the Lady had sent me something to let me know She was hearing me, that She was there with me that night. She had indeed gotten my full attention. I also knew then that all the things I was concerned about were really nothing and that they would be taken care of. What a way She had of telling me! My chuckles became a real laugh as I realized how much a part of the natural world around me I had become as I had grown in the Craft. That night, I think the Goddess laughed with me because She knew what a fantastic impact that animal had on my emotions. It was a strange and wonderful night, one that I will always remember.

Some Short Anecdotes

The following anecdotes were provided by my friend Miranda, from her own personal experiences. Although we Wiccans take our religion very seriously, we are certainly not so wrapped up in ourselves that we cannot see the humor in life's everyday situations.

Those Candles Are Dangerous

"I was doing the witche's rune—dancing, dancing, dancing—and got a bit too close to the candle in the middle of the floor. There went my skirt, up in flames. One of the other participants in the rite said, very calmly, 'I think you're on fire.' I looked down, patted out my skirt, and never missed a beat. Incidentally, the cat tried to set himself on fire that night, too.

He rolled over a few times in a playful mood and rolled right into a candle. Snuffed it out with its belly, poor thing. Must have been that kind of moon, I guess."

The Symbol of the West Is Not for Consumption

"At another time, we were getting ready for Autumn Equinox and we had made the circle with acorns and leaves. It was very beautiful. We were all sitting around munching on some goodies and talking about who would do what during the ritual. I reached over to one side, picked up what I thought was my glass, and took a drink. All conversation stopped and everyone stared at me as I took another sip and asked what they were looking at. Several mouths dropped open as someone said, very quietly and deadpan, 'You're drinking the West. The cat might not know any better, but come on now!'"

Sage Smoke Can Impact Your Lungs

"Once we were doing a cleansing ritual in the parking garage of the apartment I lived in, since someone had been stealing from the parked cars. My husband was chanting the witch's rune, while my sister-in-law and I were smudging to purify and also chanting along with him. I have a slight case of asthma and everyone else was just basically out of shape—I mean, really out of shape. Sometime during the third or fourth repeat of the rune, because of the sage smoke and our own breathing problems, the words that should have been:

Eko, eko Amalk.
Eko, eko Zamalak.

became something more like:

Eko, eko (gasp for breath).
Eko, eko (I can't breathe).

It was funny, and we all ended up laughing and wheezing a lot more than chanting; but the stealing stopped, so what can you say?"

The Fire Extinguisher

"The running joke in our Coven was that the fire extinguisher was under my sink and everyone had to know that before they entered the circle. It was a requisite, when rituals were done in my apartment, that everybody knew not only where the extinguisher was located, but also how to use it. We had one guest who didn't believe me when I said that I drilled the fire extinguisher issue into everybody's mind, so I simply told him to ask anyone. He stood before the group and said, 'So, where is the fire extinguisher?' In perfect unison, about ten people droned, 'Under the sink!'"

Chapter Summary

You hopefully have found this brief glimpse into the lighter side of our Craft meaningful, because laughter and mirth must be always be recognized as an integral part of any viable religion, regardless of its origin, and Wicca is no different. Work the rituals and rites and work the magick, enjoy your evolving relationship with the Lord and Lady, and by all means enjoy life. Are we serious about our religion? Of course we are; it is extremely important to us. Are we serious in our religion? Well, not always, because the Craft of the Wise is many things and one of those things is our ability to love and laugh at life. The God and Goddess want us to laugh and sing in our worship of Them, and They will laugh and sing right along with us.

10
Out of the Broom Closet

Wicca Is a Duly Constituted
and Recognized Religion

*W*icca is, as we have previously discussed, a legally recognized and protected religion. The First Amendment to the United States Constitution states that "Congress shall make no law respecting an establishment of religion, or prohibiting the free exercise thereof; or abridging the freedom of speech, or of the press; or the right of the people peaceably to assemble, and to petition the Government for a redress of grievances." The first and second parts in this amendment provide the keystone upon which all legal cases involving the constitutionality of Wicca have rested.

Additionally, section 1 of the Fourteenth Amendment further states that "all persons born or naturalized in the United

States, and subject to the jurisdiction thereof, are citizens of the United States and of the State wherein they reside. No State shall make or enforce any law which shall abridge the privileges or immunities of citizens of the United States; nor shall any State deprive any person of life, liberty, or property, without due process of law; nor deny to any person within its jurisdiction the equal protection of the laws." Simply put, this means that state or regional laws cannot be enacted that circumvent or violate those federal protections already guaranteed under the First Amendment.

Unfortunately, more than one thousand years of bad Christian press are extremely difficult to undo, and there are still those who look at Wicca and insist that, regardless of any court action, it is not a "real" religion. The issues surrounding the Helms and Walker Amendments of 1985 and the Fort Hood Texas military personnel witchcraft practices confrontation of 1999, which are detailed later in this chapter, are both prime examples of the fact that this mindset still exists today. I think that anyone who looks at Wicca, even with a critical eye, must admit that it has all the hallmarks of any other duly recognized or constituted religion. The Wiccan movement exhibits the hallmarks of beliefs, ritual practices, and community (meaning organized groups with a spiritual leader) that are common to every other recognized religion in the world.

Furthermore, as discussed in chapter 2, in legal actions involving the United States Court of Appeals (as detailed in and excerpted from the public records regarding *Dettmer v. Landon*), the following decisions were rendered: "Witchcraft is recognized in the United States as a legitimate religion. The District Court of Virginia pursuant to rule 52(a) of the Federal Rules of Civil Procedure has ruled that Witchcraft is a legitimate religion and falls within a recognizable religious category.

The Federal Appeals court further affirms that decision and clearly sees Witchcraft as a religion under the protection of constitutional rights. Accordingly, this court concludes that the Church of Wicca (or Witchcraft) is clearly a religion for First Amendment purposes."[1]

Adding to these arguments the fact that Wicca is included in the *United States Military Chaplain's Manual* as an acceptable religion for military personnel would seem to firmly place all rational thought in support of us when we say that we are indeed a "real" religion. We are a religion in every sense of the word, and we are entitled to full protection under the law in the performance of our rites and rituals.

What is the relationship today between Paganism and the more mainstream religions? Are we still dealing with people who exist in the mental Dark Ages, or is there enlightenment on the horizon that will allow us to practice our religion openly and without fear of attack by firebrand-wielding, anti-Pagan zealots? Is it conceivable that in the future there could be a Christian church on one corner and a Pagan temple across the street?

Let me base a response to these questions on my own personal experience. I am virtually 100 percent out of the broom closet in my practice of the Wiccan religion. In all the years that I have been open about that practice, I have yet to encounter a single person who reacted to me in alarm, backed away in terror while making the sign of the cross, or hurled profanities at me. While I do not travel the streets and byways of southern California stopping strangers on the street and waving my pentacle ring under their noses, I do come in contact with a considerable number of people during the course of each day. What is the number of negative reactions I have received? Zero, none.

I have seen some individuals stare openly at my pentacle ring for a few seconds, then simply get on with the business at hand. Others have expressed mild reactions, from raised eyebrows to a comment or question or two, but never in a derogatory sense. While I obviously cannot speak for experiences other Pagans may have had, I can state that my own experiences have led me to believe that my Pagan religion is as acceptable to the mainstream folks I deal with on a daily basis as any other religion. In other words, "It's no big deal."

Opposition

Unfortunately, this does not change the fact that people are out there who would like nothing better than to establish a Christian fundamentalist religious state in the United States, and probably resurrect Tomas de Torquemada as its head. We all know these people exist—they make their presence painfully obvious, all too often; still, I firmly believe they are very much in the minority. They are not as large a group as they would like us to believe.

Those individuals who espouse a stringent antiwitch philosophy, however, do continue to surface from time to time, as the following examples indicate. The incidents detailed in the next paragraphs represent attempts by individuals, as well as officials at varying levels of government, to restrict the practice of the Old Religion. Fortunately, in all cases these attempts failed; however, the very fact that someone even felt the need to try to curtail the religious liberties of Pagans is still a very frightening thing. It shows us that the antiwitch mindset first instilled by fundamentalist Christianity in the Dark Ages still exists, and that it exists even at the levels of government where laws could actually be formulated that would restrict or even seek to eliminate our freedom to practice the Craft.

While it is gratifying to realize that in all three cases described here we were successful in defending our religion, it also serves as a warning that the battle is far from over. Eternal vigilance is indeed the price of our religious liberty.

Helms Amendment, 1985–1986

Under United States law, witchcraft and other Neo-Pagan religions, churches, and organizations may apply for tax-exempt status in the United States, just as other religious organizations do. In 1985, Senator Jesse Helms of North Carolina and Representative Robert Walker of Pennsylvania introduced measures in both congressional houses that would have denied such tax-exempt status to witchcraft and Neo-Pagan groups. The more significant of the two was probably the Helms Amendment, given the weight that Senator Helms wields in Congress among more conservative members.[2] Both bills moved out of their respective committees on voice vote, but fortunately failed the general floor vote, even though Senator Helms tried repeatedly to attach his amendment as a rider to numerous other pieces of legislation.

On the surface, the attempt to exact such legislation, even though it failed, seemed to have little significance to most people. The amendment applied only to witchcraft and Satanism, and of the hundreds of witchcraft and Neo-Pagan groups in the United States, only a very small percentage of them had ever applied for tax-exempt status.

Both bills were opposed by the American Civil Liberties Union (ACLU) and numerous witchcraft and Neo-Pagan organizations. These organizations included the Covenant of the Goddess, Circle Sanctuary, and the Church and School of

Wicca. The Covenant of the Goddess is a tax-exempt organization located in Berkeley, California; Circle Sanctuary is an international Wicca and Neo-Pagan networking organization based near Mt. Horeb, Wisconsin; and the Church and School of Wicca are located in New Bern, North Carolina.

The ACLU, numerous Pagan and witchcraft organizations, and individual practitioners of the Craft organized a massive letter-writing and flyer campaign against the legislation that was virtually unprecedented. The Helms Amendment was subsequently defeated in 1986.

Fort Hood Military Witch Practitioners Issue, 1999

When Fort Hood became the first U.S. military installation to sanction the Wicca religion, it became an object of national media attention. In a letter to the Fort Hood commander, Lieutenant General Leon Laponte, Georgia Republican Representative Robert Barr wrote, "What's next? Will Rastafarians demand the inclusion of ritualistic marijuana cigarettes in their rations?"[3] Representative Barr was supported in his verbal diatribe by then Governor George W. Bush, who made the now infamous statement on a nationally televised interview for ABC-TV in June of 1999, "I don't think witchcraft is a religion."[4]

Fort Hood officials have not buckled under conservative pressure, citing their soldiers' constitutional rights to religious freedom. Following Fort Hood's lead, other U.S. military bases worldwide, in all branches of the armed forces, are now affording Wiccans the same right as Christians, Jews, and Muslims to hold services on military facilities.

David Oringderff, a retired major who served twenty-two years in the army, is founder and High Priest of the Sacred

Well Congregation of Texas, which sponsors the witches on Fort Hood and three other military bases. He sent Barr a response asking the congressman to apologize. Additionally, Reverend Gary Kindley, senior pastor of the First United Methodist Church near Fort Hood was quoted as saying that "although he doesn't share the Wiccan's beliefs, . . . he has found little to fear from the group."[5]

Unfortunately, not all mainstream ministers near Fort Hood share the more tolerant attitude of Reverend Kindley. The Reverend Jack Harvey sees no difference between Wicca, devil worship, and voodoo, even going so far as to suggest that members of his congregation go to services armed in case a Wiccan attempts to kidnap one of their children. Says Harvey, "I hear they drink blood, eat babies. They have fires, they probably cook them."[6]

Even though he was outnumbered by the more liberal and open-minded citizens near Fort Hood, Representative Barr would not be deterred from his crusade to ban Wiccan rituals on military facilities. He attempted to attach an amendment, known as the Barr Amendment, to one of several military appropriations acts in the House of Representatives that would have banned financial assistance to any organization advocating the practice or observance of Wiccan rituals on military installations.[7]

In July of 1999, the Barr Amendment died an ignoble death, never making it out of committee. Although Representative Barr has vowed to attempt to introduce some form of antiwitch legislation in the future, there is apparently sufficient congressional and First Amendment legal support for the presence of witchcraft as a viable religion in the military to keep this issue closed, at least for now.

School District versus the ACLU

The two attacks on Wicca just noted involved none other than elements of the U.S. government. The year 1999, however, also saw single individuals under fire from those who either did not understand our religion, or even worse, had a conscious agenda to attack it.

In October of 1998, an honor student at Lincoln Park High School, Michigan, was ordered by school authorities to remove her pentacle under threat of suspension. The honor student, Chrystal Seifferly, was an admitted witch and Priestess of Wicca and had been for several years. In March of 1999, the American Civil Liberties Union brought First Amendment legal action against the Lincoln Park School District in the court of U.S. District Judge Gerald Rosen. Judge Rosen agreed with the ACLU, declaring the student's pentacle to be a recognized symbol of the Wiccan religion. As such, the display of that symbol is protected under constitutional law.

The school district subsequently reversed itself and proclaimed that indeed the display of jewelry related to Wicca would be permitted as a religious icon and afforded the same protection as jewelry depicting a relationship with any other religion. The Lincoln Park School District was ordered to pay court costs as well as fees incurred by the ACLU attorneys.[8]

Out of the Broom Closet, Slowly

One of my Internet acquaintances provided this story involving the efforts of his Coven to come out into public view. It is reprinted here with his permission, as well as the permission of his High Priestess.

"Our Covenstead is roughly seven and one-half acres in Livingston Parish, Louisiana, which is serious fundamentalist country. Several years ago, our High Priestess decided to make our Coven public by having open ritual events and, in general, not hiding the fact that we are witches. Unfortunately, this resulted in bullets being fired through windows on occasion, a couple of incendiary devices placed in our mailboxes (made of fireworks and prophylactics), and a lot of teenagers passing by the property, usually driving very fast, hollering obscenities. Early on, there were even threats against our lives and threats that the buildings on the property would be burned down. There were several arson attempts, and we actually had to put out two fires. Once in a while, there is still the occasional trespassing incident when some kid just has to take up a dare.

"We have been very careful in how we deal with each of these incidents. While we have the right to press charges, so far we have elected not to do so. We have simply made it clear that we want the behavior stopped, but are not and will not be vindictive about it. This has slowly but surely changed the attitudes of the people in our neighborhood. They still view us with suspicion. Most still are sure we are doing something they haven't learned about yet, and would probably not approve of, but they have ceased to fear us, and we have very few incidents any more.

"This has been over sixteen years of patience, letting people get away with these provocations while we turned the other cheek. In so doing, we have earned the respect of the local authorities by calling them only when absolutely necessary and by never holding a grudge against even the people who sometimes pushed us almost over the edge. The local sheriff even has one particular deputy who now handles all complaints either about us or from us. This deputy has come to our Covenstead often to visit and have coffee.

"Again, this has taken a willingness to let some people literally take pot shots at us and make threats while we just keep smiling at them. It still hasn't totally gone away after sixteen years of being open and in the public eye, although by now, the middle of 1999, many of our neighbors seem to have finally come to terms with our presence."

A Personal Tragedy

The incidents I've described thus far turned out positively, all in all, in that our constitutional rights as Wiccans were upheld. Unfortunately, I must now describe a situation involving a personal friend that did not turn out well at all. My own personal experiences in being open with others about my religion, at least so far, have all been generally positive. We must be aware, though, that there is a real potential for a serious negative reaction to our religion, and thus there are those instances when things simply do not work out well. Unfortunate incidents that remind us all too painfully of the Christian fundamentalist mindset continue to occur. This point was brought home to me recently by events that happened to a friend of mine at work who is Pagan and studying the Druid Tradition.

At the time of this occurrence, none of my friend's family members were aware of his religion, and, in fact, it was never his intention to make a major announcement about it, preferring to keep his practice of the Craft low-key and covert. Since he was not married and did not typically interact with other family members on a close or daily basis, he felt reasonably safe in his ability to keep his Pagan religion hidden; at least until such a time that he might feel comfortable at least beginning to open the subject for discussion. Unfortunately, that was not to be the case, because while playing with his cousin's young child on the floor of the cousin's home, his pentacle necklace inadvertently dropped out of his shirt into plain view.

The reaction from the cousin was sudden and vehement. The cousin exclaimed, "My God, you're a devil worshipper!" and immediately grabbed the child away from my friend. The cousin sputtered and ranted for several minutes about devils and hell, mostly in incoherent half-sentences, before ordering my friend to leave his house. Now, my friend is not a small person and, having had extensive specialized military training, was not particularly fearful of being physically attacked, but the intensity of the verbal outburst left him no real choice. He left immediately in order to give his cousin some time to cool down and think.

Some weeks later, my friend took the chance of visiting the cousin's home again in hopes of talking the situation out and bringing it to some resolution. He rang the doorbell repeatedly, to no avail, even though he could see the cousin's car parked in the driveway. When he was about to give up and leave, the cousin appeared through a gate in the fence, carrying a baseball bat. The cousin was obviously in a high state of agitation, holding the bat in one hand while striking it repeatedly into the palm of his other hand, and visibly trembling to the point where he could not speak coherently. He lifted the baseball bat several times in a very threatening gesture while simply pointing at the street. The meaning of the gesturing was quite clear, and, in order to avoid a potentially serious physical confrontation, my friend again left, considerably shaken by the entire chain of events.

It was not until some weeks later that my friend's father, uncle, and both of their wives invited my friend to breakfast. Knowing that his cousin had talked with the rest of the family, and also being well aware that his father and uncle were both born-again Christians, my friend naturally assumed that this breakfast was going to involve some type of confrontation. He was fully correct in that assumption. As soon as they sat down to eat, the other family members immediately began a diatribe on the evils of where my friend's religion was taking him. For a while he attempted to reason with them, but soon gave up the effort when it became obvious that nothing he could say was going to have any impact on their preconceived ideas of Paganism. He left that breakfast meeting fully understanding that he would have to make a very difficult choice— he would have to choose between renouncing his Pagan religion or severing his ties with the rest of his family.

There is one family member, my friend's sister, who is still talking to him. She is at least somewhat open-minded and willing to discuss his religion without grabbing for a Bible to defend herself. She has also been somewhat of a mediator between my friend and his cousin, and it now seems that the cousin may have realized that his initial reaction was neither necessary nor warranted. The sister thinks the cousin will be calling my friend soon in order to attempt to sit down and talk about what has happened between them. This discussion will hopefully be fruitful and allow some measure of resolution to be obtained, at least between those two.

As far as the relationship between my friend, his father, uncle, and their wives is concerned, it may be beyond salvage. My friend feels that he has been given an ultimatum and indeed has made his choice already. His feeling is that if their narrow-minded and vindictive attitude is an indication of their Christian viewpoint and what it means to them to be followers of Jesus, then he indeed wants no part of them or their religion. It is extremely sad that bigotry and fear may have torn apart a family, but when one looks at the lessons of history and even at the events in our world today, all the prece-

dents and reasons for this incident are plainly there for anyone to see.

Religion is a powerful force and, when wielded by the
hands of fundamentalists of any persuasion, those who have
the attitude of "my way is the only way," someone must invariably get hurt. In this particular incident, there is some
possibility that my friend and his cousin may be able to recon-
cile, but as far as the rest of the family is concerned, probably
not. He is deeply hurt by this because he still obviously has
love and affection for the other family members.

There is a lesson in this for all of us. We can never take for
granted the reactions people will have to our practice of the
Craft. Some will react with curiosity or even happiness, some
will react with indifference, but always remember that some
will also react with anger and alarm. This is an unfortunate
fact that we, as members of a minority and persecuted religion, must understand in order to be able to deal with it.
There are indeed those who hate us and everything we stand
for; it has been that way since the Dark Ages and may never
totally change. What we can hope for in a more enlightened
age is at least a measure of understanding from the majority
of others, knowing full well that there will always be those
who will be ready and willing to pile the wood at the base of
the stake—in the name of their loving God, of course.

Even though the fundamentalists like those just described
may be in the minority, they are organized and they have an
agenda. They are determined to force their viewpoints on the
rest of us and will stop at nothing in order to achieve that
end. They will literally shout down, either vocally or in print,
any viewpoint that is contrary to their own. They will resort
to innuendo, intimidation, scare tactics, and, in some cases,

blatant lies in an attempt to force their agenda on the group as a whole. Their agenda or viewpoint becomes the only right one. Any deviation, or even discussion, of alternatives to this "party line" are not permitted, since this might undermine the authority, and thus the control, exercised by those chosen few who have set themselves up as leaders and arbitrators of what constitutes an acceptable doctrine or ideology.

I need only point to the somewhat successful takeover of the Republican party during most of the 1980s and 1990s by groups supported by the conservative Christian Coalition to emphasize this point. This is virtually a textbook illustration of how a minority of dedicated zealots can corrupt an established political organization.

It is interesting to note, though, that recent studies by various scholars seem to indicate that the strength of the mainstream Christian religious denominations now appears to be declining in the United States. By those denominations, I am referring mainly to the Catholic and Protestant faiths. Unfortunately, many of those who leave the mainstream denominations divert, at least initially, to the fundamentalist extremes.

Our country does appear to be in the beginning of a religious shift or awakening that is making us one of the most spiritually diverse cultures in the world. The impact of this shift away from mainstream Christianity may have far-reaching implications as more and more people seek and find their own unique spiritual path. Our religious composition is changing, and we will hopefully become richer and more tolerant because of that fact.

It is unfortunate that there are still ultraconservative individuals or groups within our country who actually consider us dangerous, a threat to civilization as they know it. Does the mindset of the Dark Ages still exist? In some people, yes, particularly among those who espouse an ultraconservative viewpoint. We must not lose sight of the fact that one of the things a fundamentalist or ultraconservative religious movement must have in order to survive is an enemy; someone or something they can rail against and point to as the "source of all problems," the "great evil" from which they, and only they, can offer salvation. Those who practice Wicca are still very much targets of this type of rhetoric and the occasional acts of oppression or even violence that this rhetoric spawns.

It would be a utopia if the conservative elements comprising the Religious Right wing in this country were to embrace their "enemies" as their own Bible tells them to do; but then one of their basic reasons for being would simply go away. Most religious organizations, like industrial and government bureaucracies, have a law of self-preservation in that survival of the entity is the first order of business. Given that philosophy, I find it highly unlikely, regardless of logical argument, that religious conservatives will accept Wicca in a live-and-let-live atmosphere any time soon.

There are plenty of considerations that we as Pagans must address carefully in making our decision to come out and go public with our religious beliefs. I urge each and every one of you who may be considering this step to look at those considerations honestly and thoroughly before making your decision.

Why I Chose to Come Out of the Broom Closet

I elected to reveal my practice of witchcraft publicly simply because I personally feel that the time for intentionally hiding ourselves in forests or closed rooms has come to an end. We are practitioners of a kind, gentle, and peace-loving religion that worships the attributes of nature in the person of our female divinity. We are not the bloodthirsty or depraved orgiastic fanatics all too often portrayed by the entertainment and news media. The general public has been misled about witchcraft for over a thousand years. Now, with our numbers reaching probably an all-time high, possibly in excess of one million members worldwide, we need to stand up and set that record straight.

Please don't get me wrong and assume that I am on some kind of moral crusade. I am not finding fault with the efforts of organizations like the Witches League for Public Awareness and the Pagan Educational Network (I belong to both organizations and they do the best job they can). That is not the case, nor am I on some kind of a recruitment campaign. Additionally, let me be very clear that there are good Christians out there, those who would most likely stand beside us in the interest of tolerance and understanding. Not all Christians see Wicca as the ultimate threat to Western civilization that fundamental Christianity has been trumpeting since the twelfth century.

No, my friends, this is not a crusade nor a recruitment effort. I am speaking up only in the hope that my experiences and thoughts will ignite that same fire in others of our religion. One day, in the not-too-distant future, we will stand shoulder to shoulder across this country to face those extremists and fundamentalists who would bury us in the name of their narrow-minded bigotry and say to them, "No, it ends right here and right now. We are here, we will be heard, and we will no longer tolerate your attempts at interference and control of our constitutionally guaranteed liberties. We are a force that from now on will be recognized and reckoned with.

No more hiding in the shadows, no more being afraid to worship in public, no more witch hysteria in the press. No more! Never again!"

Since our religion has been so secretive until recently, no one really knows with any degree of accuracy how many witches there are in this country or in the rest of the world for that matter. However, a quick perusal of Internet websites and services using a search engine with any of several keywords such as *pagan* or *witch* results in a listing of thousands of websites. One can only assume that we are, in this present day, a religion with literally hundreds of thousands of adherents. There is simply no reason for us as an organization of that magnitude to remain fragmented, divided, and secretive. There is no reason to sit quietly in the shadows while the right-wing religious zealots trample not only our rights but also the rights of women and other minorities into the dust of the Dark Ages in the name of religious conservatism.

We are out there by the hundreds upon hundreds of thousands. We are in the arts, the sciences, and the humanities. We are law enforcement officers, engineers, builders, doctors, and farmers. We are a legally recognized religion under the protection of the First Amendment to the Constitution of the United States, and our isolation from the rest of the religious community should and must come to an end. With the phenomenal growth of witchcraft since the 1970s and with the free and easy interchange of information afforded to us by things like the Internet, that time will come to pass and it will happen soon. It may be happening now.

Your decision to become open about your Wiccan beliefs should nonetheless be approached with caution and trepidation. Once begun, this is a decision that in most cases will be irrevocable, and the possible consequences must be carefully evaluated. There are numerous things to consider before making this decision. How you prioritize them will depend to a great extent on the degree of "Pagan friendliness" in your community and those dearest to you.

I have attempted to list the things that I considered before exposing myself and my family to the general public, but obviously the following list will vary for each individual in both content and priority.

1. Family—If some family members are unaware of your Pagan religion, how will they react?

2. Employer—Will your job security or professional standing within your career field be impacted?

3. Friends or acquaintances—Will they react negatively to your religion?

4. Vendors and service providers—Are you likely to suddenly find your favorite table at the local coffee shop "unavailable?"

5. Is there a possibility of physical violence from anti-Wiccan groups in your community?

If you can answer yes to any one of these questions, or similar questions that you can devise on your own, then prudence dictates that you reconsider your decision. Put quite simply, is it worth it? In some cases, unfortunately, the answer will probably be no, and that is a sad thing because it strikes at the very core of our religious freedoms. In all honesty, there may be circumstances that dictate that such revelations are best not made. As I have said, it is up to each one of you as individuals to analyze the possible risks and ramifications of publicly acknowledging your practice of the Pagan religion. No one can make that choice for you, and I urge you to be honest with yourself as you evaluate taking that largely irrevocable step.

You also need to consider the degree of "openness" you wish to express. Many communities are much more accommodating to practitioners of Wicca than others, and I would not recommend a stroll through many of the cities of the Baptist South while wearing a large pentacle necklace. On the other hand, an open display of Wiccan jewelry or wearing a Wiccan shirt will probably go pretty much unnoticed in more progressive cities like San Francisco or Los Angeles.

How to Do It

How do you begin to come out of the broom closet and openly discuss witchcraft? How do you break the ice and make it known that you practice a religion that was a death sentence only 300 years ago? How do you start the dialogue?

I am afraid that there is no single or simple answer to these questions. Most of what you say and how you say it will depend on your own personal relationships with those to whom you wish to acknowledge your religion. What I can do is offer the following guidelines based on my own experience and the experiences of other witches who have related parts of their own stories to me.

Just because you may have found something that brings you great joy and happiness does not mean that everybody else will share your enthusiasm, regardless of their own religious leanings. What I mean by this can probably be summed up with two guidewords that are somewhat interlocked— *selection* and *obsession*.

Be selective of those in whom you confide; not everybody you know will necessarily want to know or will even care about your religion. Their own feelings about witchcraft aside, some may treat your talking about the subject with the same warmth they would give to a salesman banging on their front door in the middle of dinner. They just might not care. It took me well over a year before I had talked with most of the people in whom I felt I could or should confide, and there are still those with whom I may never discuss the Old Religion.

By *obsession* I simply mean do not overdo it either in the number of people you initially contact nor in the level of information you impart. If you feel that you have found someone who seems to care about what you have to say, it is not necessary to launch into a lengthy discourse. Take it easy, and, if the person is really interested, he or she will be back, wanting to know more.

I suppose it would be worthwhile to mention one other guideword as long as we are on the subject, and that word is *honesty*. Why is it that you want to share this information? In my case, the reasoning was essentially twofold. I wanted to be honest and open with those whom I love and care for, and I wanted to share with them the peace and contentment that Wicca has brought me. It is important to note that my revelations were at no time done to shock or impress anyone. That is the last thing you want to do, since it does a disservice to both yourself and the deities we worship. Absolutely nothing will be gained if the intent in revealing your religion is only to draw attention to yourself.

Once you have decided that your Wiccan life is something you wish to share with others, how do you go about it? How do you start or open the conversation and get it moving in the direction you desire? Since your first remarks may well set the tone for the rest of the discussion, it is important to avoid forcing the issue. Starting the whole process by taking out an advertisement in your local newspaper and announcing that you are a practicing witch is probably not a good idea.

In some cases, when the person you wish to open up with is a close friend, it might be done by telling that person that there is something very personal that you wish to share with him or her, and go from there. Obviously, attempting this discussion in a hectic or busy environment, when others may reasonably be expected to intrude, is also not wise. Choose your location for this discussion carefully. It could be an office with a closed door, a private lunch, or at a time when the two of you can talk for some time uninterrupted.

In the event you just cannot open the discussion easily, even with a close friend, it would probably be necessary to either create some kind of an appropriate opening or wait for one to develop. Sometimes even a casual statement can suffice to get the discussion moving, such as, "I was reading this interesting book the other day. It's all about alternative religions"; or, perhaps your friend will bring up a topic that you can reasonably turn into a comment about Paganism or Pagans.

If starting the discussion on your own scares you and you just cannot seem to find the right opening, then it may be possible to resort to getting the person's attention with a physical display of our religion. A pentacle ring, necklace, or earrings will usually draw attention at some point. If you want to be more brazen, try openly reading one of the many books on witchcraft and displaying the book jacket.

Those last two situations, a contrived opening and physical displays, can come dangerously close to circumventing the *honesty* word we discussed earlier. Why should it be necessary to go to these lengths to open the conversation? If you cannot sit down with someone face to face and have this discussion, then it may be wise to evaluate your reasons for informing that person of your beliefs in the first place.

Special circumstances may exist that will leave you no choice but to use some kind of a forced opening, but I would expect those situations to be rare. The best method, by far, is to find the time to sit down with the person and talk openly and honestly. My own experiences have taught me that this is definitely the best way to communicate with others.

I'm not saying that you cannot wear Pagan or Wiccan jewelry simply because you like it; there is nothing wrong with that. In my own case, I began to wear my pentacle ring because I actually wanted to have everybody and anybody ask me about our religion. I need to emphasize, though, that my intent here was hopefully to educate others, not to shock or impress them. My desire was that they would come to me asking questions. I did not go to them wishing to flaunt our religion.

Once you have taken the first step and opened the discussion, it may become obvious rather quickly that the person you wish to share this with is not interested in the subject. In the worst-case scenario, the person may be openly hostile to the subject. In that unfortunate event, there is nothing else to do but back to off from the conversation gracefully with a shrug of the shoulders as if to say, "Well, it doesn't really interest me that much either." Dropping the discussion at this point will allow you to retain your Craft anonymity and probably save the relationship as well.

In the event the person you wish to confide in seems to be receptive to the discussion, then you can move forward slowly. Remember that it is quite likely that he or she will have no knowledge of our Craft or, even worse, knowledge obtained from slanted and biased Christian rhetoric or sensationalist tabloid publications. Therefore, there are some things you can do to prepare yourself for the initial discussion.

Be fully knowledgeable of our religion in all its aspects. Know and understand both what a witch is and what a witch is not. There are many Traditions in Paganism, and not all of them are the peaceful, nature-loving religion of Wicca. Understand this and be able to explain honestly the differences between Wicca and some of the other Pagan religions such as Voodoo, Santaria (or Santeria), and Satanism.

At all times during any discussion, remain calm and collected and stay in control. Keep your voice conversational and friendly. You do not want the discussion to become heated or adversarial. At the first sign of resistance, it would be wise to back off and drop the subject, at least until the other person has had a chance to digest what you have begun to explain.

In the event an interest or curiosity is expressed, then proceed, but do it slowly. What you will be explaining may be something of a shock and it is important to know when to stop talking and let the person ask questions. Do not attempt to deliver a lecture or an hour-long monologue on Paganism and the Wiccan contribution to modern civilization. You will be imparting information that will typically need to be considered or thought about. Do not be surprised if the other person asks you to stop and let him or her mull it around for a while.

In order to emphasize the success of dealing with people in a calm and rational manner, I would like to reiterate something my wife heard on a local talk radio show in Los Angeles just before Samhain of 1997. The disk jockeys were discussing Halloween and its history, and asked if a "real" witch would please call the program and discuss the holiday on the air. In a few minutes someone did call, a gentlemen in military service that identified himself as a Wiccan.

The discussion was quite amicable for several minutes and the caller was able to discuss the origins of the holiday at length. Unfortunately, the disk jockies finally decided to resort to the old stereotypes and began to talk about sacrifices, Satanic worship, and drunken orgies. Through all this the caller remained extremely calm, never raising his voice or using profanity. He calmly and successfully answered each of the accusations openly and honestly, and defended his Wiccan religion as a member of the armed forces by referring to the *United States Military Chaplain's Manual*, which accepts Wicca as a valid religion for military service personnel.

By the end of the on-air interview, the listening audience had been treated to a very good historical description of the Samhain Sabbat, and had heard an acknowledged witch rationally and calmly defend our religion in the face of some rather blatant attempts at provocation. I don't know if that interview made any difference in the station's ratings, but hopefully it made a difference to some of the people who heard it. Please note that the caller was both knowledgeable of his topic and calmly in control of the interview. He did not allow himself to be stampeded into a heated or argumentative debate.

There is no tried-and-true method to begin a discussion like this, nor is there a single or best way to discuss our religion with all people. All of us are unique and each one of us has a unique situation or set of circumstances. My best advice to you who may be searching for the way to communicate with others is to follow your heart. If it feels right to you, then it probably is right; and if it is meant to be, then our deities will let you know when and how. Do not be surprised if, once you acknowledge to yourself that you wish to open up to someone, the way to do so suddenly presents itself.

We must always remember that, as Wiccans, we do not attempt to recruit or convert others to our religion. Those who wish to join us will come only by their own desire, in their own recognition of the God and Goddess, and in their own time. We can impart information on our own and offer assistance if that is asked for, but we must never take it upon ourselves to attempt to dissuade someone from his or her own chosen path.

We are not and must never be evangelists. Our Lord and Lady will choose those whom They wish. If our words have the effect or opening someone's eyes or stirring the age-old memories within them, then we have simply been the messenger for a power far greater than you or I.

Chapter Summary

The purpose of this chapter has been essentially to educate and offer advice on the pros and cons of making your practice of the Old Religion known to others, particularly for those who may be relatively new to the Craft.

First, are you sure you want to do this? Carefully examine the attitudes of your community and of those with whom you wish to share your Wiccan beliefs. Remember that once this decision is made, you may find that it will take on a life of its own. Once you take even a close friend into your confidence it is quite possible that your story will begin to spread.

You must be reasonably sure that no difficulties will be brought to you or your loved ones once your practice of the Old Religion becomes known to those outside of the Craft. Carefully evaluate your own personal situation and do not begin to make this announcement until you are sure that it is reasonably safe to do so. Remember that there is absolutely nothing wrong with working the rituals in private; we've been doing that for over a thousand years.

If something negative does happen as a result of your revelations, are you prepared to deal with it? Look carefully at your family, at your educational or professional life, and be sure that those facets of your existence can withstand any ramifications that may arise as a result of this decision. Please remember that some parts of our country are not as liberal and accepting as others. If there is any doubt in your mind about your emotional or physical safety after admitting your Wiccan religion, then prudence dictates that silence may be the only option.

Secondly, look at your own attitudes and reasons why you want to make your religion known to others. If you are taking this action out of some misguided sense of recruiting others to Paganism, then you are making a mistake. Remember that we do not proselytize, and, if others wish to follow our path, they must come to that decision on their own. That is not to say that we cannot offer guidance or education—far from it. I point to this very book as an educational tool.

Never forget the oath you took at your initiation: "Love is the law and love is the bond. I swear to honor, defend, and love the Lord and Lady and all those who love Them. So mote it be." Your own ethics in taking that oath prohibit you from publicly admitting that others are practitioners of the Craft without their full knowledge and consent. If others wish to make that public acknowledgment, it is up to them and only them.

Please do not take this action in an attempt to intimidate, shock, or impress others. Wicca is a serious religion, and, although we can certainly laugh at ourselves, those of us who take our religion seriously have a hard time dealing with "one-time Saturday night witch wannabes." Those people are not Wiccan and they do not follow the Craft of the Wise. They do our deities, and the rest of us, a grave injustice.

Your reasoning for publicly revealing your practice of witchcraft must be an honest one. The desire to share your innermost feelings with loved ones or those near and dear to you, or the education of others by the refuting of antiwitch propaganda, most certainly fall into this category.

Thirdly, be prepared. Be knowledgeable of our religion and be prepared to respond to criticism and hostility. Before you even begin to consider taking the step to come out of the broom closet, it is imperative that you be as well armed with as many facts as possible. Read about the time in history when the Old Religion flourished, and the Burning Times when the Inquisition attacked it. Learn what drove people of the times to do what they did. There are many books of varying depth devoted to ancient and medieval history that describe the everyday life, politics, warfare, and sciences of the times.

Take the time to read and study the Craft, spending a year and a day with each of at least the first two levels of our religion, and become proficient at what you study. I have studied the history of Europe and been a Pagan and an initiated witch for many years and consider myself fairly proficient at Craft skills; but I am still studying history, and I feel that I have just begun to really scratch the surface of our religion. There is so much more to learn, but learning is an ongoing process that never ends.

Become a vociferous reader of all the books on Wicca you can find, either through libraries, bookshops, or mail-order book outlets. I have found Raymond Buckland's books to be excellent guides, as well as those by Scott Cunningham, Edain

McCoy, and Janet and Stewart Farrar. Read as much as possible and identify the Pagan Tradition or Wiccan Path that is right for you. If necessary, take what you feel you can use from each Tradition in order to build your own eclectic relationship with our deities.

I do not mean to imply from all this that you must obtain an advanced degree in European history or become a certified member of Wiccan clergy. That is certainly not necessary. It is imperative, though, that you amass enough information so that you can discuss our religion and the historical events surrounding it with a sense of authority and competence. That is the very best way to defend yourself and the Old Religion against any verbal attack.

My own experiences have shown that, at least in some parts of the country, an acknowledged witch is treated absolutely no differently than an acknowledged Christian. Some of the comments raised by others in the Craft have, however, indicated a lack of receptiveness. Still others have decided that silence is the best choice in order to save family feelings or friendships.

The choice each one of us makes when it comes to bringing our religion into the open must be, as I have said before, a personal one. It absolutely must be based on your own individual needs, desires, and existing personal relationships. We are all unique and all of our life situations are unique. What works for one will not necessarily work for another. Each one of us must make this decision on own own, and I urge you to be honest with yourself as you do so.

Whatever you as an individual decide must ultimately be your decision and yours alone, grounded on facts and solid information. Whatever that decision is must be based on a firm understanding of both the positive and potentially negative reactions you may encounter. If there is any doubt in your mind at all, it is probably in your own best interest to remain silent and keep your practice of the Old Religion to yourself.

Never forget that whatever you decide to do, you are never alone. The God and Goddess will always walk beside you, and every witch that ever existed lives emotionally within you. Even if you decide to practice all your life as a Solitary, never become involved in a Coven, and never confide your religion to anyone else, you are now and forever a Wiccan. That fact will never change. You practice a religion that can trace its roots into the misty dawn of antiquity, back to the Neolithic peoples of the British Isles, a religion that was already thousands of years old when Jesus Christ was born. You are a practitioner of a religion steeped in the unconditional love, honor, and trust of our Lord and Lady, and of all those who live and practice Wicca.

While some may practice differing Paths of our religion, it is the very fact that we are different and unique that makes us special. None of us will walk precisely in another person's footsteps or exactly on another person's Path, but it is that very diversity that makes us all contributors to the whole. We each have something different and meaningful to bring into the circle, regardless of our Path. We each are a different part of the God and Goddess, and that is what makes us all a part of the cosmic fabric.

I wish you all bright blessings. May your experience and growth in the Old Religion bring you nothing but happiness and joy. Merry meet and merry part, my friends, until we merry meet again. Blessed be.

---

1. Public records of the U.S. Court of Appeals for the Fourth District at Alexandria, VA, CA-84-1090-AM, in the case of *Dettmer v. Landon*, September 4, 1986. Richard L. Williams, District Judge.

2. The Helms Amendment, introduced in Congress on September 26, 1985, as SAMDT.705, reads: "No funds appropriated under the Act shall be used to grant, maintain, or allow tax exemptions to any cult, organization, or other group that has any interest in the promoting of satanism or witchcraft."

3. See Barry Shlachter, "Bothered and Bewildered: Wiccans at Hood Shrug Off Media Hubbub," *Fort Worth Star-Telegram*, 8 August 1999, final morning edition.

4. Ibid.

5. Ibid.

6. Ibid.

7. The Barr Amendment, HR2561 Department of Defense Appropriations Act, 2000 Amendment No. 1, reads: "None of the funds appropriated or otherwise made available by this Act may be used to provide assistance to the practice of witchcraft or Wicca, as defined by the encyclopedia of American Religions, on any military installation or vessel."

8. See the full text of this press release on the ACLU's website at http://www.aclu.org/news/1999/n032599a.html.

Appendix A
Classic Wiccan Texts

The Wiccan Rede (version 1)
(possibly attributed to Doreen Valienti, c. 1950)

Bide the Wiccan Rede, Ye must,
In Perfect Love and Perfect Trust.
Live, and let live,
Fairly take and fairly give.
Soft of eye and light of touch,
Speak thou little and listen much.
Heed ye flower, bush, and tree,
And by the Lady blest you'll be.
When-so-ever ye have need,
harken not to others' greed.
With a fool no season spend,
Nor be counted as his friend.

Merry meet and merry part,
Bright the cheeks and warm the heart.
True in love forever be,
Unless thy lover's false to thee.
Cast the Circle thrice about,
To keep all evil spirits out.
To bind the spell everytime,
Let the spell be said in rhyme
Deosil go by Waxing Moon,
Chanting out the Wiccan Rune.
Widdershins go by Waning Moon,
Chanting out the baneful rune.
When the Lady's Moon is New,
Kiss the hand to Her times two.
When the Moon rides at Her peak,
Then your heart's desire seek.
Where the rippling waters go,
Cast a stone and truth you'll know.
When misfortune is enow,
Wear the Blue Star on thy brow.
Eight Words the Wiccan Rede Fulfill:
An' It Harm None, Do What Ye Will!

The Wiccan Rede (version 2)

(as supposedly given to Gwen Thompson
by Adriana Porter in the 1930s)

Bide the Wiccan Laws we must,
In Perfect Love and Perfect Trust.
Live and let live,
Fairly take and fairly give.
Cast the Circle thrice about,
To keep the evil spirits out.
To bind the spell every time,
Let the spell be spake in rhyme.
Soft of eye and light of touch,
Speak little, listen much.
Deosil go by the waxing moon,
Chanting out the Witches' Rune.
Widdershins go by the waning moon,
Chanting out the baneful rune.
When the Lady's moon is new,
Kiss the hand to her, times two.
When the moon rides at her peak,
Then your heart's desire seek.
Heed the North wind's mighty gale,
Lock the door and drop the sail.
When the wind comes from the South,
Love will kiss thee on the mouth.
When the wind blows from the West,
Departed souls will have no rest.
When the wind blows from the East,
Expect the new and set the feast.
Nine woods in the cauldron go,
Burn them fast and burn them slow.

Elder be the Lady's tree,
Burn it not or cursed you'll be.
When the Wheel begins to turn,
Let the Beltane fires burn.
When the Wheel has turned to Yule,
Light the log and the Horned One rules.
Heed ye Flower, Bush and Tree,
By the Lady, blessed you'll be.
Where the rippling waters go,
Cast a stone and truth you'll know.
When ye have a true need,
Hearken not to others' greed.
With a fool no season spend,
Lest ye be counted as his friend.
Merry meet and merry part,
Bright the cheeks and warm the heart.
Mind the Threefold Law you should,
Three times bad and three times good.
When misfortune is enow,
Wear the blue star on thy brow.
True in Love ever be,
Lest thy lover's false to thee.
Eight words the Wiccan Rede fulfill:
An ye harm none, do what ye will.

The Charge of the Goddess

Listen to the words of the Great Mother, She who of old has been called Artemis, Astarte, Dione, Melusine, Cerridwen, Diana, and by many other names:

Whenever you have need of anything, once in the month, and better it be when the moon is full, then shall ye assemble in some secret place to adore the spirit of Me, who am Queen of all the Wise.

You shall be free from slavery, and as a sign that ye be free, you shall sing, dance, feast, make music and love, all in My praise.

For Mine is the ecstasy of the spirit, but Mine also is joy on Earth.

My law is love unto all beings.

Mine is the secret door that opens upon the land of youth, and Mine is the cup of the wine of life that is the Cauldron of Cerridwen, that is the Holy Grail of Immortality.

I give the knowledge of the spirit eternal, and beyond death, I give peace, freedom, and reunion with those who have gone before.

Nor do I demand sacrifice, for behold, I am the Mother of all things and My love is poured out upon the Earth.

Now hear the words of the Star Goddess, the dust of whose feet are the hosts of Heaven, whose body encircles the universe.

I who am the beauty of the green Earth, and the white moon among the stars, do call upon your souls . . . arise, and come unto Me.

For I am the soul of nature that gives life to the universe.

From Me all things proceed, and unto Me they must return.

Let My worship be in the heart that rejoices, for behold— all acts of love and pleasure are My rituals.

Let there be beauty and strength, power and compassion, honor and humility, mirth and reverence within you.

And you who seek to know Me, know that thy seeking and yearning will avail thee not unless you know this mystery:

If that which you seek you find not within thee, you will never find it without, for behold—I have been with thee from the beginning and I am that which is attained at the end of desire.

The Charge of the God

Listen to the words of the Great Father, who of old was called Osiris, Adonis, Zeus, Thor, Pan, Cernunnos, Herne, Lugh, and by many other names:

My Law is Harmony with all things.

Mine is the secret that opens the gates of life and Mine is the dish of salt of the earth that is the body of Cernunnos that is the eternal circle of rebirth.

I give the knowledge of life everlasting, and beyond death I give the promise of regeneration and renewal.

I am the sacrifice, the father of all things, and my protection blankets the Earth.

Now hear the words of the dancing God, the music of whose laughter stirs the winds, whose voice calls the seasons:

I who am the Lord of the Hunt and the Power of the Light, sun among the clouds and the secret of the flame, I call upon your bodies to arise and come unto Me.

For I am the flesh of the Earth and all its beings.

Through Me all things must die and with Me they are reborn.

Let my worship be in the body that sings, for behold, all acts of willing sacrifice are My rituals.

Let there be desire and fear, anger and weakness, joy and peace, awe and longing within you.

For these, too, are part of the mysteries found within yourself, within Me, all beginnings have endings, and all endings have beginnings.

Appendix B

General Deity and Quarters Invocations

The Call to the Goddess

I am the Great Mother, worshipped by all and existent prior to their consciousness.

I am the primal female force, boundless and eternal.

I am the chaste Goddess of the moon, the Lady of all magick.

The winds and moving leaves sing my name.

I wear the crescent Moon upon my brow and my feet rest among the starry heavens.

I am mysteries yet unsolved; a path newly set upon.

I am a field untouched by the plow.

Rejoice in me and know the fullness of youth.

I am the blessed Mother, the gracious Lady of the harvest.

I am clothed with the deep, cool wonder of the Earth and the gold of the fields heavy with grain.

By me the tides of the Earth are ruled, all things come to fruition according to my season.

I am refuge and healing.

I am the life-giving Mother, wondrously fertile.

Worship me as the Crone, tender of the unbroken cycle of death and rebirth.

I am the wheel, the shadow of the Moon.

I rule the tides of women and men and give release and renewal to weary souls.

Though the darkness of death is my domain, the joy of birth is my gift.

I am the goddess of the Moon, the Earth, the Seas.

My names and strengths are manifold.

I pour forth magick and power, peace and wisdom.

I am the eternal Maiden, Mother of all, and Crone of darkness, and I send you blessings of limitless love.[1]

The Call to the God

I am the radiant King of the Heavens, flooding the Earth with warmth and encouraging the hidden seed of creation to burst forth into manifestation.

I lift my shining spear to light the lives of all beings and daily pour forth my gold upon the Earth, putting to flight the powers of darkness.

I am the master of the beasts wild and free.

I run with the swift stag and soar as a sacred falcon against the shimmering sky.

The ancient woods and wild places emanate my powers, and the birds of the air sing my sanctity.

I am also the last harvest, offering up grain and fruits beneath the sickle of time so that all may be nourished.

For without planting there can be no harvest; without winter, no spring.

Worship me as the thousand-named Sun of creation, the spirit of the horned stag in the wild, the running wolf, the endless harvest.

See in the yearly cycle of festivals my birth, death, and rebirth—and know that such is the destiny of all creation.

I am the spark of life, the radiant Sun, the giver of peace and rest, and I send my rays of blessings to warm the hearts and strengthen the minds of all.[2]

Basic Ritual Invocations to the God and Goddess

These invocations have been taken from my Book of Shadows, with the original sources sometimes unknown, as well as from class notes collected over a period of several years. I have attempted to give proper credit to authors or originators of a particular invocation where I am aware of that author. Unfortunately, there are some examples listed here where I have no idea who wrote the original words or when they may have been written.

In many cases, as you will see here, the actual names or aspects of the God and Goddess are not used. Instead, the generic Mother, Father, Mother Goddess, Father God, or Lord and Lady are the preferred address. Specific names for the deities, or a specific aspect of Them, should really be used only if each member of the circle has agreed in advance on some specific act (such as spell work) that requires the presence of a unique aspect of the Lord or Lady. Secondly, using the generic

forms of address for the deities allows each member of the
Coven to visualize the God and Goddess in his or her own
unique way.

Example 1

Dear Lady of the night,
We open our arms, minds, and hearts to You.
All power is Yours (name of Goddess if desired),
as we ask You to join with us.
Send us Your love, Your guidance, and Your blessing.
Be with us, Lady, welcome and blessed be.

Dear Lord and consort of our Lady,
We open our arms, minds, and hearts to You.
All power is Yours (name of God if desired),
as we ask You to join with us.
Send us Your love, Your guidance, and Your blessing.
Be with us, Lord, welcome and blessed be.

Example 2

Dear Lady of Lunar Silver,
By all the thousands of names by which You are known.
You who are protectress of all the Wicca and creatrix of
*   us all.*
Silver Lady of the starry skies.
We who are Your children call You and welcome You.
We invite You to our circle, Lady.
Join with us in perfect love and perfect trust.
Welcome, dear Goddess, blessed be.

Dear Lord of Solar Gold,
By all the thousands of names by which You are known.
You who are the consort of our Lady and creator of us all.
Horned One of the forest, mountain, and field.
We who are Your children call You and welcome You.

We invite You to our circle, Lord.
Join with us in perfect love and perfect trust.
Welcome, dear Lord, blessed be.

Example 3

Gracious Goddess,
You who are Queen of the Gods,
Lamp of night,
Creatrix of all that is wild and free,
Mother of woman and man,
Lover of the Horned God and protectress of all.
Descend with Your lunar ray of power upon our circle
   here.[3]

Gracious God,
You who are King of the Gods,
Lord of the Sun,
Master of all that is wild and free,
Father of woman and man,
Consort of the Moon Goddess and protector of all.
Descend with Your solar ray of power upon our circle
   here.[4]

Example 4

Wondrous Lady of the Moon.
You who greets the dusk with silvered kisses.
Mistress of the night and of all magicks,
who rides the clouds in blackened skies
and spills light upon the Earth.
Lunar Goddess, Crescented One,
shadow maker and shadow breaker.
Revealer of mysteries past and present.
Puller of seas and ruler of women.
All-wise Lunar Mother,

I greet Your celestial jewel at the waxing of its power
With a rite in Your honor.[5]

Example 5

Blessed Lady, Mother of us all.
You who were before all humankind.
You who are our hope and inspiration.
You who have been with us from the beginning
and You who will be with us at the end of time.
Be with us now and forever, so mote it be.

Example 6

Mother Goddess,
Creatrix of us all,
Protectress of all the Wicca,
Consort of our Horned One.

Hear us across the thousands of years,
Hear us across the thousands of miles,
Be with us in this time that is not time,
Be with us in this space that is not space.

Be with us as the maiden of the night sky,
Let us grow as You grow night by night,
Join with Your children,
Blessed be, Mother Goddess.

At the end of the ritual or rite, it is necessary to thank and release the deities. The following examples will give you some insight into the structure I have used over the years, but feel free to modify or otherwise alter these words to fit your own requirements and tastes. Keep in mind that as the Goddess is always called first when the God and Goddess are both invoked, She is always released last when They are both released.

Example 1

Dear Lord and Lady,
We thank You for Your presence,
for Your circle, for Your light and love,
for night and change.
We ask for Your blessing as You depart.
Hail and farewell, Lord and Lady.
Go in power. Blessed be.

Example 2

Sky Father,
Protector of us all.
We give thanks for Your presence here tonight.
We give thanks for Your guidance and love.
Go in all power, dear God.
Hail and farewell.
Blessed be.

Earth Mother,
Protectress of us all.
We give thanks for Your presence here tonight.
We give thanks for Your guidance and love.
Go in all power, dear Goddess.
Hail and farewell.
Blessed be.

Invocations to the Quarters

These invocations have been taken from my Book of Shadows, either provided as class notes or even sometimes verbally.

Example 1

Regents of the East.
Spirits of Wind and Air.

We call Thee to this Circle.
We charge Thee to watch over and witness
these rites of (name of rite or ritual)
in this sacred space between the worlds
and in this sacred space out of time.

The phrasing for the remaining three quarters will be identical to the example of East, with the cardinal direction and element being changed to South (fire), West (water), and North (earth), respectively.

Example 2

Hail to Thee, East, powers of Air!
Blow through us and cleanse us.
Awaken that which has slept too long.
Give us the blessing of Your light.

Hail to Thee, South, powers of Fire!
Temper our sprits with Your heat.
Stoke the flame of our will.
Give us the blessing of Your strength.

Hail to Thee, West, powers of Water!
Wash us and flow through us.
Carry us swiftly through our days.
Give us the blessings of Life.

Hail to Thee, North, powers of Earth!
Dark mirror that reflects no image,
yet gazes back at us with our own eyes.
Give us the blessings of Your wisdom.

Example 3

Hail, Guardians of the Watchtower of the East,
Powers of Air.

We invoke and call You, come.
By the Air that is Her breath, be here now!

Hail, Guardians of the Watchtower of the South,
Powers of Fire.
We invoke and call You, come.
By the Fire that is Her spirit, be here now!

Hail, Guardians of the Watchtower of the West,
Powers of Water.
We invoke and call You, come.
By the Waters of Her living womb, be here now!

Hail, Guardians of the Watchtower of the North,
Powers of Earth.
We invoke and call You, come.
By the Earth that is Her body, be here now!

I personally do not like this particular type of invocation since it has the form of a command rather than a request. I feel it is somewhat inappropriate for us to be issuing commands to the Guardians or Spirits of the Four Quarters. Nonetheless, you can use this, or a modified version, if you desire.

Example 4

Spirit of the East, Spirit of Air.
Join with us and protect us in our circle.
Welcome Spirit, and blessed be.

The phrasing for the remaining three quarters will be identical to the example of East, with the cardinal direction and element being changed to South (fire), West (water), and North (earth), respectively.

Example 5

Spirit of the East, Ancient One of the Air.
I call upon You to attend this circle.
Charge this by Your powers, Old Ones.

The phrasing for the remaining three quarters will be identical to the example of East, with the cardinal direction and element being changed to South (fire), West (water), and North (earth), respectively.

At the end of the ritual or rite, it is necessary to thank and release the Spirits of the quarters. One simple way to accomplish this is presented here, but feel free to modify or embellish this example text as you desire.

Farewell Spirit of the East, Ancient One of Air.
We give you thanks for attending our circle this night.
Go in power, Spirit, hail and farewell.
Blessed be.

The phrasing for the remaining three quarters will be identical to the example of East, with the cardinal direction and element being changed to South (fire), West (water), and North (earth), respectively.

---

1. See Scott Cunningham, *Wicca: A Guide for the Solitary Practitioner* (St. Paul, MN: Llewellyn Publishing, 1988) 114.
2. Ibid, 115.
3. Ibid, 149.
4. Ibid.
5. Ibid, 125.

Appendix C
A Brief Dictionary of Pagan Gods and Goddesses

Making a detailed and complete listing of the pantheons of all Pagan gods and goddesses would be an almost insurmountable effort. There are literally thousands of deities associated with the various Traditions and Paths that comprise the overall scope of those religions we identify as Pagan under the definitions presented in chapter 1. There are, however, two excellent reference sources, *The Witches' God* and *The Witches' Goddess,* both by Janet and Stewart Farrar, that give a comprehensive listing of Pagan deities worshipped throughout the world. I strongly recommend both of these volumes to anyone even remotely interested in studying the various Pagan religions.

Even when it comes to identifying the deities associated with Celtic Wicca alone, the task can become formidable since again there are hundreds of deities worshipped by Scot, Welsh,

Irish, British, and Brython Pagans. I think it is important to note here that I am including the Neolithic Brythonic influence in this mix, even though these deities are not originally Celtic. The Brythonic deities were those worshipped by the Neolithic builders of such monuments as Stonehenge and predate the influx of the Celts into the British Isles by thousands of years. As far as we can tell, though, the original Brythonic pantheon seems to have been pretty much absorbed by, and amalgamated with, the Celtic, resulting in the pantheon worshipped and served by those who today follow the Path of Celtic Wicca.

There are several works available that attempt to address the identification of only Celtic gods and goddesses. *Celtic Myth & Magick* by Edain McCoy is quite good, and I recommend it to those who find themselves drawn to the Celtic Paths. While some practitioners of the Craft have pointed out flaws in McCoy's work, I generally find her identifications of the gods and goddesses who make up the overall Celtic pantheon to be quite adequate, at least as a starting point.

My purpose in writing this appendix is not to provide a thoroughly detailed description or identification of all gods and goddesses who make up the Celtic Pagan pantheon, nor simply to repeat the work done by the Farrars and McCoy. The list I present here is a tabulation of the deities generally associated with my Tradition and Path, those deities my Coven either invokes or at least recognizes as part of our spiritual lives. I offer it only as a short and simple guide, a starting or reference point, for those who are drawn to this or a similar Path. I emphasize again, as I have throughout this book, that what I present for your reading should always be considered to be a place to begin your own studies. Nothing presented here should be considered to be the complete and final authority or source.

Argante

A goddess of healing in both Welsh and Brython pantheons. Argante is called upon for aid in spells related to recovery from illness or injury.

Arianrhod

A goddess of reincarnation. She is symbolized by the Wheel of the Year. Arianrhod is a full moon goddess aspect and represents the power of the female through fertility. In Welsh mythology, Arianrhod is the daughter of Don, the Great Mother Goddess.

Boadicea, or Boadicca

Although not truly a goddess but a historical figure raised to mythical proportions, Boadicca can be invoked as a patron of strength and courage. As a female figure, She is generally called upon by a woman who needs Her power to overcome a possibly frightening test or challenge.

Brighid, also Bridget, Brigit, or Brid

As Brid, She is the great Mother Goddess of Ireland, some-times also going by the name of Dana in that aspect. She is a goddess of fire and forge, thus one of craftsmanship and especially of metalworking. As Bridget or Brigit, She also represents the mother aspect through fertility of the womb of both woman and earth, as well as the fertility of inspiration. She is also worshipped as a goddess of protection and healing and can be called upon in virtually any spell or magick involving those endeavors.

Cerridwen

Goddess of the Cauldron of Knowledge, She is another aspect of the Mother Goddess in both Welsh and Scot pantheons, exhibiting all phases of Maiden, Mother, and Crone. Also known as a patron goddess of arts and letters, She can be invoked as an inspirational muse as well as a giver of knowledge. Her counterpart in Irish mythology is probably Bridget, with both goddesses having their origins as Mother Goddess as far back as the Neolithic Brythons, at which time They may have been one and the same.

Cernunnos

Cernunnos is typically known as the Father God in both Welsh and the Southern British Isles pantheons, as well as those of mainland Europe, where He may have originated. He is the consort of either Brigantia (the British version of Bridget) or Cerridwen. As Father God, His symbol is the sun and He is worshipped as the male or Lord counterpart to our Lady in Her lunar aspects.

Dagda (The)

He is probably the Irish equivalent of Cernunnos, or Father God, and consort to the goddess Bridget. The Dagda possesses a bottomless cauldron of plenty and, with His war club, He can either slay men or bring them back to life. Dagda is sometimes portrayed in a comical pose with a full belly and dancing on short, stumpy legs. He is the ideal deity for male practitioners to invoke when strength or cunning is needed to meet challenges.

Danu, or Don, Dana

Another aspect of the Great Mother in the Irish pantheon, Dana is also sometimes given the position of Maiden in the Triple Goddess assembly when Bridget assumes the role of Mother.

Epona

She is a horse goddess of primarily the southern England Celtic pantheons and eventually became the patron goddess of cavalry of the Roman legions posted to Britain. Her symbol, as She rides a mare, can be found etched and carved into many Roman military shrines throughout the British Isles. Her worship was eventually taken to Rome itself by returning legionnaires.

Eri

A virgin goddess who submitted to the love of a sun god, Eri represents the feminine power of creation and can be related to any Mother Goddess moon image. She can be invoked for spells or rituals involving pregnancy, birth, or in any endeavor where something new is to be unveiled.

Habondia

A goddess of prosperity and plenty, Harbondia actually may have Her roots in the original Celtic Paganism of Western Europe prior to the Celt incursion into the British Isles. Harbondia is an excellent goddess to invoke for fertility or harvest rituals, or for prosperity magick.

Lugh, or Llew

He is the son of Arianrhod and the personification of the sun god or hero god as warrior, lover, and master of all skills and crafts. Known as Llew of the Long Arm or Llew of the Strong Hand, the Irish name Lugh and the Welsh Llew may actually relate to the same god. He is generally the sacrificial deity worshipped at the Lughnassadh festival and represents the harvest fruits being returned to the earth for rebirth. In this aspect He represents reincarnation.

Mabon

Initially represented as a sun god, Mabon eventually became associated with the Underworld theology of the Celts as King of the Dead and is now worshipped as a god of fertility and harvest. He is another of the Celtic deities adopted by the Romans, and His rituals are celebrated at the Sabbat that bears His name.

Morrigan (The)

The Morrigan is a war goddess representing the darker side of our religion and, as such, She is not to be invoked lightly. She has three very separate and distinct aspects under the names of Badb, Macha, and Nemain, representing war, death, and destruction, respectively. Morrigan is usually seen washing blood from the clothing and weapons of fallen warriors or as circling over the field of battle calling to the dead to come to Her. Legend says that if you see any aspects of Morrigan before taking the field of battle, you will not survive the conflict.

Oghma, or Ogma

A god of eloquence and language, Oghma is generally portrayed as an old man dressed in a lion skin and leading His listeners by golden chains attached to their ears. Oghma is generally credited with giving the written alphabet to the Celts in the form of straight lines etched about a central line to form consonants and vowels. This is typically referred to as the oghamic or ogamic alphabet, not to be confused with the various forms of the runic alphabet that came later.

Rhiannon

Although generally identified as a death goddess, Rhiannon is also associated with fertility, and at one time may have been referred to as a sun goddess. Rhiannon is also an excellent goddess to invoke with magick aimed at repelling enemies or seeking to provide protection for yourself or loved ones.

Turrean

Generally seen as a patron goddess of small animals, particularly dogs, Turrean is the goddess to invoke when working with dog Familiars or when caring for sick or injured pets.

Appendix D
Shops and Sources

Pagan Shops

The two sources given here provide a good starting point for identifying Pagan, Wiccan, or occult suppliers who currently have websites on the Internet. Additionally, I am sure there are many shops or outlets of Craft supplies that do not advertise on the Internet but can be found in the telephone directory of any moderate-sized city.

http://www.monmouth.com/~queen/sources.html
A compilation of Pagan, Wiccan, and other occult resale shops or stores. The list is alphabetical, first by state, then by foreign country. This is an excellent source for locating shops in any geographical area.

http://www.witchvox.com/network/shops
A compilation of Pagan, Wiccan, and other occult wholesale shops or stores. The list is alphabetical, with both states and foreign countries intermixed. This is an excellent source for locating shops in any geographical area.

Periodical Publications

The three publications listed below are ones I have found to be of excellent and diverse quality. I am sure there are other publications available that are probably as good as these, but this will at least give you a starting point if you are looking to subscribe to a Pagan or Wiccan publication.

Circle Sanctuary
(608) 924-2216
circle@mhtc.net
http://www.circlesanctuary.org
P.O. Box 219
Mt. Horeb, WI 53572

Pagan Dawn
http://www.paganfed.demon.co.uk/pagandawn/pf_pd.html
The Pagan Federation
B.M. Box 7097
London WC1N 3XX
England

Reclaiming
P.O. Box 14404
San Francisco, CA 94114

Classical and Medieval Arms and Attire

Museum Replicas Limited
(800) 883-8838
P.O. Box 840
Conyers, GA 30012

The Nobel Collection
(800) 866-2538
P.O. Box 1476
Sterling, VA 20167

Edged Weapons and Accessories

The Edge Company
(800) 732-9976
P.O. Box 826
Brattleboro, VT 05302

Atlanta Cutlery
(800) 883-0300
P.O. Box 839
Conyers, GA 30012

Bibliography

The listings in this bibliography represent a small sampling of reference materials, works, and sources available from my own bookcase. I have found these sources to be the most useful in evolving my own Wiccan learning and as historical reference works. The titles may give you some idea of the depth of information one can easily and quickly draw upon in a study of the Craft or its related history.

I have attempted to provide a brief description of each entry and have offered some personal comments where I thought they were warranted. These comments are mine alone, however, and some readers may not agree with them, so I urge you to read as much as possible, become as informed as possible, and then make your own decisions. Additionally, most Pagan or occult shops usually have at least a modest book selection on hand or can suggest any of various publishing catalogs where Craft-related, mail-order reading materials can be purchased. These establishments can be found in the phone directory of any moderate-sized city, and are usually listed under *occult* or *New Age*.

For those with access to a computer, I suggest you access the websites of book wholesalers, such as http://www.amazon.com, http:// www.borders.com, or http://www.barnes& noble.com. These websites offer literally hundreds of thousands of book titles and have internal search engines that enable you to locate books by author, title, or subject matter. I have personally found these all to be excellent sources of books related to almost any form of Paganism or its related history. There are also literally thousands of websites on the Internet related to all forms of Paganism. A quick search of the Internet using the Yahoo search engine recently yielded over one thousand hits for the keywords *Pagan*, *Wiccan*, and *witch*.

This bibliography is broken into three sections: Websites, Books of General and Historical Interest, and Books on Wicca and Witchcraft. Take your pick and go where your path of inquiry leads you.

Websites

American Civil Liberties Union

http://www.aclu.org

(See your local phone directory for the address in your area.)

The ACLU is dedicated to the legal protection of all civil liberties by mounting challenges to potential infringements of those liberties in local, state, and federal courts. Of significant importance to Pagans recently are the ACLU's actions during 1998 in spearheading the defeat of the federal establishment of government-sponsored and mandated Christian teachings as part of public school curricula under the misnamed Religious Freedom Amendment. In 1999, the ACLU was the leader in legal actions culminating in overturning a school district decision in Michigan that prohibited the wearing of pentacle jewelry by students.

Celtic Studies Resources

http://members.aol.com/lisala/index.html

A good reference source of Celtic myth and legend, with links to various technical and lay documents and sources.

Covenant of the Goddess (COG)

http://www.cog.org

P.O. Box 1226W

Berkeley, CA 94701

Officially, the major recognized Pagan organization within the United States, probably representing the majority of formal Covens, and a valuable networking connection for those Covens who become associated with COG. Personally, I have found the COG membership officials somewhat difficult to contact, and it appears that this organization is also much more supportive of and oriented toward Covens than Solitaries.

Earth Religion Rights

http://www.journey1.org/rights

This is an excellent companion source to the Freedom Fighters web page in that it lists a multitude of support organizations with links to many websites, including names and e-mail addresses of local or regional representatives of various Pagan organizations.

Freedom Fighters

http://members.aol.com/runes3/freedom.htm

A web page of resources and links devoted to organizing individuals into effective tools to combat the dogma and stereotypical definitions attached to many Pagan religions.

Moon Phase Calendar

http://www.googol.com/moon

A printable tabulation of lunar phases and dates allowing the user to input the desired month and obtain moon phase information for the days of that month.

Mythological and Sacred Traditions

http://mythinglinks.org

Although this website of mythology, lore, and sacred traditions was developed for graduate students in the Mythological Studies Department at Pacifica Graduate Institute, all others interested in these subjects are also warmly welcomed here by the author.

Pagan Educational Network (PEN)

http://www.bloomington.in.us/~pen
P.O. Box 1364
Bloomington, IN 47402

I believe that PEN is one of the better organizations devoted to dealing with the issues of public awareness and education regarding Paganism and Wicca, in particular. Their quarterly publication, *Water*, is an excellent compendium of what actions are being taken by PEN members to counter antiwitch sentiment and pronouncements in both print and television media.

The Pagan Federation

http://www.paganfed.demon.co.uk/

The Pagan Federation is based in the United Kingdom and is an excellent resource for all Pagan activities there. Their publication, *Pagan Dawn*, is also a valuable resource.

Rambling with Raven

http://annex.com/raven/wiccans.htm
Raven Scott's website. Includes the article "Who Is Wiccan?"

The Symantec Rhyming Dictionary

http://www.link.cs.cmu.edu/dougb/rhyme-doc.html

An invaluable resource for those who may be somewhat rhyme-challenged. This website offers various search routines for any word you input and provides literally thousands of corresponding words that rhyme.

Witches League for Public Awareness (WLPA)

http://www.celticcrow.com
P.O. Box 8736
Salem, MA 01971

Founded by Laurie Cabot, WLPA has the same avowed aim of public education and awareness of Craft issues as PEN. In my personal opinion, however, PEN seems to be somewhat more proactive in this arena than WLPA. I understand, though, that WLPA has undergone somewhat of a restructuring in the past few years and may well be equally as effective as PEN.

The Witches Voice

http://www.witchvox.com/

This website offers the absolute latest information related to modern-day witchcraft and the activities of the Neo-Pagan global community. The Witches' Voice now offers over 1,300 meticulously crafted pages of information related to the modern Pagan community. This website is updated on a daily basis.

Books of General and Historical Interest

Abbott, Geoffrey. *Rack, Rope and Red Hot*. London: Pincers Headline Publishing, 1993.

A description of the various tools and techniques of torture and execution as they were applied from approximately the Dark Ages through the 1700s, although those instruments and techniques of torture and interrogation typically associated with the Inquisitions are not singly identified.

Caesar, Julius. *The Conquest of Gaul*. Translated by S. A. Handford. Book VI. London: Penguin Books, Ltd., 1951.

Castleden, Rodney. *The Stonehenge People*. London: Routledge & Kegan Paul, Ltd., 1987.

Covering the period of 4700 to 2000 B.C., this work is an invaluable aid in understanding the religion and culture of the Neolithic inhabitants of the British Isles, and also gives interesting insights into their everyday lives. Livestock handling and crop raising are discussed, as well as the possible commercial and social interconnections between the various tribes or clans. An excellent companion book to Castleden's *Stonehenge Revealed*.

Green, Miranda, et al. *The Celtic World*. London: Routledge Publishing, 1996.

A detailed study of Celtic arts, religion, organization, and everyday life. Probably a mandatory reference work for those interested in Celtic history. This work is not restricted to the Celtic inhabitants of the British Isles, but also discusses the Celtic culture in a much broader scope, including the continental European influence.

Guest, Lady Charllote. *Mabinogeon.* 1906. Reprint, Mineola, NY: Dover Publications, Inc., 1997.

This is a translation of some of the original bardic oral tales of Welsh rulers and knights dating to around A.D. 950. These eventually formed the basis for the Arthurian legends as first written in about 1136 as the work of a Welsh chronicler, Geoffrey of Monmouth.

Hoffman, David. *Holistic Herbal.* Rockport, MA: Element Books, Inc., 1996.

An excellent basic book on many herbs and their uses. Details ailments and the appropriate herbal remedy, and cross-references both for easy access to the information.

Jenkins, Elizabeth. *Mystery of King Arthur.* New York: Barnes & Noble, 1996.

Discusses the myths and possible truths surrounding the Celt warrior king known today as Arthur, and of his uniting of the clans of southern England against Saxon invaders between the fourth and fifth centuries A.D.

Laing, Lloyd and Jenny. *The Picts and The Scots.* Gloucestershire: Sutton Publishing, 1993.

A study based on recent archaeological findings of the origins of the Pict and Scot peoples and of their interrelations. A good working guide to understanding the evolution of both cultures.

McCoy, Edain. *Celtic Myth & Magick.* Saint Paul, MN: Llewellyn Publications, 1997.

Contains short but detailed descriptions of the Celtic Sabbat calendar and holidays, an excellent section on Pathworking, and a very detailed dictionary naming each god and goddess in the pantheon along with descriptions of each deity's function and family tree. This is one of the most detailed works I have seen on Celtic deity identification.

Rolleston, T. W. *Celtic Myths and Legends.* 1897. Reprint, Mineola, NY: Dover Publications, 1990.

Sommerset-Fry, Peter and Fiona. *History of Ireland.* New York: Barnes & Noble, 1988.
   A history of Ireland and Irish rulers, with the first six chapters of particular interest to Celtic Pagans since they cover Irish history from 6000 B.C. up to the 1600s.

Souden, David. *Stonehenge Revealed.* London: Collins & Brown, Ltd., 1997.
   A rather exhaustive evaluation of Stonehenge, as well as numerous adjacent barrows and cursuses, describing the astronomical alignments of these various sites to both lunar and solar events. This book is quite detailed, with many drawings and photographs, and is an extremely good work for anyone with an interest in understanding some of the meanings of Stonehenge and its related structures.

Stewart, R. J. *Celtic Gods, Celtic Goddesses.* New York, NY: Sterling Publishing Co., 1990.
   A description of the various Celtic pantheons, and renditions of the stories surrounding the deities and their relationships with the land and the Celtic people.

Plaidy, Jean. *The Spanish Inquisition.* New York: Barnes & Noble, 1994.

The history of the Inquisition in Spain under Queen Isabella and King Philip II, and an excellent account of the tyranny of the Spanish Inquisition and of the Inquisitors themselves, such as the infamous Tomas de Torquemada. The Spanish Inquisitors were fanatics in their belief that physical pain in its most extreme form was a viable method to bring heretics and heathens into line so that all would accept the established religious dogma of the Church.

U.S. Government. "Religious Requirements and Practices of Certain Selected Groups." In the *United States Military Chaplain's Manual.* Washington, D.C.: U.S. Government Printing Office, 1988.

Books on Wicca and Witchcraft

Adler, Margot. *Drawing Down the Moon.* Boston: Beacon Press, 1979.

An in-depth look at the evolution of the Pagan movement of the twentieth century. Includes numerous interviews with Pagans and witches of various Traditions and Paths, dispelling the evil and dark connotations all too frequently assigned to our religion by mainstream media and publications. In my opinion, this is a mandatory addition to the library of anyone interested in witchcraft.

Buckland, Raymond. *Complete Book of Witchcraft.* Saint Paul, MN: Llewellyn Publications, 1975.

An excellent "how to become a witch" book, with rituals and rites easily workable in either a Coven or Solitary environment. This work is complete with questions at the end of each chapter and takes the reader step by step through the basics of learning how to be a witch.

———. *Witchcraft from the Inside.* Saint Paul, MN: Llewellyn Publications, 1995.

An interesting dissertation on the revival of witchcraft in the United Kingdom and the United States, with significant historical content. The work does not contain ritual information, but offers excellent material on Craft background.

Cantrell, Gary. *Out of the Broom Closet.* Parkland, FL: Upublish, Inc., 1998.

The author's personal account of stepping out of the broom closet and making his practice of Wicca known to others. The legal, emotional, and spiritual rationale the author considered before making this step are discussed, as are the reactions he received from friends, family, and coworkers. A valuable guide to others who may be considering taking this same step.

Cunningham, Scott. *Living Wicca*. Saint Paul, MN: Llewellyn Publications, 1993.

An excellent reference work for the Solitary practitioner of Wicca, and a companion book to Cunningham's *Wicca: A Guide for the Solitary Practitioner*. This book is a valuable tool in the bookcase of any witch.

————. *Wicca: A Guide for the Solitary Practitioner*. Saint Paul, MN: Llewellyn Publications, 1988.

An excellent starting book for the Solitary practitioner of Wicca. Discusses rituals and rites, and delves into the philosophy of our Craft. Another of those works that should be at the top of the list of any beginner who is serious about learning the Old Religion.

Farrar, Janet and Stewart. *The Pagan Path*. Custer, WA: Phoenix Publishing, 1991.

A very good work on the basics of Paganism, describing what it is and what it means to be a Pagan today. I believe this is a book that belongs on any Pagan's or witch's reading list. I recommend it to any beginners looking for someplace to start. Some of the material is more Coven-oriented than Solitary-oriented, but overall the book is excellent.

————. *The Witches' God*. Custer, WA: Phoenix Publishing, 1989.

————. *The Witches' Goddess*. Custer, WA: Phoenix Publishing, 1989.

Two companion books that go into great detail describing Pagan deities from around the world, as well as some of the rituals used to invoke and honor them. These two volumes are a must for any serious student of the Craft.

Farrar, Stewart. *What Witches Do.* Custer, WA: Phoenix Publishing, Inc., 1971.

Describes Wiccan and witchcraft rites and rituals in detail, and is a good "how to" book, although it is more Coven-oriented than Solitary practitioner-oriented.

Fitch, Ed. *Magical Rites from the Crystal Well.* Saint Paul, MN: Llewellyn Publications, 1984.

A compendium of rituals and spells suited for use by Solitaries or Covens. Includes interesting thoughts by the author on the meanings of the various rituals. The work also contains one of the few references I have seen to another code of conduct which many Wiccans I am acquainted with also seem to embrace. This is the Witch's Rede of Chivalry, also sometimes known as the Old Code, which I have mentioned several times in my own book.

McCoy, Edain. *Entering the Summerland.* Saint Paul, MN: Llewellyn Publications, 1996.

This work is devoted to understanding death and dying from a Pagan perspective, as well as dealing with the grief of those left behind. Various rituals and rites associated with the passage into Summerland are also described. This is an excellent work, particularly for those who may have older loved ones and may be looking for solace in the event of a pending death of those loved ones.

———. *The Sabbats*. Saint Paul, MN: Llewellyn Publications, 1994.

This work is, in my opinion, one of the finest I have seen on the meanings and explanations of our Sabbats. The book does not contain specific ritual information, but each Sabbat is explained in great detail, including foods and beverages to be served as well as games and offerings typically associated with each Sabbat. This is not another "how to be a witch" book, but is more of a working aid to assist the novice or beginner in understanding the meanings behind the Sabbats. A must for the bookcase of any Pagan.

Morrison, Dorothy. *In Praise of the Crone*. Saint Paul, MN: Llewellyn Publications, 1999.

An excellent guide for the older woman be she witch, Pagan, or simply one who has interest in reaching her inner self for recognition of her abilities. Although geared for the woman of menopausal age, this book is still a good source for women of all ages.

Murray, Margaret. *The God of the Witches*. Oxford: Oxford University Press, 1970.

Although Murray's theories concerning a widespread witch cult throughout Western Europe during the Middle Ages have been somewhat discounted by many present-day scholars (but not all), this work still gives valuable insight into how our Craft might have grown. Interesting reading, if nothing else.

Orion, Loretta. *Never Again the Burning Times*. Prospect Heights, IL: Waveland Press, Inc., 1995.

A relatively good dissertation on witchcraft and Western shamanism, and the types of people who practice our religion, including demographic breakdowns. It is not, however, an in-depth work on the Inquisition or other witch trials, as the title seems to indicate at first glance.

Pajeon, Kala and Letz. *Candle Magick Workbook*. New York: Carol Publishing Group, 1991.

A reasonably well-written book on the basics of candle magick. Many aspects of candle magick are discussed, as is the relationship of color and the elements to the art of magick. Each chapter is followed by a short quiz to test your knowledge, and there is ample room provided to accommodate notes or personal comments.

Simms, Maria Kay. *The Witch's Circle*. Saint Paul, MN: Llewellyn Publications, 1996.

An excellent "how to" book for the beginning student of Wicca, either as a Solitary or Coven member. This work is a valuable complement to Buckland's *The Complete Book of Witchcraft* or to any of Cunninghams works.

Skelton, Robin. *The Practice of Witchcraft Today*. Secarus, NJ: Carol Publishing Group, 1997.

Quite a well-rounded book on witchcraft, and its rituals and basic philosophy. A good "how to" work with numerous boilerplate rituals and spells in the workbook sections. The book is an easy read, the spells are easily understood, and the material is well suited to the novice practitioner.

Watson, Nancy. *Practical Solitary Magick*. York Beach, ME: Samuel Weiser, Inc., 1996.

A very good text on practical magickal applications. This is not, however, a ritual book with ritual or rite descriptions, but one that takes the reader through the various steps of working the magick. Not necessarily a work, in my opinion, for a novice or beginner since there is little ethical or spiritual awareness content provided.

Wood, Robin. *When, Why . . . If.* Dearborn, MI: Livingtree Books, 1996.
    This is one of the finest works on witchcraft ethics that I have come across in my own reading, and, in my opinion, it should be a required volume for any beginner or novice witch. It should be one of the first books suggested as soon as the beginner indicates a serious intent to pursue work in the Craft.

Glossary

ACLU
The American Civil Liberties Union. A legal organization dedicated to defending a person's civil rights or constitutional liberties against local, state, or national government intrusion.

Agnostic
A person who may not necessarily believe in one supreme being, but does not totally deny the possibility, either.

Agrarian
A society based on agriculture.

Alpha State
One of the first states of relaxation for meditation, similar to deep daydreaming.

Altar
A physical place or object for religious ceremonies, or for holding the tools of worship.

Anglo-Celtic
The Celtic clans of southern England and Wales who inhabited and settled in these parts of the British Isles between 1000 and 500 B.C.

Atheist
One who denies the existence of God or gods.

Black Magic(k)
Any ritual or spell performed to hurt or harm someone or cause damage.

Book of Shadows
A witch's book of rituals, spells, and incantations.

Broom Closet
A slang term for keeping one's Pagan religion or practice hidden from public view.

Celt
Any of the originally Indo-European peoples of Central Europe, or their descendants, who were spread throughout most of Europe by about the first millennium B.C.

Cernunnos
The great male deity of the Celts, consort of the Earth Mother, and usually represented as having the horns of a stag.

Cerridwen

A female deity of the Celts, the Welsh-Celtic Earth Mother, and keeper of the Cauldron of Knowledge.

Christian Church

The Catholic Church of the first through the fifteenth centuries A.D.

Coven

A group of witchcraft practitioners, usually thirteen in number, but not necessarily limited to this number of members.

Craft

The short version of the word *witchcraft*.

Dark Ages

The period in Western European history from approximately A.D. 500–1500, characterized by an outlawing of secular thought and total control by the Christian Church.

Druid

A priest or priestess of the Celtic clans, a learned teacher and healer. The Druidic priesthood of the Celts was also responsible for verbally committing clan and tribal history to memory and reciting that material as stories or sagas for the rest of the clan.

Eclectic

Taking only what is wanted or needed, or taking the best from several contributions to make a new whole.

Equinox

The time of year when the Earth's tilt on its axis places the sun directly over the equator. This occurs twice each year, once in March and again in September.

Etruscan

An ancient civilization existing in the northern portions of Italy, what is now Tuscany, possibly of Greek origin. The Etruscans were eventually conquered by Rome in about 600 B.C.

Heathen

A member of a religion that does not acknowledge Christianity, Judaism, or Islam.

Heretic

One who refutes the dogma of the Christian church.

High Priest/ess

A man (High Priest, also abbreviated as HP) or woman (High Priestess, also abbreviated as HPs) who has completed several formal degrees of advancement since initiation, or through experience has amassed a similar body of witchcraft lore, and has been elevated by desire of all members of a Coven to be the spiritual and ritual leader of that Coven.

High Sabbat

The four major Sabbats of the Wheel of the Year: Imbolc, Beltain, Lughnasadh, and Samhain.

Inquisition

Medieval Church court for trials involving witches, heretics, and Pagans. Instituted by Pope Gregory IX in A.D. 1233, it existed through about the late seventeenth century A.D.

Lugh

God of sun, light, and warmth in the Welsh-Celtic pantheon, celebrated at the Sabbat of Lughnasadh.

Magick

A term used to denote spells or other magical acts performed by a witch, ending with the letter *k* to differentiate it from the magic of stage performances or entertainment.

Matriarchal

A society or religion with a female head or chief.

Mirror Book

A witch's personal account of his or her growth and evolution as a witch.

Monotheist

A religion based on a single deity.

Old Religion

The worship of Pagan gods and goddesses, and of the Pagan holidays.

Pagan

Any follower of a non-Christian and usually multideity religion.

Pantheist

A religion based on multiple deities, each of whom have essentially equal powers and equal stature within the universe.

Pantheon

A description of the family of gods and goddesses making up a Pagan religion.

Patriarchal
A society or religion with a male head or chief.

Pogrom
An organized and usually state-sponsored attack against a religion or a way of life, with the ultimate aim of eliminating it.

Polytheist
A religion based on multiple deities with one supreme deity, the others being subordinate to that one.

Path
Any of the various subforms of a Pagan religion, usually within an established Tradition and having specific guidelines for its adherents.

PEN
Pagan Educational Network. An organization devoted to disseminating truthful information regarding Pagan views and philosophy.

Pentacle
A five-pointed star displayed on a Pagan altar or robe, or worn on the body as jewelry, with the five points representing the elements of earth, air, fire, water, and spirit.

Priest/ess
A man (priest) or woman (priestess) who has completed a course of study such that he or she has been initiated as a witch.

Proselytize
Initiating a conversion of someone to a new doctrine or religion, usually by rather forceful and intimidating methods.

Ritual Robe

Any garment worn by a witch during the performance of a ritual or spell, usually loose-sleeved and hooded.

Santaria (Santería)

A Pagan religion having its roots in Cuba and parts of South America, in which animals are ceremoniously sacrificed in order to cast spells and to determine the future.

Satanism

A Path or Tradition of the Pagan religion that acknowledges Satan as God.

Stonehenge

A megalithic monument of standing stones on the plains of southern England, built about 5000 B.C. by the indigenous inhabitants of the British Isles.

Symbology

A method of writing or marking using recognized symbols to convey information.

Theology

Any religious doctrine or philosophy.

Torquemada

Tomas de Torquemada. A Dominican monk appointed Grand Inquisitor in 1487 by Pope Innocent VIII. Torquemada devised extremely harsh procedures for the Spanish Inquisition.

Voodoo

A blend of Catholicism and African Paganism practiced typically in the islands of the Caribbean.

WLPA

Witches League for Public Awareness. This organization is devoted to the dissemination of the truth about witchcraft and to countering the biased claims of religious conservatives.

Index

ORDER LLEWELLYN BOOKS TODAY!

Llewellyn publishes hundreds of books on your favorite subjects! To get these exciting books, including the ones on the following pages, check your local bookstore or order them directly from Llewellyn.

Order Online:
Visit our website at www.llewellyn.com, select your books, and order them on our secure server.

Order by Phone:
- Call toll-free within the U.S. at 1-877-NEW-WRLD (1-877-639-9753)
  Call toll-free within Canada at 1-866-NEW-WRLD (1-866-639-9753)
- We accept VISA, MasterCard, and American Express

Order by Mail:
Send the full price of your order (MN residents add 7% sales tax) in U.S. funds, plus postage & handling to:

Llewellyn Worldwide
P.O. Box 64383, Dept. 1-56718-112-0
St. Paul, MN 55164-0383, U.S.A.

Postage & Handling:
Standard (U.S., Mexico, & Canada). If your order is:
  Up to $25.00, add $3.50
  $25.01 - $48.99, add $4.00
  $49.00 and over, FREE STANDARD SHIPPING
(Continental U.S. orders ship UPS. AK, HI, PR, & P.O. Boxes ship USPS 1st class. Mex. & Can. ship PMB.)

International Orders:
Surface Mail: For orders of $20.00 or less, add $5 plus $1 per item ordered. For orders of $20.01 and over, add $6 plus $1 per item ordered.

Air Mail:
Books: Postage & Handling is equal to the total retail price of all books in the order.
Non-book items: Add $5 for each item.

Orders are processed within 2 business days. Please allow for normal shipping time. Postage and handling rates subject to change.

Magical Rites From the Crystal Well
ED FITCH

In nature, and in the earth, we look and find beauty. Within ourselves we find a well from which we may draw truth and knowledge. And when we draw from this well, we rediscover that we are all children of the Earth.

The simple rites in this book are presented to you as a means of finding your own way back to nature; for discovering and experiencing the beauty and the magic of unity with the source. These are the celebrations of the seasons; at the same time they are rites by which we attune ourselves to the flow of the force: the energy of life.

These are rites of passage by which we celebrate the major transitions we all experience in life. Here are the Old Ways, but they are also the Ways for Today.

0-87542-230-6
160 pp., 7 x 10, illus. $12.95

Wiccan Warrior

Walking a Spiritual Path in a Sometimes Hostile World

KERR CUHULAIN

"*Being a warrior is not about fighting. It's about freeing yourself of limitations so that you can be truly creative and effective in life.*" In the current Wiccan community, many archetypes present themselves: Maidens, Mothers, Crones, Healers, Magicians—but rarely Warriors. *Wiccan Warrior* is the first book to show the average Pagan how to access the Warrior archetype within. It demonstrates how to follow a path that is essentially the Wiccan Rede in action: "*An it harm none, do what thou wilt.*"

Written by a Wiccan police officer and martial artist, *Wiccan Warrior* combines personal insights and real-life anecdotes with ritual, magick, energy work, meditation, self-examination, and self-discipline. It is about taking responsibility for your actions, knowing that a true Warrior wins most of his battles with his head, not his hands.

1-56718-252-6
216 pp., 6 x 9

$12.95

Witchcraft

Theory and Practice

LY DE ANGELES

Here is a manual to the theory and practice of Witchcraft aimed at the serious student; specifically, the practicing Witch. It is written conversationally, talking to the individual, as though the student was being trained through the author's coven.

It takes the trainee step-by-step through the stages of the work and leaves nothing undone. It is a comprehensive textbook for both solitary and group practice, covering the philosophy, the disciplines involved, the meaning and practice of ritual, applicable alternative studies, and the attitudes required for successful spellcrafting (sorcery). It specifically implies that a Witch does have certain psychic powers, either inherent or that can be developed. The depth in *Witchcraft: Theory and Practice* enables it to be read more than once and also used as a Grimoire.

1-56718-782-X
6 x 9, 288 pp., softcover $12.95

(